AF412236

# INNOVATION AND EMPIRE IN TURKEY

*To my beloved wife, Tûba*

# INNOVATION AND EMPIRE IN TURKEY

## Sultan Selim III and the Modernisation of the Ottoman Navy

TUNCAY ZORLU

Tauris Academic Studies
LONDON • NEW YORK

Published in 2008 by Tauris Academic Studies,
an imprint of I.B.Tauris & Co Ltd
6 Salem Road, London W2 4BU
175 Fifth Avenue, New York NY 10010
www.ibtauris.com

In the United States of America and Canada distributed by
Palgrave Macmillan, a division of St. Martin's Press
175 Fifth Avenue, New York NY 10010

Copyright © 2008 Tuncay Zorlu



ISBN: 978 1 84511 694 1

A full CIP record for this book is available from the British Library
A full CIP record for this book is available from the Library of Congress

Library of Congress catalog card: available

Printed and bound in India by Thomson Press India Limited
camera-ready copy edited and supplied by the author

# CONTENTS

# LIST OF TABLES

# ACKNOWLEDGEMENTS

I wish to acknowledge the assistance generously given by the following institutions: The Turkish Academy of Sciences; the Ottoman Prime Ministerial Archives at Sultanahmet; the Naval Museum and Archives in Beşiktaş; the Turkish Archaeological Museums Library at Gülhane; the Public Record Office in London; the School of Oriental and African Studies; the Greenwich Maritime Museum; the London School of Economics; the IRCICA (Research Centre for Islamic History, Art and Culture).

I am specifically grateful to the following people who kindly provided me with books, articles and addresses as well as insight into the intricacies of the subject: Prof. Rhoads Murphey from the Ottoman, Byzantine and Modern Greek Studies Department at the University of Birmingham; Kate Fleet from the Skilliter Centre for Ottoman Studies at the University of Cambridge; Prof. Daniel Panzac from the University of Aix-en-Provence, Paris; Prof. Stanford Shaw from Bilkent University; Prof. Murat Çizakça from Bahçeşehir University; Prof. Ali Ihsan Gencer, Prof. Idris Bostan, Prof. Feza Günergun, and Assoc. Prof. Mustafa Kaçar from Istanbul University; Prof. Zafer Toprak and Prof. Selim Deringil from Boğaziçi University.

I feel indebted to Prof. Ekmeleddin İhsanoğlu, former general director of the Research Centre for Islamic History, Art and Culture (IRCICA), and presently the Secretary General of the Organization of the Islamic Conference (OIC), who, from the very beginning of

this study, encouraged and supported me to work on the subject. My special thanks go to Prof. Günhan Danışman from the History Department of Boğaziçi University. He not only played an active role in my choosing the subject, but also read and discussed my drafts, and encouraged me during the course of this book.
I also feel indebted to I.B. Tauris Publishers, specifically editors Lester Crook, Elizabeth Munns and Rasna Dhillon for their patience and kindness during the creation process of the present book.
Finally, I would like to acknowledge warmly the spiritual, material, and intellectual support of my wife, family and friends: without them, this book would never have been produced.

# PREFACE

*Innovation and Empire* aims to draw attention to one of the most important gaps of the Ottoman history: naval technology, which has generally been taken up as an incidental field within the broad spectrum of economic history, or as a discourse intermingled with heroic narrations or tales of pirates and glorious captains.

This book focuses on Selim III's efforts (1789–1804) to create a new Ottoman navy as an extension and climax of the modernisation attempts in the aftermath of the Çeşme Incident (1770), with reference to the new shipbuilding materials, structures and methods, supported by foreign technicians as well as native dynamics.

The present book utilizes mainly archival documents in the Ottoman Prime Ministerial Archives in Istanbul and the Public Record Office in London. These primary sources providing factual data are supported by a large spectrum of secondary sources, including recent publications and periodicals. Therefore, it aims to introduce the field to the academic community and to provide substantial data to prospective students of Ottoman naval technology. This book, considering the rising importance of interdisciplinary studies in historiography, also aims to provide historians studying the history of Ottoman modernisation with new types of data, with its technical terminology and *sui generis* jargon.

# 1

# EVOLUTION OF THE OTTOMAN NAVAL TECHNOLOGY UP TO THE REIGN OF SELIM III

### The transition to sailing vessels: Reasons and consequences

Ottoman sea power is a subject of study encircled by prejudices and biases, which are difficult to sort out and can lead the student of naval history to confusion and incorrect results. One of them appears in a bid to limit the Ottoman sea power to a short period between Pîrî Reis and Barbarossas, representing the intellectual and ignorant/illegitimate aspects of the Ottoman sea power, respectively. The second one tends to show the Ottoman Empire as a land-based military power, ignoring the importance of the navy and attributing to it a secondary role. The assessment of the sea power in connection with naval campaigns only and the exclusion of maritime trade constitute a third bias. The final prejudice envisages that the Ottomans never adapted to or developed the technology necessary to become a sea power.[1]

It is beyond the capacity of this work to attempt to clarify all the points raised by Brummet. What we intend is to help elucidate the state of naval technology of the time. In order to obtain a more accurate picture of the technological assessment of the Ottoman sea power, one should first deal with the question of the transition from oared to sailed ships, which is a widely discussed question within academic circles.

There is no doubt that the Ottomans did not abandon their classical ships all of a sudden. They followed a course of naval modernisation that was conservative and slow in some periods, but rapid in others. In this context, the Ottomans' first attempts at the construction of sailing warships dates back to the time of Mehmet the Conqueror, who ordered a galleon of 3,000 tons in imitation of similar vessels in the Venetian, Genoese and Aragonese navies. However, this vessel sank at launch. In the following centuries Ottoman shipbuilders made attempts at building sailing ships, which failed mostly due to the lack of technological know-how. In the reigns of Bayezid II, Selim I and Süleyman I, galleons similar to Venetian caravels were built, but later abandoned because of their impracticability in the absence of wind.[2] Although the appearance of the first galleons in Istanbul is said to have occurred as early as the 1580s by some historians, it is most probable that ships constructed before 1644 were mostly hybrid vessels, such as *kalite*, *göke* and *burton*, with both oars and sails, and originally employed to protect the convoys, functioning as transporters or corsairs and cruising against enemy ships.[3]

The first Ottoman galleon planned as a battle ship was constructed in 1644.[4] In May 1648, in the fourth year of the Crete campaign, the Ottomans seemed to have begun to realise the importance of galleons and somewhat hesitantly discussed their advantages over galleys.[5] However, the systematic construction of galleons was initiated under the grand vizier Merzifonlu Kara Mustafa Pasha and Kaptan-ı Derya Gazi Hasan Pasha.[6] It would not be an exaggeration to say that the galley type of oared ships, which had been the backbone of the Ottoman navies throughout the sixteenth and in the first three quarters of the seventeenth centuries, only came to be replaced by large sailing ships in the last quarter of the seventeenth century. However, the period between 1682 — the year referring to the beginning of the systematic adoption of sailing ships — and 1770 — the year marking the devastating defeat of the Ottoman fleet at Çeşme — witnessed the symbiosis of the oared and sailed technologies. In that period, the Ottomans occasionally left the new sailing ships, preferring the traditional oared ships. This hesitation and indecision lasted until 1770.

In the aftermath of the defeat of 1770, the balance tilted considerably in favour of sailing ships as part of the modernisation process accelerated by Cezayirli Gazi Hasan Pasha, which culminated with the reign of Selim III thanks to the developments in naval warfare, artillery and technical know-how in navigation throughout the world.

By the late eighteenth century, oared ships had become obsolete and almost disappeared, leaving their place to new types of ships for good. The number of galleys fell to 15 in 1701 and remained at this level until the 1760s. Eventually, their previous functions as the backbone of the Ottoman navy was abandoned and their duties were restricted to scouting, patrolling the coasts and the islands of the Aegean, and sometimes towing the sailing vessels.[7]

Although we are deprived of the full account of the motivations and rationale behind the reluctance of the Ottomans to adopt sailing ships, several factors such as the supply of shipbuilding materials, the Ottomans' long rivalry with neighbouring Venice and geographical conditions might supply a satisfactory explanation.

First, it is important to realise that the shipbuilding sector, regardless of any specific period, has an important shortcoming: slow change. The reason behind this is multi-dimensional. To begin with, naval technology requires huge investments in construction, equipment and personnel that could be achieved only by state power to a great extent, leaving other entrepreneurs outside. Second, the high cost required for training personnel in new equipment and technologies is a formidable undertaking. Finally, difficulty in finding suitable construction sites delays the adoption of new technology. Most of these obstacles seem to be surmountable by today's huge firms, whereas in those times they were almost impossible to overcome by any power but strong states themselves.

The matter of the supply and availability of materials, such as timber, required for building a ship was of major importance. It is true that the amount of timber was dramatically reduced in Kocaeli province towards the end of the seventeenth century due to the intensive harvesting during the sixteenth and seventeenth centuries. The timber available from the Kocaeli region fell from the amount required to construct ten galleys to the amount necessary to build seven. However, timber sources still existed in the inner regions of Anatolia.[8] So although it has been argued that the decline in timber supplies was one of the reasons behind the Ottomans' reluctance to adopt galleons[9] before the seventeenth century, this theory is not applicable to the period in question. Indeed, Kocaeli or Iznikmid and the surrounding areas were still the main sources of timber for the intensive naval construction movements in the aftermath of the Çeşme Incident and in the reign of Selim III. Beside the Kocaeli region, Midilli, Kazdagi, Canik, Taşoz, Rumeli, Megri, Rhodes, Kidros, Cide, Misivri, Ahyolu, Segen, Ayna Island, Gemlik, Gümülcine, Karaağaç, Bolu, Mudurnu, Âbâd Yaylası, Elmacık Dağı, Sarı Ot Dağı, Samsun, Sinop, Inebolu, Meset, Faacas, Bartın, Akçahisar and other areas were also active in supplying timber for shipbuilding. Towards the end of the eighteenth century, Ottoman lands and specifically Albania and the Black Sea region,[10] with their abundant and high-quality oak wood, came to be centres of attraction for England and Russia, in addition to providing timber for the Ottoman navy.

The second factor in the Ottomans' slowness in adopting galleons involved the Ottomans' prolonged rivalry with Venice. Venice was a major naval and commercial rival sharing the same geographical market with the Ottomans. The Porte had fought its first sea war against Venice in 1416.[11] Even in the sixteenth century, the Ottoman and Venetian naval arsenals had much in common.[12] Operating in the same geography compelled them to observe each other closely and to seek ways to have a greater share of the benefits of the competition. It was also the cause of their technological similarities. Long wars, commercial and technological exchanges, being obliged to cope with the difficulties of the same geography made them similar in many respects. It was difficult for either to change its well-rooted galley tradition, regardless of the possible negative outcomes, as doing so might have put it into a disadvantaged position in the face of its rival. In addition, adopting new technology meant new expenses, know-how and expertise. All these factors caused them to cling to the traditional vessels, which seemed more practical within the geography in question. This prudent attitude continued until this relatively peaceful geography was disturbed by the naval forces of the Atlantic powers in the seventeenth century.[13]

In dealing with the transition question, a problematic approach emerges in the overestimation of galleys in the face of glorious galleons irrespective of the geography and time in which they operated. This attitude tends to oversimplify and to ignore the complex web of conditions intertwined in accounting for the Ottomans' reluctance to give up their oared vessels. In this context, the third factor suggests that the preference of traditional oared vessels stemmed, to a great extent, from the circumstances of their physical geography rather than from their rivalry with neighbours. The Ottoman Empire was surrounded by seven seas when it reached its zenith in the sixteenth century. The Black Sea and the Sea of Marmara were almost under absolute control. The Aegean, eastern Mediterranean and Red Seas were effectively controlled, but occasionally challenged. Finally, the Persian Gulf and the Indian Ocean were zones of conflict in which Ottoman influence was evident.[14]

Under these geographical conditions, galleys had many advantages, making them practical and economical. First of all, they were powered by oars, which freed them from dependence on fair wind on calm days. Galleys also served, in mixed fleets consisting of oared and sailed ships alike, as tow vessels when galleons became becalmed and crippled. Another advantage of the galleys was their speed and manoeuvrability. They were able to operate close to the shore and were not visible from a great distance, thanks to their low structure in the freeboard and shallow draught. These were important features for the ships of the period, considering that their crews worked as pirates as well.

In addition to these advantages, the Ottoman Mediterranean fleet was superior to its rivals in its ability to draw on the vast human and material resources of a geographically united empire. It was also under the control of a centralized, military government that could exploit them efficiently.[15] This geography naturally brought about some constraints imposed by such phenomena as tides, prevailing winds and other natural forces, which defined the role of the Ottoman State in this respect. Therefore, war galleys rather than galleons remained the most suitable vessels to wage naval wars and to gain possession of the bases and islands that would lead their masters to control the sea routes.[16]

The practicality of oared vessels in naval warfare was another reason behind their long dominance. During sea battles, the Ottomans were skilled at the time-tested techniques of ramming and boarding, for which galleys were well suited. Therefore, it was difficult for the Ottomans to give up these vessels for new ones, which would require a whole new way of manoeuvring in battle. Above all, galleys were amphibious forces, using their ordnance against targets ashore, covering landings and debarkations, re-supplying missions and functioning as siege batteries against coastal fortresses.

For sound technological and tactical reasons, heavy ordnance was used effectively from the bows of galleys before it was from the broadsides of sailing ships. Large cannons could be accommodated on the earliest main centreline mounts on war galleys. Being simple in construction, these mounts did not require any major modification of the galley's hull. However, the addition of bow artillery made war galleys even better suited than before for amphibious raids and skirmishing. In the course of time, galleys had assumed a role as floating siege battery. In economic and geographical terms, galleys stood for the efficient use of good heavy ordnance. The Mediterranean rulers of the early sixteenth century were not faced with the choice between the war galley and sailing ship, but with how to get the most out of a limited quantity of good artillery.[17]

Another important point regarding the transition from oared galley to sailing galleon is offered by Guilmartin, who suggests that the transition was directly bound up with economic factors. The earlier galleons of relatively small size fell short in the course of time in transporting the increasingly large amounts of goods, and therefore the first Ottoman galleons were used for transporting large amounts of merchandise rather than for naval campaigns.[19]

Another factor that worried the naval circles was of economic and psychological origin. War galleys provided useful employment for about 600–700 oarsmen and 250–300 seamen/soldiers.[xix] The adoption of galleons would necessitate the employment of foreign technicians, which would lead to the unemployment of a great number of crew and arsenal workers knowledgeable in constructing, rigging and using oared ships. This, in turn, would cause the falling out of favour of the traditional Muslim sailors, who had contributed greatly to the glorious naval victories in the past and were respected by the common people.[20]

It is true that the galleys had some shortcomings both as a type of ship per se and in comparison with sailing vessels. Their elongated forms and shallow draughts made it difficult for them to withstand storms. Therefore, as a rule, the Ottoman imperial fleet did not put to sea until *nevruz*, the vernal equinox, and returned to its base in October or the beginning of November. Another disadvantage of the galley was the inverse proportion between the size of the ship and number of crew on it. There were 200–300 crew and six to ten officers on an average galley. Hence, the consumption of victuals reached enormous amounts, which created storage problems. Since space was limited on a galley, provisions had to be restricted accordingly, which led to their early exhaustion. In order to compensate for this shortcoming, the Porte arranged for separate ships to go to pre-arranged coastal points to fetch supplies. However, this was not an efficient solution when distances were great and the sea route was insecure. This system accounts for the failure of the Ottoman navy to dominate the western Mediterranean. Additionally, the use of green and unseasoned timber as well as undersized adzes used to cut and shape timbers were technical disadvantages impairing the ships.[21]

The Ottomans were not completely ignorant of the galleon tradition. They had been in contact since the mid-sixteenth century with Algerian sailors,[22] who had long used sailed vessels as well as oared ones.[23] During the first half of the seventeenth century, Ottoman North Africa made a substantial contribution to the imperial navy, participating in its campaigns with sailing vessels.[24] It is known that the Grand Vizier Merzifonlu Kara Mustafa asked the North African corsairs for information about sailing ships in the early 1680s. Also, it is claimed that it was the North Africans who might have suggested taking on a Muslim convert shipbuilder from Leghorn who, in 1682, launched the first Ottoman sailing ship at the *Tersâne-i Âmire*.[25] Another indicator supporting the Ottomans' early contact with sailing ships was their Indian Ocean policy, resulting in a virtual withdrawal from that ocean. Between 1517 and 1554, the Ottomans had confronted Portuguese sailing ships in the Indian Ocean. Some sources report the construction of 20 large sailing ships as preparations for the campaign.[26]

As for the short- and long-term consequences of the transition question, many changes took place in such areas as shipbuilding technology and economy, naval warfare, the role of the human factor and so on.

The shift from classical oared ships to sailed ships changed and redefined the role of the human factor as well, as the transition called for the exchange of oarsmen for sails and warriors for guns. In Cipolla's words, 'it meant the exchange of human energy for inanimate power.'[27] However, this did not mean the disappearance of men on board. The changing factor was the manning strategy. Oarsmen were replaced by free sailors, Janissaries and ironsides (*cebeliler*) with marines and a new body of naval and petty officers. The crews on Ottoman warships consisted of Janissaries, Muslim rowers and sailors, Christian oarsmen and sailors, prisoners of war and convicts. According to the recruiting system, when manpower was needed for ships, judges sent a portion of this requested manpower from the provinces. Some others were provided from among imperial slaves and convicts, and finally from labour markets in return for a payment called *bedel-i grifte* (payment for the hired men). The minimum cost for hiring a man was at least 1,500 *akçes* for a season. The number of Christian crew was much greater than that of Muslims. However, Muslims earned more than Christians (318 vs. 242 *akçes* per campaign), leading to wage discrimination based on religion, while it did not exist in the arsenal. This can account for the relative scarcity of Muslim sailors and insecurity about Christian crew during naval campaigns.[28]

Contingent upon the increase in the number of sailing ships and their growing size, the following years witnessed a rise in the number of crew as well. For instance, the number of crew on a flagship increased from 600 to 800 in 1699, to 1,470 in 1738 and decreased to 1,207 in 1815.[29] This last figure, e.g. 1,200 crew on the three-decked *Selimiye*, was during the reign of Selim III.[30] Then a new manning system imposed by these huge warships shifted the classical tasks and division of labour on the oared vessels as well.

The limited number of tasks on the oared vessel was replaced by many different duties and functions on board the sailing ship. These new ships had to be sailed and fought on simultaneously, which was a complicated matter requiring a great number of skilled men and a complex division of labour. Among the various occupations were steering, administration, victualling, gunnery, craftsmen (carpenters, caulkers, sail makers, etc.), religious leaders (*imam*), surgeons, longboat crew, mariners, sailors and so on.[31] The manning strategy, beside its advantages, placed a new economic burden on the navy. The victualling and accommodation of the increasing number of skilled crew and salaries of naval and petty officers meant new expenses that were aggravated by the increasing employment of foreign technicians, engineers and officers in the naval works, especially from the 1770s onwards.

The development of firepower was probably the most determining consequence of the transition. The beginning of the widespread use of cannons on ships in the sixteenth century was a watershed with respect to its revolutionary impulse in the course of naval warfare and technology. Earlier naval wars had been in the form of land wars waged on floating ships. With the introduction of galleons, naval warfare came to be a battle between ships instead of between individual soldiers. Fighting powers shifted their focus from killing or wounding the adversary to smashing the hulls and rigging of the adversary ships. Galleons could mount whole rows of huge cannons on several gun decks along each side. The weight of one alone would have capsized the lighter galleys. Therefore, the appearance of heavy artillery in Mediterranean naval battles soon made the galley obsolete. Despite their slowness, galleons could stand off and pound the relatively fragile galleys to pieces at long range before the galleys could even get in close enough to fire their small cannons, let alone grapple and board.[32]

### The state of the Ottoman navy from the Çeşme incident up to the ascension of Selim III to the throne

The year 1682 marked the systematic adoption of galleons by the Ottoman state. Thanks to the reforms of Grand Admiral Mezzamorto Hüseyin Pasha, several imperial edicts and regulations that referred to the organisations of the sailors and mariners were promulgated in 1701. The most important one was the creation of a new kind of post: *Kapudâne*, which corresponds to Grand Admiral. The *Kapudâne* held the first rank in the command of a sailing ship before the *Patrona* (naval official second in command) and the *Riyâle* (naval officer third in command). Their appointments and dismissals were regulated by strict rules according to meritocracy. These reforms soon proved successful.

Ottoman galleons achieved success in the second Morean War in 1714–18. They maintained their superiority in the Mediterranean Sea until the outbreak of hostilities with Russia in 1769. A period of approximately 50 years between the second Morean and Russian wars were free of any serious naval involvement.[33]

The destruction of the Ottoman fleet by the Russian one — which consisted of 15 *kapaks*, six frigates and other small crafts — in the bay of Çeşme on 6 July 1770 exerted a shocking impact on the Ottoman navy. The cost was huge: 11 ships of the line, six frigates, six three-masters, seven galleys and 32 others were burned by the Russian fleet; a sailed ship and five galleys were captured; out of 15,000–17,000 men, 5,000–6,000 were captured, wounded or killed. Although this defeat has been attributed by scholars to the weakness of the Ottoman fleet, it was actually caused by the tactical, administrative and strategic mistakes made by Grand Admiral Hüsameddin Pasha, who, despite the opposition of Cezayirli Hasan Bey (later Pasha), locked the fleet into a narrow bay at anchor side by side, allowing the enemy to attack with fire ships.[34]

Ironically, in the long run the Çeşme disaster contributed greatly to the awakening of the Ottoman reform movement in naval affairs. The reform movement started with the appointment of the energetic Gazi Hasan Pasha as Grand Admiral. Barracks (*Kalyoncular Kışlası*) were built at Kasımpaşa in order to train and discipline unruly sailors, and the men were paid a certain salary. These efforts paved the way for the emergence of the *Kalyonculuk* as a separate corps in the naval arsenal. Foreign naval engineers were employed in naval works. Under the guidance of French shipbuilders such as Le Roy and Durest, new ships were constructed on European lines. In order to provide technical training to naval officer candidates, the *Hendesehâne/Hendese Odası* (Chamber of Mathematics) was established at the *Tersâne-i Âmire* on 29 April 1775. Baron de Tott, Campbell Mustafa Aga and a Frenchman named Kermovan played important roles in the formation of this institution. On 5 November 1784, this school moved to a new building composed of a few rooms around the *Tersâne Zindanı*, which was constructed by Ataullah Efendi, the superintendent of the naval arsenal, expanded into a full-fledged school for naval engineers with both native and foreign teachers.[35]

Thanks to these reforms, the Ottoman navy began to develop rapidly. However, foreign observers tended to understimate its power, some describing a general picture based on individual examples, others portraying in numbers. For instance, Joost

Frederic Tor, the secretary to the Duch ambassador Van Dedem in 1785, mentioned the deplorable state of the Ottoman navy, citing the example of a ship on the stocks on the island of Lesbos that had been waiting for repair for one and a half years. He also described the uselessness of the Ottoman transport vessels at Çanakkale and the ruinous condition of the Dardanelles fortresses.[36] Although these comments might have been true to some extent, when compared with the Ottoman and other European sources it is clear that they were biased and inaccurate. Examples contradicting Tor's claims can be checked against the reports and observations of travellers and ambassadors, of which mention of a few will suffice. M. Bonneval's report of 22 April 1784 presented concrete data and threw considerable light on the condition of the Ottoman navy at the time.[37]

| Table 1. Condition of the Ottoman navy (22 April 1784) | | | | | | |
|---|---|---|---|---|---|---|
| Rates of the ship | In good condition | In bad condition | Confirmed ships (rigged out) | Unconfirmed ships (not rigged out yet) | On stocks | Construction site |
| Line of the battle: | | | | | | |
| 2 (74 guns) | | 1 | 1 | | 1 | Istanbul |
| 12 (64 guns) | 8 | 4 | 4 | 8 | | 10 Istanbul |
| 1 Rhodes | | | | | | |
| 1 Bordeaux | | | | | | |
| 10 (54 guns) | 8 | 1 | 4 | 5 | 1 | |
| 24 | 16 | 6 | 9 | 13 | 2 | |
| Source: PRO. FO 95/8/14 (25 April 1787), pp. 862–63. | | | | | | |

As shown in Table 1, the line-of-the-battle ships and frigates were the main contemporary forces while old galleys were still effective. In the following years, the replacement of these galleys by various man-o'-war ships would be witnessed. The following three tables, which indicate the state of the Ottoman navy on 25 April 1787, refer to the above-mentioned transition.[38]

Table 2. State of the Ottoman navy (25 April 1787)

| Type of ships | Their number |
|---|---|
| Galleys | 6 |
| Bomb ketches | 8 |
| Gun-boats carrying a 24-pounder and a mortar of 10 inches | 21 |
| Ships of the line | 9 from 70 to 76 guns<br>10 from 60 to 66 guns<br>7 from 50 to 54 guns<br>Total 26 |
| Frigates | 14 from 32 to 40 guns<br>10 from 24 to 30 guns<br>Total 24 |
| Sloops | 10 from 16 to 20 guns<br>30 from 8 to 12 guns<br>Total 40 |
| Of all types | 25 |

Source: PRO. FO 95/8/14 (25 April 1787), pp. 862–63.

Table 2 shows clearly that classical Ottoman galleys had become obsolete, leaving their place to sailed ships with bigger gun and fire capacity. Another striking point can be observed in the increase in the types of ships.

Table 3. Types of ships on the stocks and their gun capacities (25 April 1787)

| Type of ships on the stocks | Their guns |
|---|---|
| Ships of the line | 2 of 74 guns<br>2 of 64 guns<br>2 of 54 guns |
| Frigates | 2 of 40 guns |
| Total | 8 |

Source: PRO. FO 95/8/14 (25 April 1787), pp. 862–63.

Compared to Table 1, Table 3 indicates that the gun capacities of the ships were the same as in 1784. It seems that 40–74 guns were preferred with respect to the manoeuvrability of ships. This range was common in the navies of the world during the period.

As for the geographical distribution of ships, Istanbul appears as the leading place, with 56 ships; the Mediterranean as the second, with 39 ships, and the Black Sea as the third, with 30 ships. The striking point in Table 4 (see below) is the increasing number of sloops. Forty in number, these small sailing warships prove that the Ottomans planned to benefit from their manoeuvrability in battle. It can be argued that these 125 naval ships were the harbinger of the deterrent Ottoman naval force of the future.

| Table 4. Geographical distribution of the Ottoman navy (15 April 1787) | | | |
|---|---|---|---|
| **Repartition of the Ottoman navy** | | | |
| **Type of the ships** | **The Mediterranean** | **The Black Sea** | **Istanbul** |
| Ships of the line | 10 | 5 | 11 |
| Frigates | 5 | 8 | 11 |
| Sloops | 20 | 4 | 16 |
| Bomb-ketches | 2 | 2 | 4 |
| Gun-boats | 2 | 11 | 8 |
| Galleys | | | 6 |
| TOTAL | 39 | 30 | 56 |
| Of all denominations | 125 | | |

Source: PRO. FO 95/8/14 (25 April 1787), pp. 862–63.

In 1789, when Selim III ascended the throne, the Ottoman navy consisted of 18 galleons, 24 frigates, six *kırlangıç*, ten *şehdiye* (a type of two-to-three-masted sailing warship of 23–35 *zira* in length), eight *şalope* (sloop), 24 *bülbülce*, *çamlıca* (a type of *şehdiye*), *kerpe* and *Rum tırhandili* (a type of Greek light boat), all amounting to 90, irrespective of the active, inactive or size. On the biggest galleons were 600–750 crew who had mainly been transferred from merchant ships[39] and were far from being properly trained, and therefore were backward in comparison with the contemporary technology.[40]

# 2

# DEVELOPMENTS IN OTTOMAN SHIPBUILDING TECHNOLOGY IN THE LATE EIGHTEENTH AND EARLY NINETEENTH CENTURIES

The development of a sound naval technology required a powerful administration, a well-organised division of labour, plentiful material and skilled human sources, suitable geographical conditions, technical know-how and efficient channels of information. The Ottomans were luckier than many other nations with respect to these priorities. The geography in which they lived was generous enough to provide the raw materials required for naval technology. There was a well-organised division of labour starting from the felling and transportation of timber to the construction and launching of a ship. Neighbouring coastal areas were rich in skilled human power, though foreign technicians, engineers and officers could be employed in case the domestic technical know-how was insufficient. Technological developments were closely followed through with such methods as sending ships to assess enemy harbours, count the anchored ships and observe the state of their rigging, construction and repair facilities. Beside these, accounts of travellers and merchants, diplomatic and consular representatives and their paid agents, foreign officers, engineers and technicians working for rival countries constituted the official and relatively more reliable sources of information. More importantly, prize ships, wreckages and ships offered by foreign countries as gifts[1] and wreckages in general no doubt allowed the Ottoman naval technicians to examine the technical properties of the enemy fleets in order to create their own to overcome the shortcomings of their shipbuilding and navigational technologies.

This chapter examines some of the more important technological developments in the Ottoman navy. The main materials used in the construction of ships in the late eighteenth century, the process of shipbuilding, the introduction of copper sheathing of ships, the introduction of new tools, equipment and machines used in naval works, the construction of new shipbuilding structures and auxiliary forms, and developments in naval gunnery in the time in question are among the leading themes taken up here.

## The main materials used in the construction of ships in the late-eighteenth-century Ottoman Empire

The main materials for shipbuilding generally were supplied in two ways. First, the provinces that were rich in some materials delivered the required amounts to the naval arsenal in Istanbul to be stored for future use, or these provinces sometimes constructed one or two ships as part of their tax. This kind of tax was called *avârız*, while the method was named *ocaklık*. Second, the Ottomans also had recourse to the method of purchasing these materials from traders and producers during the preparations for naval campaigns. Among the main materials required for the construction of ships were timber, heath, iron, nail and bolts, copper, lead, sailcloth, pitch and tar, paint, tallow, resin, hemp, rope, wire, sulphur, oakum and ballast.

### *Timber (Kereste)*

Until the second half of the nineteenth century, wood continued to dominate as the main construction material since metals had not assumed much importance yet. A three-rated vessel (mounting 65–79 guns), for instance, in England cost roughly 1,000 pounds per gun, so a 74-gun vessel, for example, cost approximately 70,000 pounds. Half this figure was for timber, one-tenth for masts and one-seventh for the sail and rigging. Thus, the price of building lumber was of primary importance: its scarcity and cost were the determining factors in naval construction.[2]

It seems that the Ottomans, with their abundant timber sources, were luckier than most of the northern states, which were forced to look for overseas timber sources in order to carry out their maritime trade and wage war against their enemies. The Ottoman archives provide information about the timber sources, its transportation to the construction sites, its various types and quantities, as well as some domestic and foreign transactions for its supply.

The construction of new ships in an unexpectedly short time after the destruction of the Ottoman fleet at Lepanto (*Inebahtı*) in 1571 and in Çeşme in 1770 cannot be accounted for by anything but the ample timber sources and well-organised timber administration. Ottoman sources, in general, indicate that the types of timber used in shipbuilding and related naval works were mostly oak (*meşe*), pine (*çam*), elm (*karaağaç*), fir (*köknar*), larch (*melezçam*), chestnut (*kestane*), hornbeam (*gürgen*), ash tree (*dişbudak*), *kayacık* tree, lime tree (*ıhlamur*), *gökez* and *pırnar/pırnal* (Quercus ilex, holly oak, holm oak) trees.

European countries such as France and England, suffering from shortages of timber, sought ways to acquire this material from the Balkans and the Black Sea. France, previously prevented by the Porte, in order to secure the timber for masts from the Black Sea, followed a cunning policy and eventually succeeded to some extent by commissioning some French technicians and engineers in the construction of ships in the Imperial Naval Arsenal.[3]

Likewise, the British government asked for permission from the Porte in order to cut oak trees in the forests in Albania.[4]

Considering the financial crisis the Porte suffered, Aldair, the British minister to Istanbul, made applications for ship timbers and proposed to the Grand Vizier a loan providing that Turkey permit the export of oak for the British navy. The consent was eventually secured.[5] In the following years, British interest in and need for Albanian oak seems to have continued.[6]

Among the timber sources of the Ottoman navy in the late eighteenth century were Midilli, Kazdağı (*koğuşluk* pine),[7] the province of Canik,[8] Taşoz (oak, elm), Rumeli (oak, elm),[9] Megri, 60 miles from Rhodes, Biga (*pırnar* tree/treenail/*kavilya*[10]), Iznikmid (hornbeam/*gürgen lata, kemerelik lata-i kebîr-i çam, piraçol-ı kebîr-i meşe*,[11] *felenklik* and *kızaklık*[12]), Kidros, Cide (timber for masts), Misivri, Ahyolu, Segen, Ayna Island (oak),[13] Gemlik,[14] Domaniç

(large pine timbers for *kemerelik* and *lata-i kebîr*), Gökâbâd (tim-
ber for *lata-i kebîr, mangatsa* and *kemerelik*),[15] Gümülcine,
Karaağaç,[16] Bolu, Mudurnu, Âbâd Yaylası, Elmacık Dağı, Sarı Ot
Dağı (oak for *koğuş* and *lata* timber),[17] Seferihisar, Mihaliçcik,
Günyüzü, Gökçedağ, Beypazarı, Bergama, Tuzla, Ayvalık,
Karahisar, Kurupazarı, Kozak, Soma, Kırkağaç, Akyazı, Darıçayrı,
Sarıçayır and Bidayic.[18]

As of 1803, the best and cheapest timber, both for shipbuilding
and other purposes, came from the Black Sea region, from Samsun
and Sinop and several other places down to Akçahisar. In the first
two places, there were regular dockyards. Therefore, the best markets for the purchase of timber were Inebolu, Meset, Faacas, Bartın
and Akçahisar. These places were frequented by Russian ships,
laden with iron, an article much in demand along that entire coast.
Timber also came from Galatz in Rumelia, particularly in quantities
suitable for masts. The fir trees of Asia were of a superior quality
and cheaper than the ones in Europe, but they were harvested in
smaller quantities because of the difficulty of floating rafts from the
Asian coast against the winds and current, both of which were
favourable to the transportation of timber from the Danube to the
Bosphorus.

For foreign states, the purchase of timber was at all times more
efficient with the assistance of a *firman* from the Porte, but it was
possible to get it done without such aid, by forging understandings
with the different Ottoman commanders and by making regular
payments to them. As the newly admitted foreign ships were to be
exempted from custom house visits, the timber trade in large spars
and masts could be carried on independently of the Ottoman government.[19]

The size of the timber changed according to the size of the ship.
For instance, 60 large timbers of 40, 34 and 32 *zira* (75 cm) for
masts were required for a three-decker under construction at the
naval arsenal on 18 October 1797. The local authorities were
odered to search for and provide these masts from Kidros and
Cide.[20]

Timber was used in a variety of works related to shipbuilding.
Beside its use in the construction of masts, yards, planks,[21] keels,
knees, hulls, broadsides, rudders, tillers and water barrels, timber
was also used for the production of pulleys. Especially ash tree,

*kayacık* and elm trees were needed for that purpose.[22] Timber was essential in the construction of tools and equipment used in naval works and dry docks as well. In 1795–96 a certain amount of *teknelik elvah-ı ıhlamur kalas* (timber for hulls), *sütun orta çap meşe* (oak for average columns), *kanatlık elvâh-ı çam* (pine plates for wings), a sack of *ambar sandal* (timber for boats), *kumluk sakadiye* and some others were provided from the *mahzen-i çûb* (timber store) for the construction of two workbenches (*destgâh*), a wheel with a clamp (*mengeneli çarh*) and some other tools.[23] Furthermore, timber for yards (*serenlik kereste*) was used in the production of cannon moulds in Hasköy in the beginning of September 1795.[24] There is evidence indicating that 500 pieces of elm tree provided from the province of Salonica were needed for the production of gunstocks to be used on the three-deckers, galleons and frigates in 1796–97.[25]

Timber was named in many ways. The regions from which it was supplied and the part of the ship in which it was used were two important references in naming the timber. In a register book (*defter*) dated 22 July 1803 that shows the timber bought from a certain Kosta, we come across the following names: *Kara sağir, çam tahtası* (pine wood), *çifte kanatlık, bostan oluğu, çifte bordalık, çifte çam tahtası, çifte kalas, on iki arşın lata* (thinnish board of 12 *zira*),[26] *on iki arşın kebir çam* (12 pieces of large-sized pine timber), *çifte mane, kestane agacı tahtası* (timber of chestnut tree), *Rumeli omurgası* (timber for the keel from Rumelia), *Kidros omurgası* (timber for the keel from Kidros), *Bartın kanatlığı, Karasu tahtası* (timber from Karasu), *Fındıklı dolabı*,[27] *Fıstıklı koğuşu*[28] and so on. In addition to these types were the following ones used in Sinop: *asdar* (pine), *barbelik, barbe-i kebîr, baryalık-ı kebîr, bedel koğuş kablı, bedel koğuş çam kablı, çubuk çam, diyame-i sağîr* (any tree), *diyame-i kebîr* (any tree), *döşek, döşek mişe kütük* (oak), *ecnâs-ı çam* (pine), *felenk, fındık çubuğu* (*tecne çubuğu*), *katene, kazıklık* (hornbeam for stakes), *kızak, koğuş* (pine), *koğuş-ı çam* (pine), *kütük* (log), *kütük-i mişe* (oak log), *iskelelik* (timber for building wharves), *ırğad-ı sağîr* (elm for pulleys), *ırğâd-ı man-ula, latakına, levm-i yar, makaralık-ı kebîr* (big sizes of elm log for pulleys), *makaralık-ı sağîr* (small sizes of elm), *makas direk* (fir for masts), *mertanlık kürek, mülk, omurga* (keel), *tahtalık* (pine wood), *tahtalık-ı çam* (pine wood), *taslak kürek, tiyame-i sağîr, üsküce, küyeşte, varyozluk* (elm for the production of heavy hammer), *varyalık, yarpalık, seren direği* (*gökez* tree for yards) and *seren-i sağîr* (timber for small yards).[29]

Most of these types are mentioned in a document dated 21 March 1797 as well, with some additions including *Tırhandil-i kebr-i çam, yeke-i dümen, ser kütük, çatal bükme, çatal kazık, kemerelik lata-i kebir-i çam* and so on.[30] To give an idea about the required timber and its types for a new galleon of 55,5 *zira* constructed on 15 November 1783, some 500 pieces of timber were needed. Among them were *bodoslama-i baş, bodoslama-i kıç, pare-i bodoslama-i baş, asdar-ı bodoslama-i baş, asdar-ı bodoslama-i kıç, akreb-i baş, kanad-ı kalyon, pare-i kanad-ı kalyon, pıraçol-ı akreb-i kıç, karina, asdar-ı karina,* and *bükme çatal.*[31]

As for the system of measurements used in the wood trade and in the building of naval ships, *zirâ, arşun, kadem, karış, kulaç* and *umk* were the basic units. Out of these measures, *zirâ* and *arşun* were equal units of length, while *kadem* was for width. In measuring the width of the timbers, *karış* and *kulaç* were used, while *umk* was used for their depth.[32] It is important to note that some French measures of length were also used. For instance, at the end of Mahmud Raif Efendi's book entitled *Tableau des nouveaux rēÉgle-ments de l'Empire Ottoman*, pictures of ships constructed by French engineers were measured in French *pic*, corrresponding to the Ottoman *arşun/arşın.*[33]

### Heath (Funda)

Consisting of various types of small trees, heath was burned to dry out boats, galleys and galleons when their hulls were first constructed. It was also used during the caulking process. Towns such as Üsküdar, Çengel, İstavroz and Kuzguncuk were among the main suppliers of heath.[34] There were more than 500 kinds.[35]

### Raw Iron (Âhen-i Hâm)

In the late eighteenth century, iron, both raw and processed, was used in many forms in the Ottoman navy. Mostly coming from Samakoçak/Samakovcuk[36] and Ayna (or İne) Adası,[37] it was generally stored in and delivered from the *mahzen-i surb* (store for iron pieces, nails, copper pots, lead plates, hemp, cords, barrels, sail, awning, anchor, cannon, lamp and paper).[38]

The Imperial Mint (*Darphâne-i Âmire*) also stored, processed and delivered iron when the need arose. Raw iron was mainly used in the manufacture of common anchors (*lenger*), warping anchors[39] (*tonoz demiri*), nails, hands/cranks (*akrep/kol*), bolts and screws, rings, axes, sledgehammers (*balyoz/variyoz*), sledgehammers for fids[40] (*variyoz-ı kaşkaval*), chisels, shovels, torches (*meşale*), rings for water barrels (*çember-i macana-i âb*), axles (*mil*), forks, tongs, levers (*manivela*), augers/drills for guns (*burgu-i top*), hooks for gunports (*kanca-i lumbar*), hooks for threefold purchase[41] (*kanca-i firaşkon*), hooks for cat david/catheads (*kanca-i griva*), hooks for boats (*kanca-i sandal*), cannons, some joints and parts of gun-stocks, common chains, chain plates of backstays (*landa-i pater-aça*), hawses (*gomana*), stoves (*ocak*)[42] and so on.[43]

In addition, raw iron was affixed, in plates, to the inner sides of the ship hulls to isolate fires from the broadsides of the ships[44] as well as to fasten joints in the construction and repair works.[45] Finally, iron imported from Samakov, Sweden and Hungary was also used in the production of steel in the naval arsenal by engineers.[46]

### Nails and bolts (Mismâr and Civata) used in naval works

Nails were produced by ironsmiths by smelting of a variety of substances. Nails made of wood, iron, copper and a copper–zinc mixture might be used, depending on the structure of the ship. For instance, copper nails were used to fasten the copper planks onto the bottoms and hulls of the ships. Under the conditions where the use of pure copper was not possible, nails produced from the copper–zinc mixture were preferred in 1795–96.[47] A decree by Kaptan-ı Derya Küçük Hüseyin Pasha to Murâbıtzâde Hasan, the governor of Rhodes (13 October 1792), illustrates why certain materials were preferred for producing nails and bolts. The nails and screws used in the fastening of the imperial galleons, since they were all made of raw iron, caused ships to be heavy as well as increased the consumption of iron. Moreover, iron nails rusted, damaging the timber of the ships' hulls. He recommended that, if, as was done on the ships of the Christian states, pegs called *kavilya* made from the *pırnar* tree were used instead of iron and if they were fastened to the timber at certain intervals, decay would be prevented. Being made of wood, the pegs would fit snugly into the timber of the hull of the ships. So, three sizes of wooden peg samples were sent and the production of 10,000 from each sample was ordered for the naval arsenal.[48] Later correspondence in 1796–97 shows that wooden pegs were preferred to iron nails and that the mountains in the province of Biga were rich in *pırnar* trees.[49]

*Funda/Fonda* coal (*funda kömürü*) and *hark-ı nâr* (a substance used in the melting process) were used to melt and pour the raw iron into moulds for the production of nails and some other iron tools to be used in the construction of frigates and galleons.[50] The cast nails were filed when necessary.[51] Bolts were used in the construction of galleons as well. Ironsmiths utilised pine coal for this purpose. This coal was provided from Midilli, Molva and Kalonya for a galleon being constructed in Midilli in 1793–94 at its current value.[52]

In discussing the importance of nails for naval constructions, it is worth noting that the Swedish engineer RhodéÈ was commissioned to construct a nail-production workshop in October 1805. He and his translator were assigned a monthly salary of 750 *kuruş* in total.[53]

Among the types of nails and bolts produced were *mismâr-ı basdika-i sağîr* (nails for snatch blocks of small size), *mismâr-ı basdika-i kebîr* (nails for snatch blocks of big size), *mismâr-ı mesâmîr*, *mismâr-ı kostanyola*, *cıwata-i piraçol* (bolts for fastening knees), *cıwata-i karîne* (bolts for the bottom of a ship), *kavilye* (treenails, pegs), *mismâr-ı atîk* (nails removed from old ships),[54] *mismâr-ı üstâdiye*,[55] *mismâr-ı yâş*,[56] and *mismâr-ı nühâs* (copper nails).[57] Beside them, others such as *mismâr-ı kalafat* (caulking nails), *şumârî*, *şayka*, *çubuk*, *Trabzon*, *Samakov*, *Lofça*, *Zağra*, *şişe*, *büzürk* (big size), *meyâne* (medium size), *bölme*, *pedavra*, *taş* (stone), *kalafat-ı tulumba* (for caulking conduits), *zevrak* (boat), *kayık* (boat), *baskı-i kayık*, *kalay* (tin), *mertek* (beam), *gevele-i tahta*, *gevele-i körpe*, *gevele-i kuşak*, *sağış-ı büzürk*, *sağış-ı meyâne*, *taban* (base), *çatı*, *sağrı*, *meyâne-i hurda* (scrap nails of average size) and *çâr-kûşe* (square) can be mentioned.[58]

### Raw copper (Nühâs-ı Hâm)

Copper was used in the construction and equipment of the Ottoman ships in a variety of ways. In the late eighteenth century, it was mainly used in the cladding of ships against shipworms, for the nails and some joints of the ships, and for onboard equipment[59] such as pots and pans and other kitchen utensils and the cans for storing gunpowder and paints. It was also used in the production of cannon-loading tools such as cannon ladles (*kepce-i top*) and ramrods (*harbe*). Beside domestic sources, raw copper was provided from foreign locales. We know that it was occasionally purchased from Russian traders when the need arose.[60] It was processed in a *haddehâne* (processing house) before use.

### Lead *(*Kurşun*)*

Stored in the *mahzen-i sürb*, the *Cebehâne* (Armoury) or the Imperial Mint, *kurşun* was used as raw lead, bullion or plates after being cast in moulds and processed. To exemplify, it was mainly used in the making of the hawseholes of chain cables (*gomana delikleri*), as complementary material to the copper cladding of the ships, in the making of tools and equipment, in producing the sets for naval flags, in the construction and mending of the outer gates of the big dry dock, in producing the touch-hole of muzzle-loaders (*falye deliği*)[61] and in making bullets for rifles.[62]

In a petition of 1790–91, Cebecibaşı stated the need for providing 700 *kantars* of lead bullion from the Imperial Mint, to be used on the imperial galleons that would sail off for a campaign next year and for casting lead for the needs of the ironsmiths and sets for naval flags, since there was no lead bullion left in the arsenal of Enderun/the Palace School.[63]

In the sixteenth century, lead was generally provided from Rudnik, Novo, Kratova, Serbrenice and Olowa in Rumelia as well as from Gümüşhane, Keban and Ereğli in Anatolia. In the seventeenth century, Üsküp emerged as one of the main sources of lead.[64]

Some shipbuilding materials, including ten lead plates, were demanded for the imperial galleons under construction on 8 July 1792 from *Cebehâne-i Âmire* via Kapucubaşı Altıkulaçzâde El-Hâc Hüseyin, the governor of Kastamonu and the official in charge of the construction of a galleon in Sinop.[65]

Lead plates were used in the holes of the chain cables (*gomana delikleri*) of galleons and frigates as well. For the lead plates to be used in this way on a galleon being constructed at the naval arsenal and on a frigate being built in Rhodes, 1,000 *vukıyyes* of bullion lead were required on 4 March 1793.[66] For that purpose, 3,023 *kıyyes* (80 *akçes* per *kıyye*) of 200 lead plates were bought and delivered to the *mahzen-i surb*.[67]

Also, Bozkır mines produced lead for the Imperial Mint and the Imperial Naval Arsenal. Lead was transferred to the Alaiye wharf and then to the arsenal via either imperial or private ships.[68] It was needed as a complementary material in the copper sheathing of the ships as well. Thirty-two and 34 *vukıyyes* of large lead plates were demanded for the *Ejder-i Bahrî* on 9 October 1796.[69]

In order to manufacture 156 lead plates, 4,872.5 *vukıyyes* of raw lead provided from the *mahzen-i surb* were cast in moulds by the *Kurşuncubaşı* (the chief official in charge of providing and processing lead) in 1797–98. The cost for the casting process was 243.5 *kuruş* in total at six *akçes* per each *kıyye*.[70] Eighty-two large lead plates (2,939 *kıyyes* of raw lead) at six *akçes* per *kıyye* were provided by the *mahzen-i surb* via el-Hâc Mehmed Ağa, the chief lead provider, in 1797–98 for naval ships.[71]

Lead was also used in the construction and mending of the outer gates of the big dry dock in 1800.[72]

Regarding the casting of lead in the circular shapes (*göz kurşunları*) for the holes of chain cables (*gomanas*) of the naval galleons, 627 *kuruş* were paid as the casting cost for 9,947 *kıyyes* of lead in 1801–02.[73]

In the year 1803, 200 *kantars* of lead were demanded for the equipment and fitting out of the three-decked *Mesudiye* galleon and some other ships. But considering the 140 *kantars* of lead (costing 3,542 *kuruş*) given in the previous year, this time 150 *kantars* of lead at 23 *paras* per *kantar* (total 3,795 *kuruş*) were allotted to these ships.[74]


### Sailcloth (Kirpas)

Sailcloth was a type of cloth woven from canvas and used in the production of sails and awnings of sailing vessels. The province of Gelibolu, the Dardanelles (Çanakkale), the island of Negroponte (Eğriboz), Egypt, the Aegean coasts, Benefşe and Cyprus were the main sources for the raw materials of sailcloth in the seventeenth and eighteenth centuries.[75]

It has already been discussed how the transition from the traditional oar-powered galley type ships to the galleon type sailing ships created a huge demand for sailcloth. Mehmet Genç shows clearly that this demand increased from 140,000 *ziras* in 1774 to 300,000 *ziras* in 1803.[76]

In order to meet this increasing demand for sailcloth production from the late seventeenth century onwards, the state established a large workshop (*Kirpâshâne*) attached to the Imperial Naval Arsenal in 1709 and gave its management to an entrepreneur called *bezcibaşı* (chief official in charge of cloth production), who undertook the supply of the navy in peace years with 30,000 *ziras* and in war years with 200,000 *ziras* of sailcloth. After 1750 the private weaving of sailcloth was prohibited and a monopoly granted to the *bezcibaşı*. It became a complete state monopoly after 1825.[77]

In some cases, the Porte sought sailcloth material from Russia. On 27 September 1797, the Porte purchased 83 rolls of thick Russian sailcloth from a Russian trader called Dimitri at a cost of 30 *kuruş* per roll. The total cost amounted to 2,490 *kuruş* and this money was paid from the allotted part of the Imperial Mint.[78] In 1803–04 Aydın, Tire, Gelibolu and Boğazhisar were the leading sailcloth providers.[79]

Selim III's reforms envisaged that all the sails, ropes and equipment belonging to frigates and other ships would be stored in hangars. Ship commanders were responsible for the proper sewing or fixing of sailcloth.[80]

Ottoman archival documents of the eighteenth century often mention the names and types of sailcloth. For instance, a document of 1790–91, with the title 'der sefîne-i trabago süvari-i Sinan oğlu Hasan Reis' ('A trabacco ship commanded by Sinan Oglu Hasan Reis'), demonstrates that green sailcloth was used in the stern part of the ship. It is apparent from the same document that the ship in question carried 40 used (*müstamel*) sailcloths as back-up. In 'defter-i sefine-i trabago süvari-i Salih Reis' ('A trabacco ship commanded by Salih Reis'), another type of green sailcloth used in the stern part of a ship as well as 40 spare ones are mentioned. Green sailcloth in the stern and 40 spares also appear in 'sefine-i trabago süvari-i Ülgünlü Yusuf Reis' ('A trabacco ship commanded by Ülgünlü Yusuf Reis'). In 'defter-i pirgandi-i Mahmud Paşa süvari-i Ahmed Reis' ('The register of Mahmud Paşa ship commanded by Ahmed Reis) are listed green sailcloth in the stern and two types of spare ones: five *kirpas-i bogaz* and ten *kirpas-i beyaz* (white sailcloth)[81]

Some other documents mention the use of sailcloth on ships as well. In 'defter-i mühimmat-ı *Cabbâr-ı Bahrî* süvari-i Fettah Kapudan ('The register of the inventory of the ship *Cabbâr-i Bahrî* under Fettah Kapudan's command') of 6 July 1790–91 is noted green sailcloth, and among the ship's spare equipment were 60 *kirpâs-i kârhâne*, ten *kirpas-i buhar*, 30 *kirpas-i beyaz* (white sailcloth) and 30 *kirpâs-i mustamel* (used sailcloth).[82]

### *Pitch and tar (*Zift *and* Katran)

Pitch and tar were among the materials necessary for caulking ships. They were mostly provided from Midilli as well as the Edremid and Gümrü regions of Kapudağı.[83] Sometimes pitch and tar were purchased from local and foreign traders at current market prices.[84] Sinop also provided these materials in the middle of the eighteenth century. Both pitch and tar were generally used in putting on the *iskarmoz* (tholepin/futtock)[85] and the head of nails during the caulking process.[86]

The Ottomans used Swedish tar as well. On 1 September 1796, 20 barrels of Swedish tar (at a cost of 26 *kuruş* per barrel) and 11 barrels of red paint (at a cost of 25 *kuruş* per barrel) were purchased by the *Kaptan Pasha* for the Imperial Navy. The total cost was 795 *kuruş*.[87]

Kazdağı, Alaylı and Ereğli appeared among the sources of tar in 1803–04. In one instance, for 2,500 *kantars* of tar coming from Kazdagi, 7,500 *kuruş* were paid. At another time, payment of 4,760 *kuruş* was made for 1,587 *kantars* of tar coming from the Alayli and Eregli regions, including the freight.[88]

Ottoman documents indicate the preparations for the construction of a pool for storing tar (*katran havuzu*) at the *Liman Mahzeni* within the naval arsenal in 1804–05. The cost for such expenses as mounting the gate of the pool and materials such as stakes, timbers and the examination of a suitable place for laying the foundation was expected to be 7,553 *kuruş*. In order to meet the cost, 5,000 *kuruş* in cash was requested from the *Hazîne-i Âmire*.[89]

### *Paint (*Boya)

Paint was used mainly to protect certain parts of the ships from bad weather conditions and to increase their durability. Among the materials of paint in the seventeenth century were *sülügen-i İngiliz* (a British type of red paint that was put on newly placed iron sheets as a coating material), *senderus* (glue and oil extracted from the copal tree), *bezir yağı* (linseed oil), *jengâr* (poisonous green rust on copper), *istîfdâç/üstübeç* (white lead used to obtain the desired paint thickness) and *siyah tutkal* (an infusable elastic substance composed of gomelica, rubber and neft).[90]

It is understood that for the flags and banners of *Arslan-i Bahri*, boarded by the *Kaptan Pasha*, and of some other ships, a certain amount of paint was needed. Expenses for paint, silk and sewing amounted to 1,339 *kuruş* in 1795–96.[91] Eleven barrels of red paint were purchased from a Swedish ship at 25 *kuruş* per barrel in 1796–97.[92]

Coloured dyes were used for drawing some patterns and embroideries on the ships as well. The total money spent on *elvan boya* (coloured dyes), *ruğan-i bezîr* (linseed oil), *altın varak* (golden sheets) and some other materials to be used in adorning and decorating the naval ships for three months amounted to 6,187 *kuruş* and 9 *para* on 14 November 1802.[93]

### *Tallow (*Don Yağı/Revgân-ı Pîh*)*

Tallow was produced via melting and then freezing the internal hard fats of animals. It was mostly used for manufacturing candles and soaps as well as greasing ships during the caulking process.[94] It was used in a mixture together with soap to coat the hull during cleaning[95] and to light candles and clean the pitch from caulkers' hands.[96] In the late seventeenth century, 600 *kantars* of tallow were provided from Boğdan as *ocaklık*. Sometimes it was bought from merchants.[97] Albania, Eflak[98] in the seventeenth century, and Varna and Galatz[99] at the turn of the nineteenth century appeared among other sources of tallow. It is understood that tallow was used in greasing the ships and their slipways (*kızak*) during the launching process. For this purpose, 500 *vukıyyes* of tallow was demanded on 18 October 1797 for a galleon whose construction was almost complete in Bodrum. During the launching of a frigate constructed in Limni, 293 *kuruş* were paid for 553 *vukıyyes* of tallow.[100]

### *Resin* (Reçine)

Resin is a thick, sticky substance produced by pine trees. It was used for hardening the pitch, for caulking and for spreading on the part of the ships below the waterline in a mixture with tallow. It was provided from Mediterranean islands such as İskiri, İskolar, İşkeron and İşkopolos in the second half of the seventeenth and early eighteenth centuries. In 1702–03 people living on İşkopolos Island were ordered to prepare 1,000 *kantars* of resin per year to be used during the caulking process of the ships.[101] Beside these places, Eğriboz (the island of Negroponte, Evvoia) and Çamlıca produced resin.[102] On 19 October 1792, 3,000 *kantars* of resin were demanded from Eğriboz and neighbouring areas. The judge of Eğriboz sent 800 *kantars* of resin on the ship of a foreign merchant. When it arrived in Istanbul, 44 *kantars* were missing. The remaining 756 *kantars* of resin were put into the *mahzen-i sürb*. One hundred and fifty *kuruş* were paid for 750 *kantars* of resin.[103]

### *Raw hemp* (Ham Kendir)

Raw hemp was used mostly for producing rope (*ispavli*). The Aydın region was an important supplier of raw hemp. Two thousand and five hundred *kantars* of hemp were ordered from the governor of Aydın, Hüseyin Bey, on 17 February 1793.[104] Raw hemp coming, for instance, from Aydın, was processed in a place called *Darağacı* (Gallows) by workers called *resenci* and *alatcı esnafi* (rope makers), and then was sent to the specified storage facilities on 28 September 1794.[105] In addition to the Aydın region, Tire also supplied raw hemp for the Imperial Naval Arsenal. It is recorded that for 3,500 *kantars* of raw hemp, 20,000 *kuruş* were paid in 1803–04. Sinop appears among the suppliers of hemp and wire in the late seventeenth century.[106] In addition to these sources, Russian traders provided raw hemp for the arsenal.[107]

### *Rope* (Resen), *wire* (Tel) *and* İspavli

There was a class of artists dealing with the production of rope at the Imperial Naval Arsenal. They usually worked in the empty sheds near *Darağacı* and processed raw hemp and other raw materials to produce various kinds of rope for the ships.[108] As seen in 1797–98, rope makers were paid a further 3,000 *kuruş* in addition to the previous 2,000 *kuruş* in return for their production of Frank wire (*tel-i Frengî*) and rope.[109]

Wire was generally produced in Canik or bought from traders. A document of 1792–93 says that *ocaklık tel* (wire obtained through the method of indirect taxation) was a bit thicker and of mediocre quality, while that of the traders was thin and of good quality. When the workers were asked what the reason for this difference was, they cited the low wages. Therefore, the authorities ordered the balancing of the wages between the producers of the two types in order that wires be durable.[110]

### Sulphur *(Kükürt)*

Sulphur was one of the chemical substances used in greasing ships. It was usually stored at the *mahzen-i sürb*. On 23 January 1790, there were 33,000 *vukıyyes* of sulphur in *Cebehâne-i Âmire*.[111] Since there was no sulphur left in *mahzen-i sürb*, 2,000 *vukıyyes* of sulphur were demanded from the *Cebehâne* in 1797–98.[112]

### Oakum *(Üstübî)*

Oakum, a caulking material, consisted of flax, hemp and pieces of worn-out rope and was used to fill gaps between the timbers of hulls before the process of tarring and applying pitch.[113] In addition to the storage facilities at the naval arsenal,[114] Cairo was one of the most important sources of oakum in the late eighteenth century. In 1791–92 the Porte demanded from Egypt 250 *kantars* of oakum for the construction of a galleon in Bodrum.[115] Mahmud Raif Efendi also pointed out the importance of oakum for caulking. Because of negligence in previous years, Ottoman ships had constantly taken in water. Therefore, the *Kaptan Pasha* had 200 trained caulkers brought from Egypt. He had a large barracks constructed for them and supplied them with food and clothes. This remedy became successful, since the ships stopped taking in water, even if they stayed at sea for three or four years.[116]

### Ballast *(Safra)*

Ballast is a load of such materials as stone, sand and mine that is put into the bilges of sailing ships to provide balance. In Ottoman times, it was loaded on and emptied from the holds of ships through a porthole called a *safra lumbarı*.[117] Ballast was removed from ships before they were taken into the docks for caulking and repair in order to reduce the weight.[118] It consisted of a layer of loose stones, called 'shingle', spread on the top of flat blocks of iron called 'pigs'. This weight kept the ship upright and balanced. However, it also posed a health risk, because everything drained into it. On some French ships, dead men were buried in the ballast.[119] In some extreme cases, in addition to stones and soil, large cannons or even men were put into the holds of galleons.[120]

Ballast was thus an important material for galleons. Low-quality ballast could cause a ship to corrode and sink. Imperial edicts were issued to forbid the use of low-quality ballast and encourage the supply of high-quality materials. For instance, an imperial edict of 23 December 1792 addressing the notables of Praviște and Drama noted that, since the ballast used on imperial galleons consisted of stones and soil, when it met with rain, it became mud and caused the corrosion of the ships. Therefore, it was decided that the soil to be put in the ballast areas on ships should be cast and made from mines of local origin in order to prevent hazards and increase efficiency. Three hundred thousand *vukıyyes* of ballast stone would be produced according to the samples sent to the above-mentioned places. Ballast made of *helon* would be prepared in three classes by the sample: 20, 31 and 40 *vukıyyes*, at a price of five *akçes* per *vukıyye* and 25 *akçes* for each 100 *vukıyyes*. The prepared ballast would be transferred to Kavala wharf first, then to Istanbul via ship.[121] The total cost and freight were planned to be 13,000 *kuruş*. Half of this would be paid after delivery.

### The process of shipbuilding in the late eighteenth century

*Tersâne-i Âmire* on the Golden Horn was the main assembling centre, where ships were constructed, completed, equipped and rigged. The dockyards in the provinces generally constructed only the hulls, while other places furnished a certain amount of ropes or sailcloth.[122] This was a general division of labour. The eighteenth-century shipbuilding process throughout the world is, by and large, applicable to the Ottoman realm. Timber was felled and transferred, through local administrators, to the stores (*mahzen-i çub*) at the Imperial Naval Arsenal. Mainly, the *çekeleves*[123] of individual traders or of the state were used for transportation, and this was carried out before the winter.[124]

Seasoning seems to have been an ignored or neglected process, although a vital one for the longevity of a ship. Long-lasting wars and the urgent need for a powerful navy in the late eighteenth century were no doubt at least some of the reasons behind this trend. Some foreigners criticised the Ottomans' methods of both felling timber without paying the necessary attention to choosing the proper types of timber for naval construction and felling the timber in any of the four seasons of the year irrespective of the proper time.[125] This criticism, however, should be assessed with some reservation, considering the many Ottoman imperial edicts ordering local authorities to cut and send specific and high-quality timbers, as well as some foreign documents mentioning the high-quality timbers.

During the construction process before launching, different masters could construct different parts of ships, depending on their skills. For example, engineer Mustafa Hace was commissioned in the construction of the cutwater (*talimar*) of the bow, caulking and building of the stern and the upper part of the stern of a galleon under construction on 5 September 1797. He was given some measurements (*endâze*) to work with. After the completion of his part, other builders were employed in the launching. We learn that Nikola, an architect in Bodrum, and his brother Arem were temporarily commissioned in launching the galleon in question.[126]

The ships, completed on land to a great extent, were put on stocks or slipways for launching. The time between the putting of a vessel on stocks and the launch might depend on the supply of the required materials necessary for the completion of the ship in water.[127] With regard to this issue, a document dated 14 December 1799 says that a galleon of 59 *zira* was constructed and almost readied for launching on Rhodes by Hasan Bey, the governor of Rhodes. Following the launching, a considerable amount of money was then required in order to complete the construction of some unfinished parts.[128]

To sum up the process of shipbuilding in the Ottoman Empire, following the procurement of the required timber, first were the sternposts, second the keel and third the planking. After that, nails and screws were used as fastenings to keep them firm. Painting and details of timberwork followed. The construction process ended after the completion of the flooring, interior furnishing and sails.[129] Ottoman warships, like the ones in Europe, were composed of several decks. These can be listed from the top down in the following sequence: open deck (*açık güverte*), main deck (*palavra*), middle deck (*orta kat*), gun deck (*top ambarı*), orlop deck (*tavlon*) and lower orlop deck (*kontratavlon*)[130]

As for the physical disadvantages attributed to the Ottoman man-of-wars by foreigners, it is said that they had intervals between decks higher than was usual in European ships, in order to allow the crew to wear their high and elaborate headgear. This point is considered to have been a sacrifice to military fashion and rendered the vessels very high and thus less stable and unable to carry great quantities of sail without being in danger of capsizing.[131]

The eighteenth-century Ottoman vessels are also said to have been cumbersome, massive and bulky, with excessively high poops, superstructures and rigging as well as to have an unsound structure. A violent storm could break up a ship due to the excessive distances between the main beams. The use of soft wood and the failure in the application of regular caulking to the underwater planks were the main reasons leading the Ottoman ships to be unusually porous and prone to taking in water.[132]

Therefore, in order to decrease these disadvantages, Cezayirli Gazi Hasan Paşa lowered their decks, rendered their sterns less lofty, raised their masts and provided better tackling and a more regular gunnery in the third quarter of the eighteenth century.[133]

## The introduction of copper sheathing into the Ottoman navy

Ottomans seem to have been aware that the copper-sheathing technique, when it first appeared in Europe in the second half of the eighteenth century, had offered significant advantages. Among them were protection from wood-eating worm; the creation of a surface on which external weed and shellfish could not grow; an increase in sailing speed that not only reduced voyage times but made navigation easier, since if a vessel could move in light winds it was less liable to drift on ocean current; the applicability of copper sheathing to any shape or size of hull; providing an outer skin of copper protecting the hull to some extent; holding caulking materials in position; and reducing maintenance costs between voyages.

The disadvantages, such as high material and application costs, the risk of galvanic action and the deterioration of iron fastenings, and the fact that a coppered vessel could not be grounded in harbour without considerable risk to the sheathing and thus was restricted to harbours with water at all tides,[134] could not prevent the Ottomans from adopting this technology. However, some of these disadvantages were unknown to them initially. The Ottomans learned about these as a result of prolonged naval experiences. Thanks to academic work from the 1950s onwards, the nature, type and properties of the molluscs and crustaceans hazardous to the timbers in the seas surrounding Turkey have been identified.[135]

There is considerable evidence indicating the existence and application of this technology in ships built specifically in the reign of Sultan Selim III. There were at least 40 ships that were sheathed with copper between the years 1789 and 1802, mostly galleons, frigates and corvettes. This figure must have been higher considering the imperial edict issued in 1795–96. Indeed, it shows that the application of copper sheathing to ships proved to bear good results and it led the Sultan to order the authorities to try hard to outfit the remaining ships using this technology.[136] *Firmans* ordering the copper sheathing of ships were issued repeatedly. For instance, in a *firman* dated 1795–96, copper sheathing and painting were ordered for river ships (*ince donanma gemileri*)[137] when they were at anchor.[138] Following the copper sheathing of *Arslan-ı Bahrî* and *Şehbâz-ı Bahrî*, the same application was ordered in 1795 for *Pertev-i Nusret, Ejder-i Bahrî, Âsâr-ı Nusret, Bahr-i Zafer* and another three-decked galleon under construction. The estimate amount of raw copper required for all five ships was around 60,000 *kıyyes*. Since this process required casting very thin copper sheets processed twice, the copper coming from Gümüşhane would not be suitable; instead, that from Kastamonu or Ergani would be needed. It seems that copper-sheathing technology was limited to warships at the time.[139]

Mahmut Raif Efendi described copper sheathing in his account as well. He wrote that all the shipmen shared the idea that copper sheathing was the best way to protect ships. He noted that three ships, a three-decker of 67 *zirâ* and six *kâne*, a frigate of 55 *zirâ*, a corvette of 37 *zirâ*, and a boat (*filika*) for the Sultan were launched in a single day, which was something previously unseen.

The year before (1797), all of them had been sheathed with copper, and more ships were to be sheathed in 1798.[140] Therefore, it would not be misleading to regard most of the ships, especially warships constructed after 1795–96, copper-sheathed. Also, the prize ships and the ones received as presents would increase the number of shipped that were copper-clad at the time.

The earliest document found during this study indicating the Ottomans' application of the copper-sheathing technique dates back to 1792–93[141] In that year, the Ottoman government ordered the copper sheathing of a new galleon, and copper merchants were ordered to prepare copper planks on certain models. Once the copper sellers saw the model, they declared that the production of the model was different and would be more difficult than the one they had used previously, and therefore it would require more labour and money. Then the merchants were presented with lumps of unrefined copper for the production of the copper plates for the sheathing of the galleon in question. They were given 55 *akçes* per *vukıyye*, whereas it had been 35 *akçes* in the past. However, since the new technique required the use of copper nails, which were expensive, they found a solution by producing a new type of nail made of raw copper and zinc (*rûy-i mâye*) mixed in equal proportions. In order to test the efficiency of the new nail, they first produced five or ten test nails. After applying them to the copper plates, the authorities were convinced that the new method would work, so copper merchants were commissioned to cast this mixture in return for 50 *akçes* per *vukıyye*. It is noteworthy that such a decision was taken with the collaboration of the port commander (*liman reisi*), the chief architect (*başmimar*), the chief augerer of the naval arsenal (*tersane burgucubaşısı*) and copper merchants (*bakırcı esnafı*). The raw materials were provided by the state from the *mahzen-i sürb*.[142]

On 30 August 1795, 5,000 *vukıyyes* of raw copper were demanded urgently from the *Darphâne-i Âmire*[143]. For the copper sheathing of a three-decked galleon under construction at the naval arsenal, 10,000 *vukıyyes* of raw copper were required on 20 October 1801. Since there was not enough copper at the *mahzen-i sürb*, it was provided by the *Darphâne-i Âmire*, two-thirds of it low quality and one-third high quality. The cost, 6,666.5 *kuruş*, was met by the *seferiyye akçesi*.[144]

It seems that copper sheathing caused further changes in the structure of materials used in the construction of ships. It was noted on 14 September 1796 that it was a tradition that bearing pintles (*inecikler*) mounted on the rudders of the imperial galleons were made of iron. However, this traditional application was changed with an imperial edict ordering the introduction of copper sheathing of the ships constructed at the *Tersâne-i Âmire* and other sites outside of Istanbul. From then on, the former iron bearing pintles of the sheathed ships were replaced by ones made of bronze (*tunç*). Four *vukıyyes* of tin (*kali*), 32 *vukıyyes* of raw copper (*nühâs-ı hâm*) and 64 *vukıyyes* of zinc ferment or alloy (*rûy-i maye*) were needed for every 100 *vukıyyes* of bronze bearing pintles. Also, one *kıyye* of *hark-ı nâr* was required for every ten *vukıyyes* of the product. It seems that new regulations were applied to a new frigate under construction on Limni on the same date. It was declared that eight bearing pintles for rudders (465 *vukıyyes*) would be produced by Dimitri, the chief founder at the *Tersâne-i Âmire* on 3 September 1796.[145] The Ottoman authorities continued the copper-sheathing applications in the following years. On 3 January 1806, 30,000 *kıyyes* of copper were demanded from the *Darphâne-i Âmire* for the re-sheathing of five naval ships with copper plates (*nühas tahta*) and the repair of the copper elements of some other ships at the naval arsenal.[146]

### *The supply of copper for sheathing and its process*

Copper was an important strategic material. Its sale to foreign countries was forbidden and it was almost completely used by the state. The *Darphâne-i Âmire*, *Tophâne-i Âmire* and *Tersâne-i Âmire* were the main institutions using copper intensively.[147] The supply of enough copper for the sheathing of the ships was an important matter for the Ottoman navy. The Ottomans' main sources of copper were the mines in the regions of Ergani and Keban.[148] The raw copper was sent from these regions to storage facilities at the Imperial Naval Arsenal in Istanbul via land or sea routes. If the sea route was to be used, raw copper was first processed (*tabh ve tesviye*) in Tokat,[149] before being transferred to the Samsun wharf via carriages provided from the province of Canik and its surrounding villages, such as Kavak and Ezine Pazari, and then ships departed with copper bound for Istanbul. If the land route was to be chosen, copper was sent to the Iznikmid port (today's Izmit) before being processed in Tokat and then transported to the Imperial Naval Arsenal in Istanbul on ships. The Ottoman government commissioned the local administrators such as *muhassıl* (tax collector), *maden emini* (superintendent of mines), *kadı* (judge), *ayans* (local notables), soldiers and other notables through imperial edicts to operate the supply system.[150] The Tokat–İznikmid route was used until 1795, after which the Tokat–Samsun–Istanbul route had been preferred.[151] Sixty thousand *vukıyyes* of copper were allotted to the sheathing process as well as tools and equipment to be used on ships on 3 November 1796.[152] To have a general idea of the copper consumption, in 1797–98, 800,000 *kıyyes* of copper per year would be sent for the cannons to be constructed in Tophane and Haskoy and for galleons to be built at the *Tersâne-i Âmire*.[153]

*Mikyâs-ı Sefâin* (*Measurements of Ships*), a book translated by Diyarbakırlı Abdülhamid from an unknown writer in the beginning of the nineteenth century, shows that the number of copper plates of 28 and 32 *vakıyyes*, for sheathing the careen of a three-decker galleon with 120 guns, was 4,738. This figure was 3,850 for a three-decker *kapak* with 80 guns, 3,206 for a *kapak* with 74 guns, 1,390 for a frigate with 28 guns and 1,463 for a corvette with 18 guns.[154]

As it is judged from another document dated 1 September 1796, for the ships to be covered with copper, 29 *akçes* were to be paid per *vukıyye* and five *vukıyyes* of *hark-ı nâr* would be mixed with every 100 *vukıyyes* of copper. These wages were limited to the copper to cover ships only and were not valid for copper to be used for other equipment.[155] To give an idea about the amount of copper needed for ships, a document gives significant information. Although it does not give specifically the amount necessary for a single ship, it gives the total amount for a group of ships. It is understood that for two galleons (the *Seddülbahir* and the *Kaplân-ı Bahrî*), a new frigate and a few new corvettes, 63,000 *vukıyyes* of raw copper were given from the Imperial Mint from Fabruary 1799 to April 1799, during the time Seyyid Mustafa was the Superintendent of the Imperial Naval Arsenal. When this amount did not suffice, an additional 66,000 *vukıyyes* were given from the Imperial Mint between February–March 1800 and 1801. Ten thousand *vukıyyes* of copper were also given on 1 December 1800. The document states that those last 10,000 *vukıyyes* of copper cost 6,666.5 *kuruş*.[156] It also states that 10,000 *vukıyyes* of copper and copper nails were needed for a galleon of 63 *arşın*.[157]

The need for copper for the production of plates continued in the following years, with the Imperial Mint as the main supplier. Twenty thousand *vukıyyes* of copper were demanded from there. The *Tersâne-i Âmire* Treasury met the total cost, 15,833 *kuruş*.[158]

The copper that arrived at the storage facilities was further processed in the *haddehâne* (processing house) or some other places to obtain thin copper plates suitable for sheathing the bottom parts of the ships (usually under the water line). The *haddehâne* was a very important place for the processing of raw copper, and different tools were used to produce thinner copper planks.[159]

The Ottomans were aware of the suitability of nails made of copper or copper–zinc (*rûy-i mâye*) alloy for fastening the copper plates onto the hulls of the ships. It seems that this consciousness stemmed from trial and error rather than the knowledge of electrolytic reaction, which was something unknown even to the European countries in the 1780s.[160]

Copper and brass for sheathing the hulls or bottoms of the ships and for the construction and production of some other materials and equipment were sometimes obtained from other countries.

Two tables, prepared by John Glover, Pro-inspector General of the Imports and Exports of Great Britain on 21 March 1800 (Inspector General's Office, Custom House, London), refer to the year 1799 and the British copper and brass trade with other countries, including Turkey. The first table is an account of the quantity of wrought copper exported during that year. It shows that, by the Declarations of the Merchants Exporters, the average price of wrought copper exported in the course of 1799 was £. 6. 9s. per cwt, and accordingly, at that rate, the total value of the copper of 97,125 cwt, 2q., 7lb. was £. 626,459. 19s. 6d. Turkey, as a wrought-copper importer from the UK, is seen to have been above average (100 cwt, £.530). The second table, prepared by the same person, shows an account of the quantity of brass and plated ware exported during 1799 and states the real and nominal value thereof. It also distinguishes the countries to which the same has been exported. Here the average price of wrought brass exported in the course of 1799 appears, by the Declarations of the Merchants Exporters, to have been £. 7. 14s. 8d. per cwt, and accordingly, at that rate, the total value of the brass of 77,033 cwt 3q. 16lb. was £. 595,728. 15s. 5d. The plated ware was always entered by the merchants ad valorem, consequently the nominal value and the declared value were the same. In this second table, Turkey, as an importer of wrought brass and plated ware, is seen to have been above average (122 cwt 1q. and £. 522) as well.[161]

## New methods, tools, equipment and machines used in naval works

### *New galleon-launching method*

Until the second half of the seventeenth century, the galleons were constructed in hangars or sheds called *göz* or *çeşm* (shed), completed on land and then launched to sea. This method required the launching of the completed ships into the sea and putting the ships needing repair on stocks. Therefore, it was by nature a complex process requiring the employment of a great number of workers.[162] Apart from its economic disadvantages, the main drawback of this method was the fact that it caused the collapse of the bottom of the ship to as much as seven to eight *kanas*[163] due to the fact that during the launching process, the weight of the stern was transferred naturally onto the bow. French engineer Le Brun introduced a new method to overcome this problem. He suggested the launching of the galleons after the completion of their hulls on stocks up to their gunports. The rest of the ship would be completed in the sea, thereby reducing the pressure on the timbers during launching. This was a good solution to the problem, although it still caused a collapse of two to three *kanas*, which had to be fixed while the ship was in the sea during the construction of the rest of the ship, from gunports upwards. Le Brun applied this method first to a 59-*zira* galleon, most probably *Arslan-ı Bahrî*, in 1794–95, with the participation of the Sultan.[164] Le Brun's method was carried on for nearly 40 years.[165] Four ships, a three-decker of 67 *zirâ* and six *kâne*, a frigate of 55 *zirâ*, a corvette of 37 *zirâ* and a felucca (*filika*) constructed for Selim III were set to sea using this method.[166]

### *The introduction of the logbook and new navigational instruments*

The tradition of keeping logbooks (*seyir defteri* or *seyir jurnali*) started in 1796–97. During this time, logbooks covering naval and navigational regulations (*kavâid-i bahriye*) were given to the ships. All the captains carried Pirî Reis' *Kitâb-ı Bahriye* (the Book of Sea) as a guidebook, and they were responsible for completing and commenting on this precious book according to their own observations.[167] Additionally, the crew of a warship had to carry navigational equipment in order to find their route and geographical locations and to sail the ship into the intended country in safety. Among this equipment were compasses (*pusula*), sounding leads (*iskandil*) for measuring the depth of the sea[168] and hourglasses (*saat-i rîk/kum saati*). Most of this equipment can be found in the inventory of a frigate that was led by Fettah Kapudan.[169] Beside these instruments and books, some other tools were employed on the naval ships. It is known that the *Kaptan Pasha* ordered Alexan, a Russian trader, to provide newly invented maps, compasses and Frenk *fuğlas*[170] on 2 April 1801. In order to meet the expenses, 4,001.5 *kuruş* were paid from the *İrâd-ı Cedîd Hazinesi*.[171]

Some tools and instruments left by the late Râtıb Efendi and bought by the state for the Mühendishâne Library on 23 November 1801 include some navigational devices as well. On a list published by Beydilli, *rub' tahtası* (quadrant), *gemi pusulası* (ship compass), *gönye maa tahta* (set square with wood), *çâr kûşe pusula* (square compass), *pergâr-ı tâm* (a pair of compasses), *musavver kebîr kürre-i semâ* (big illustrated celestial globe), *akrebli ve ibreli basîtei âfâkî* (elevation wood with hand and needle), *müteharrik nemçekârî pusula* (moving compass of Austrian type) and many other tools, along with maps delineating the fortified and strategic sites and books related to navigation, shipbuilding and maritime commerce can be seen.[172]

### *The introduction of a new provisioning and central kitchen system*

A new provisioning system, providing the cooks of ships with wood, salt and oil sufficient for the entire voyage at the expense of the Treasury, was first installed on a new ship of the line, the *Bahr-i Zafer*, in 1794. All food was delivered to the captains, and the old practice of distributing the rations for each voyage to the men in their own homes in advance of sailing was abandoned. In central kitchens and allotted dining quarters, common meals began to be served at regular hours by cooks who were paid by the Treasury.[173]

Some argue that this provisioning system was applied not only to the *Bahr-i Zafer* but also to the *Humây-i Zafer* at the same time, in 1793–94.[174] This new procedure influenced future ships. There was a kitchen system on most naval ships that were launched in 1794. This system provided not only regular nourishment for the crew, but also eliminated the clutter and disorder that prevented cannons from firing efficiently because of the presence of the crew's private stoves (*maltız ocakları*).[175] Copper was adopted for general cookery and the decks were consequently cleared of an immense number of little independent fires contained in earthen pans, by means of which every man, or self-formed association, used formerly to prepare his own meals.[176]

Additionally, in order to eliminate the risk of fire, iron plates were affixed to the inner sides of the ships where the common galley stoves were located.

Another problem was also removed by the new system: that of the shops and stalls formerly established by individual seamen on lower gun decks, which rendered the cannon unmanageable and frequently inaccessible.[177]

These developments and regulations were observed by foreign states and applauded. The provisioning system especially was regarded as effective and close to the regularity in Christian navies.[178]

### *New mast machines*

Within the framework of the improvement works of the Ottoman navy in the aftermath of the Çeşme Incident, Baron de Tott had led the construction of a 120-*kadem* workbench for masts in the Imperial Naval Arsenal. Under Selim III, two new mast machines were constructed and put into operation in the arsenal in 1795. It is certain that it increased the speed and efficiency of the operations by which masts were prepared for ships.[179] This information is partly verified by Mahmud Raif Efendi's mention of a certain tool used for erecting masts into the ships and being in good working order in the arsenal in 1798.[180] The information given by Mahmud

Raif Efendi is in parallel with that in an Ottoman document dated 28 July 1802. The document tells about the need for repair of a crane (*macuna*) formerly used for fitting masts onto imperial naval ships. On the same date, the crane became worn out; its floor sank into the sea to the extent of one *zira* and the pillars of the crane collapsed. It was decided that refractory stone (*seng-i âteşî*) of one *zira* would be placed on the floor of the crane in order to get a solid footing. Plans were made to replace the pillars with massive, solid supports reinforced by iron and lead ties afer proper examinations. The estimated cost was 1,800 *kuruş*.[181] On the same subject, Hovennesyan mentions a wheeled and multi-cogged *maçuna* of Frenk invention before 1794 and says that thanks to that machine galleon masts were easily erected.[182]

Despite the information at hand, the types and working order of these machines is unknown, as is whether these machines were used in making masts or in erecting them only. However, it is known that Le Roy, a French shipbuilder in the service of the Ottoman Empire between 1784 and 1788, had established a structural design enabling the easy fitting of ship masts into their proper places with the aid of a lever, when he worked in the capacity of shipbuilding expert in the PyréÈnéÈes in 1765 before his arrival in Istanbul.[183] The machine described above might have been of the same kind.

### *Newly invented fire pumps/conduits* (**Ateş Tulumbası**)

Before the period under examination, fire pumps were used both on land and ships to put out fires. When they became worn out, they were repaired or renewed. In general, in addition to ships having pumps to discard the water that had penetrated the wooden-hulled ships,[184] there were many ships of the time that carried a pair of elm pumps placed just forward of the main mast. The suction principle was essential for the operation of these pumps, which drew water directly from an inlet at the side of the ship up through holes bored via single trunks of the elm tree. Hence, these pumps were not for removing water from the bilges, but to draw water from the sea, which was then delivered, under pressure, through outlets on the upper deck or the lower deck for putting out fires or washing the decks.[185] Most probably, the Ottomans used similar fire pumps to put on their ships.

In 1793–94, 14 fire pumps and 15 hoses loaded on Ottoman ships became worn out in the course of time and some needed repair while others needed replacement by the *Tersâne-i Âmire tulumbacıbaşısı* (the chief official in charge of supply and delivery of the pumps and related equipment). Among the items of 15 fire pumps were *prinç tas*[186] (brass bowl), *prinç çatal* (brass fork), *prinç burmalı mesarlar, prinç pulları* (brass washer), *lehim için nişadır ve kalay* (ammoniun choloride and tin for soldering), *prinç ağızlıklar ve eklemeler* (brass mouthpieces and accessories), *kavis-li* (curved hose), *demir-i ham* (raw iron), *kömür* (coal) and *sandık*[187] *ayak ve kolları* (legs and levers of coffer/pump). The total cost for the pumps and 15 hoses was 3,269 *kuruş*.[188]

The authorities, anxious to avoid accidents, were opposed to using these different pumps in the place of the ones to which there were accustomed. Therefore, on 8 November 1797, the fire pumps formerly misused or those required repair were fixed, arranged properly and readied for an emergency. Fire pumps provided from the *Tulumbacı Ocağı* (Fire Department) at the naval arsenal only (not the ones on the ships or the ones required during the caulking process) were to be used in fires on land. The hoses and pipes were also to be fixed, or renewed if necessary.[189]

Nonetheless, documents show that the Ottomans were in search of new fire pumps to be used in naval services. They seemed keen to adopt newly invented fire pumps from foreign countries. Engineer Selim (formerly Baily) was commissioned to go to England in 1803–04 by Kaptan Hüseyin Pasha and during the administration of the governor of the Imperial Naval Arsenal, Aziz Efendi, to learn the construction and manufacture of a newly invented fire pump (*ateş tulumbası*), for the gates of the large dry dock at the Imperial Naval Arsenal.[190]

*First enquiries about the purchase of steam engines, water raising and evacuation pumps from England*

One of the most important developments at the turn of the nineteenth century was the Porte's request in 1805 for a steam engine from England to be used in the dry dock at the naval arsenal. England's leading role, especially in shipyard construction, port technology and related branches, made it a technical exporter to the Ottoman Empire as well as to many other countries.[191] The first steam engine of the British navy was installed at Portsmouth for emptying dry docks in 1797.[192]

The Ottomans were aware of the developments in England and eager to acquire the technology. A British document (21 December 1805, Tarabya), written by Arbuthnot to the secretary of state, refers to the Ottoman government's request from the British government for a steam engine to be used at the naval arsenal to empty the large basins in which the ships of war were careened and repaired. The British authorities assessed and discussed this demand. They estimated that two of the basins were capable of containing a first-rate ship at the naval arsenal, that there were no tides in the harbour of Istanbul and that there was a considerable depth of water close to the shore. Therefore, in all probability, an engine of 30 horse would be sufficient. It seems that the aspect that preoccupied them the most was the difficulties and expense linked to the use of this engine. They thought that the difficulties would chiefly arise from the 'ignorance of the Turks of the proper erection and management of mechanical powers and from their being total strangers to the use of all complicated machines'.[193]

The British government requested information on how many and what kind of persons should be sent to Istanbul to oversee the erection, employment and repairs of the steam engine. It also asked for how long the Turkish government wanted to hire the steam engines and what wages as well as what additional expenses would be occasioned by the sending out of a large supply of spare screws, hikes, valves and pistons. The correspondences show that the British carefully considered such matters as the legality or illegality and prohibition of the export of the steam engine and possible objections to the idea of instructing foreigners in the use of this machine.

Mr. Hamilton's letter, dated 11 December 1805, shows that the Porte's request for the steam engine dated back to December 1803, when the Porte had enquired into the possibility of buying a steam engine through Mr. Baily. Baily had furnished the British authorities with the specifications of the dry docks at Istanbul, such as the dimensions of the docks, the height to which the water would be raised and the expenses.[194]

Baily had been commissioned to travel to England in 1803–04 by Kaptan-ı Derya Hüseyin Pasha and during the administration of the governor of the Imperial Naval Arsenal, Aziz Efendi, in order to learn the construction and manufacture of a newly invented fire pump (*ateş tulumbası*) for the gates of the big dry dock at the arsenal.[195]

In 1803 the height to which the water would be raised was 39 feet. The steam engine was prepared to work two pumps, each three feet in length. With such pumps, 12 feet would be required to empty the docks. Hamilton's letter shows that the specifications given in 1803 were changed later on, and the machine requested in 1805 turned out to be a different engine with different specifications.

As a result of the following correspondences between the British and Ottoman authorities, royal engineer Captain Squire explained the result of his enquiry into the specifications of the steam engine requested by the Porte:[196]

Dear Sir,
I have made enquiry respecting steam engines as you desired, the result is, that a good engine of Boulton and Watts construction, of the power of 30 horses for pumping water, will cost about 1200, to which must be added the cord of pumps if of large diameter, about 700 (1200+700=1900).
A rotative engine of the same power, suited to other purposes than drawing water, will cost about 1700.
Ditto- of the power of 20 horses ..................... 1300.
The above price is for engines finished in the common way, but I suppose it would be right, considering it in all points, then it should be higher finished, and in some parts more expensively than common engines are, which may add from 1 to 200 to the expense. There will also be some difference in the price of the pumps, according to the height the water is to be thrown, and the diameter of the pistons.
The above price is exclusive of fixing – and I suppose a person from this country must be sent to fix it, and set it going-
I shall wait on General Morse this day, and at the same time call on Mr. Hamilton and leave..., and hope I shall then so hoping as I fear it will be the only opportunity I shall have... from the coast as I intend to set off on Tuesday .
Most Sincerely yours,
Captain Squire
Royal Engineer
Mr. J. Renmil
27. Stamford Street
S... Road

Mr. Hamilton, in his corresponding letter, points out the ensuing factors:

December 2nd 1805
Mr. Hobson
In the forementioned paper Mr. Renmil states that the price of the steam engine required for the Porte would be £3222 delivered in London – In addition to which Mr. Renmil informed Mr. Hamilton that two persons should be sent with it to teach the use of it for at least one year at the expense of £250 for each: To this must be added the freight expenses.
The engine would be made in three months. The Mr. Bailey mentioned in Mr. Renmil's letter is a renegade Englishman, with a suffice knowledge of mathematics and mechanics to pass for a good mechanical engineer among the Turks: he is very much in confidence.
Mr. Hamilton

Unfortunately, the results of the correspondence and later developments to this end are unknown. However, it is possible to infer what happened from Tann's article on the international diffusion of the Boulton and Watts engine. Tann gives the lists of the orders and enquiries for the Boulton and Watt engine and says that it had not begun in, for example, Turkey, South Africa or Australia by 1825, although a basic knowledge of the technology of the engine had arrived.[197] Aksoy states that from 1856 onwards, steam-driven pumps were put into operation to evacuate water from the dry docks and that, until that date, a kind of a chain pump was used in the construction of dry docks at the Haliç Tersanesi (Golden Horn Dockyard).[198]

It is also reported that 12 mules (ester) were ordered from the mîrâhur-ı evvel[199] to operate the wheel to be fitted and adjusted in order to evacuate water through a temporary gate (âriyet kapusu) excavated for the new dry dock under construction in 1807–08.[200] Therefore, we can deduce from this information that the Ottomans had used animal power to evacuate water from the dry docks, before resorting to steam power. The memoirs of a leading British engineer, who came to Istanbul in 1839, support this point. According to him, the dry docks in the Tersâne-i Âmire were emptied through elevators operated by animal power instead of modern pumps.[201]

Consequently, the Porte's search for and enquiries into the steam engine, which was a fresh innovation in the third quarter of the eighteenth century, can be regarded as an attempt to keep up with the Western technology. They also show that the traditional water-emptying methods used by the Ottomans fell short of meeting the urgent needs of the navy, since the early and quick evacuation of a dry dock was vital for the caulking, maintenance and construction of ships.

### *The construction of a stone furnace for casting bronze bearing pintles and sheaves*

An order issued in 1796–97 states that bronze bearing pintles (*tunç inecikler*) and sheaves (*tunc zebanlar*), which were used for imperial galleons to be sheathed with copper, were to be melted in a pot and manufactured in a hearth (*ocak*) where copper planks were produced.[202]

Because of the lack of a separate furnace (*furun*) particular to this process, they were first cast in the form of a few pieces and then assembled and manufactured in the above-mentioned hearth located at the Imperial Naval Arsenal. It is said that these equipments proved dangerous in use. Further, the new three-decker galleon under construction was quite a large one, so the small bronze sheaves (*tunc makara zebanları*), which had been manufactured previously for smaller galleons, would not fit. It was therefore deemed necessary to build a new separate stone furnace for a constant and perpetual application of the art for bulky pieces.[203]

An examination book (*keşif defteri*) for the feasibility of the construction of the stone furnace was prepared after some research. In the book, the excavation of the construction site in question, the measures and specifications of the construction and separate parts of the building, and the materials required for the construction were all stated in detail. The building was to have a brick roof, a wooden floor, a small storage area for tools and equipment, and stonewalls. Additionally, such materials as refractory stones (*seng-i ateşî*), *küfegî* stones, Swedish iron, slop, iron beams and Horasan lime were used in the construction of the furnace.[204]

### *Newly invented furnaces and hearths for the imperial galleons*

A document dated 4 September 1801 indicates some copper equipment and other tools to be used in the newly invented furnaces (*furun*) and hearths (*ocaks*), which were put in order and delivered to the allotted places via the *Liman Reisi* and the *Kaptan Pasha* for the requirements of the imperial galleons. The document states that the cost of the production of the equipment and tools was 9,656 *kuruş*, exclusive of the raw iron provided by the *mahzeni sürb*.[205]

### *Iron equipment of new invention*

Relating to the equipment of the imperial navy, a document dated 1803–04 refers to newly invented equipment (*âhenî çilingirkârî mühimmat*) made of iron and its manufacture. It states that the total cost was 7,468 *kuruş*, excluding the raw iron from the *mahzen-i surb*, which cost 1,971 *kuruş*.[206]

### *Newly produced steels*

From a *takrir* (official petition) dated 1792–93 by Mustafa Reshid Efendi, it is understood that a certain engineer (*mühendis beyzâde*, probably French shipbuilder Le Brun) produced a kind of steel from the Samakov, Swedish and Austrian (*Nemçe*) iron. When introduced to the Ottoman experts, it turned out that the steels produced from Swedish iron were handier and superior to the others because of the toughness of the Swedish iron.[207]

### *Newly invented ground gunstocks, mechanical cranes, new darağacı structures and blocks/pulleys*

A document dated 1800–01 reveals that an urgent need had emerged for the construction of a mechanical crane (*macuna/maçula maa cerr-i eskâl*) to raise and lower the newly invented ground gunstocks (*zemîn kundakları*), which were used in transporting the cannons cast at the Imperial Cannon Foundry (*Tophâne-i Âmire*) and the Hasköy cannon foundry (*Hasköy Tophânesi*) to the Corps of Bombardiers (*Humbaracı Ocağı*), in lifting from the wharf and transferring the big shell mortars (*humbara havanı*) of 65 and 36 diameters, and in loading the same mortars (*havan*) on the gunstocks (*kundak*). It seems that the authorities believed that this construction would lessen the transport cost paid for the porters as well as make the process easier. The same document shows that an English-made mechanical crane,[208] which had been formerly received by the Porte, had been taken as an example in the construction of this new one. There are reported to have been two other cranes, which had been built by Ragıp Efendi in 1798–99.[209] Mahmud Raid Efendi wrote that the construction of a *maçuna* with perfect wheels had been started and its completion was expected soon.[210]

For the construction dates of earlier cranes, various dates are given for various cranes. According to the information given in *Hadîkatü'l Cevâmi* (The Garden of Mosques), the construction of pillars called *macuna* was started in the middle of the month of Muharrem in 1189/1775, down at the shore of the *Tersâne-i Âmire*, in a straight line with the *Zindan* (prison), and completed in 1775 under the supervision of Hasan Pasha.[211] As understood from an inscription of Yesârîzâde Mustafa Izzet's, Hasan Pasha's crane soon became useless because its legs began to rot in water.

A *darağacı* was constructed in the time of Küçük Hüseyin Pasha, in 1794–95. Earlier cranes had been called *darağacı* in the Imperial Naval Arsenal[212] and ships, after being launched into the sea, were towed beneath them for rigging out.[213] Earlier *darağacı* structures had been made of wood and had needed renewing or fixing every eight to ten years. This meant high costs. Therefore, towards the end of 1794, all of the former *darağacı* structures were pulled down and three new stone ones, for caulking, were constructed side by side.[214] Another source indicates that the *darağacı*, which was a three-legged flitch beam used for transferring the heavy materials of ships such as guns and rigging as well as for tilting the ship hulls sideways during the maintenance of the bottoms of the ships, was replaced by a new *darağacı* composed of three leggs of iron pipe on 2 August 1794.[215]

French engineer Le Brun is reported to have built two new cranes that had hands as well. However, they are said to have been old-fashioned, operated with big pulleys.[216]

Tezel, without giving any date, but most probably referring to the middle of the eighteenth century, contends that there were a crane and a crane machine (*macuna makinesi*) in front of the Camialtı building. He adds that a crane was thought to exist in the late eighteenth century.[217]

Tutel notes that the crane in Daragaci at the Camialtı Arsenal was built in 1790.[218]

Regarding the blocks (*makara*) used on the Ottoman ships to lift heavy materials, they were mostly made of the trunks of ash (*dişbudak*), *kayacık* and elm trees (*karaağaç*).[219] The same types of trees were used in Europe in block making. The parts of the block were the shell of elm or ash, the pin of lignum vitae (*peygamberağacı*), greenheart or iron, and the wheel of lignum vitae.[220] Various types of blocks with Santo sheave[221] were purchased from Galata traders to be used on the Ottoman galleons, for instance, the *Bâdi-i Nusret* in 1797–98.

The number of blocks used on ships changed between 940 and 399, depending on their size. For example, it was 940 for a three-decker galleon with 120 guns, and 848 for a frigate with 28 guns and a corvette with 18 guns.[222]

A register book of various kinds of blocks with Santo sheave, which had been purchased from Galata traders via Idris Kapudan, elucidates the technical aspects and types of the blocks. Among 87 blocks of different types costing a total of 283 *kuruş* were *demir sabanlı üç dilli makara* (three-sheave block with iron stroop), *demir sabanlı iki dilli makara* (two-sheave block with iron stroop), *iki dilli kancalı makara* (two-sheave block with hook), *kancalı torno makara* (single block with hook), *demir sabanlı makara-i bastika* (snatch block with iron stroop), *kancalı makara palanga-i güverte* (hooked block of deck tackle), *üçer dilli makara-i vasat* (middle block with three sheaves), *ikişer dilli makara i vasat* (middle block with two sheaves), *makara-i torno* (single block), *iskota makara* (sheet block), *palanga-i borina-i makara* (bowline tackle block), *makara-i bastika* (snatch block) and *makara-i mütenevvia* (miscellaneous blocks).[223]

In addition, sheaves for pulleys were mentioned in correspondences with England. To exemplify, a document dated 1793–94 and showing the list of military stores requested from England by the Ottomans included 10,000 sheaves for pulleys made of wood called 'Legno Sato'. Out of this amount, 2,000 were requested in the largest size, 3,000 in middle size and 5,000 in small size. Regarding the price, it is understood that as this article had never been brought for sale from England before, an evaluation would be made and a price fixed on arrival. It seems that the Porte wanted to have the sheaves either as ready-made or in return for a sufficient quantity of wood to be fabricated in the arsenal.[224] This information is very important for determining the date that the first sheaves for pulleys were imported from England. As illustrated above in the Ottoman documents regarding the mechanical crane, it seems that the trade of sheaves for pulleys and mechanical cranes from 1793 onwards was lively between the two countries.

We come across information of sheaves for pulleys ordered from England in 1799–1800 as well. Ottoman documents refer to Ismail Ferruh Efendi's report about the Porte's demand for sheaves for pulleys from England. It is understood from his report that in England sheaves for pulleys (*makara dilleri*) were made from a tree called 'Limbo Santo', which was found only in America and was useful in manufacturing pulley equipment (*makara takımı*). Ismail Ferruh Efendi advised and discussed the ways of transporting the material to Istanbul. In this context, he also mentioned possible insuring for secure transportation.[225]

As for the block-/pulley-making technology used in England in the years in which the Ottomans were in close contact to locate for and purchase the required products, it can be said without any hesitation that it was a very important sector for the sailing navy. Towards the end of the eighteenth century, the inspector general of naval works, Sir Samuel Bentham (1757–1831), made a study of the problem of wood-working by machinery and registered a patent, which included planing machines with rotary cutters to cut on several sides of the wood at once, the preparation of dovetail joints together by means of conical cutters, and veneer-cutting, mortising, and moulding machines. Considering the approximate 10,000 pulley blocks required for the Admiralty per year, Bentham was involved in the organisation of their manufacture. This method was costly because it was made by hand, except for the initial roughing out of the shells with a circular saw and the turning of the sheaves on the lathe. In the following years, Sir Marc Isambard Brunel (1769–1849) and other shipbuilders, bridge builders and engineers developed this technology to have more complicated and mechanised systems.[226]

### *The cleaning and deepening of the Samsun Harbour*

A British letter dated 14 April 1781, by Sir Robert Ainslie (1766–1838), the British ambassador to Istanbul, to the secretary of state, the Earl of Hillsborough, notes that a ship of 50 guns and a frigate of 32 had been loaded with machines and left Istanbul carrying workmen and engineers to be employed in cleaning and deepening Samsun Harbour as well as in building piers to make them capable of receiving and sheltering ships of war. The document indicates that this was a much desired event, as there was not a single harbour for that purpose on the Asian coast of the Black Sea. Ainslie reported that he had heard that the above-mentioned group had discovered the foundations of ancient piers that had existed in the Roman era, and that after examination they were judged to be perfectly sound.[227]

The method and the machines used in this work are unknown. However, it is understood that dredgers were used in the cleaning of Kağıthane and Sütlüce passes in the Golden Horn in the eighteenth century.[228] Actually, the dredging machine, a bucket wheel for the cleaning of the port, went back to as early as the fourteenth century. In the course of time, these machines were perfected, and by the seventeenth century were found in almost every port. They had a scoop at the end of a long shaft. This was the power shovel, which remained in use until the nineteenth century.[229] Applications by the contemporary European states show similarities. Regarding the methods of deepening rivers, canals and harbours, various techniques and machines were used. Among them were the removal of silt in suspension, the use of scoops, ladle dredgers, grab dredgers, wheel dredgers, chain dredgers or bucket dredgers.[230]

## The construction of new shipbuilding structures and auxiliary forms

### *The extension of the area of the naval arsenal*

Following the collapse of the old walls surrounding the *Tersâne*, which had been nothing but a barrier before development, a great part of the area formerly included in Aynalıkavak Kasrı was added to the complex through work carried out by Küçük Hüseyin Pasha in 1802–03. Thanks to this development and the pulling down of the seaside buildings of Aynalıkavak Kasrı, the *Tersâne* obtained the area urgently required for new improvements. This also facilitated the relations between the workers in the *Tersâne* and the sailors in Kasımpaşa.[231]

### *The construction of the* Nühashâne, Haddehâne *and new* haddes

Regarding the copper sheathing of the ships, mention has already been made[232] of a document dated 1 May 1796 that indicates the establishment of a new copper processing house (*Nühashâne*) within the body of the *Temurhâne* to process the copper to be fastened onto the hulls of the ships as well as to prevent the waste of copper formerly prepared in the *Humbarahâne*. This new copper processing house was planned as a four-walled room with three furnaces. The process of the exploration and determination of the construction site was carried out by the chief architect (*Mimar aga*) on the instructions of the *Tersâne-i Âmire Emini*. It can be traced through the construction notebook (*keşif defteri*) of 29 April 1796, written by Mehmed Arif Bey, *Ser Mimarân-ı Hassa*. The site chosen was near the *Temurhâne*. The building was surrounded by stone walls on three sides and had a perfect roof. There was a high room inside the building for the residence of the workers. Beneath the ground floor, there were a shop and a coal cellar. The building had a large gate as well as the necessary tools and components. There were two foundry workshops between the *Nühashâne* and the *Temurhâne*. Its estimated cost was 4,470 *kuruş*.[233]

A document dated 30 June 1803 gives information about the *Haddehâne* near the *Âlât Meydanı* (the Rope Square) in the Imperial Naval Arsenal, stating that the chief gunpowder expert, Arakel, manufactured a pair of newly invented large iron *haddes* to level copper plates for sheathing the imperial galleons in the time of Kaptan-ı Derya Hüseyin Pasha.[234] Although the use of the first *hadde* machines is generally ascribed to the reign of Mahmut II, those manufactured by Arakel might be considered to have been the prototypes of the later machines. Additionally, information showing that Arakel finished the *hadde* wheels to be used for gunpowder production at the Azatli Baruthanesi in 1803 supports this idea.[235] Unfortunatelly, it is not known if these *haddes* were fully manual, as in previous years, or semi-mechanical.

Regarding the later operations concerning the foundation of this *Haddehâne* building, an excavation was carried out and the foundation was reinforced with new pillars of washed black *küfegi* stones (*yunmalı seng-i siyah-ı küfegî*). New tools and wheels were constructed for better use of the *haddes*. The total cost was 8,828,5 *kuruş*. The above-mentioned document also refers to the reconstruction of the foundry, which was in a state of disrepair. In the foundry, near the *Âlât Meydanı*, a stone hearth (*kârgir ocak*) had collapsed. Therefore, under this stone foundary, a stone-grilled quay (*kârgir ızgaralı rıhtım*) of two *ziras* was filled and encircled by a wooden fence on three sides. Its interior walls of refractory stone (*seng-i ateş*) were connected with iron beams. Brick, pure mortar and whitewashed copper were applied. Its measures were three *ziras* in length, 2/60,000 in area, seven *ziras* in height and two *ziras* in foundation. In the same foundry, a small furnace (*ocak*) for casting bronze nails was constructed. The structure was encircled with walls of refractory stone (*seng-i ateş*) and whitewashed with slop (*çömlekçi çamuru*), and its measures were two *ziras* in length, 2/7,200 in area and 1,5 *zira* in height. It is understood that the 480 columns and 600 units of woods for the construction of a roof over the mentioned furnace were required. In the same foundry roof tiles, new rafters (*mertek*) and girdle (*kuşak*) were provided, and a balcony (*balkovan*) was fixed. Expenses for porterage and the transport crane, along with other expenses, were 6,000 *kuruş*.[236]

### New shipbuilding forms and new sheds for gunboats

Two new shipbuilding forms were built at Hasköy and two at Ayvansaray, allowing the construction or repair[237] of nine large ships at the same time in Istanbul and its vicinity. New sheds were also constructed at Kağıthâne to store the gunboats and other small craft of the fleet and protect them from the elements when they were inactive.[238]

### The construction of the sailhouse
### (Kirpâshâne/Yelkenhâne)

As a natural result of the transition from oared to sailed ships, at the beginning of the eighteenth century, a sailhouse, or *kirpashâne*, was established within the body of the *Tersâne-i Âmire* in order to make high-quality sailcloth in large quantities for the Ottoman galleons, whose number had increased dramatically. This facility underwent repairs and restorations in the 1760s and was enlarged in 1770.[239] During the reign of Selim III, a new and larger sailhouse was constructed by İsmail Hulûsî Efendi in 1795–96 in Darağacı at the Imperial Naval Arsenal.[240]

### *The construction of the* Endâzehâne *(ship-modelling house)*

An *endâzehâne*[241] was constructed on 30 May 1800 for the purpose of determining the measures and drawings of galleons to be constructed in the big dry dock and for storing the related materials. One out of the three rooms of the granary (*zahire ambarı*) near the dry dock was allotted to the *endâzehâne*, while the remaining two constructed were to be used for storing foodstuffs as before. The vice-chief architect (*mimarbaşı vekili*) and Tersâne Emini Efendi carried out the examination of the buildings and measurements and they decided that if the room allotted to the *endâzehâne* was separated, being three *ziras* higher than the roof from the room next to it via a stone wall of 15 *arşın* in heigth and one *zira* in width, it would be protected from all the other stores. In addition, the boxes for foodstuffs in the room would be collapsed, and a higher floor with three small rooms underneath for the engineers would be made. Additionally, large windows and doors would be fitted for the construction of two stores if needed. The debris of the boxes of foodstuffs and the columns under them would be used to lessen the possible cost. The total cost was expected to amount to 5,665 *kuruş*.[242]

### *The construction of new stone caulking places*

The caulking of ships was an important matter. There was no class of caulkers peculiar to the Imperial Naval Arsenal. Ships took in water because of the lack of care. To overcome this serious problem, the *Kaptan Pasha* brought 200 skilful Arabic caulking masters from Cairo. Large barracks were constructed behind the arsenal, where they were fed, clothed and accommodated well. As a result of their work, the ships became stronger so that they did not take in water despite three to four years sailing in the sea. To further improve the system, a second caulking place was constructed so that more than one vessel could be caulked at the same time. Both structures were made of wood and required renewal or fixing every eight to ten years, which was expensive. Around 1798, both wooden structures were pulled down and three stone (*kârgir*) caulking platforms were constructed in their place.[243]

### *The construction of an anchor house* (Lengerhâne)

Anchors were, most often, forged in the naval dockyards and made up of pieces of iron scrap welded together. These pieces were heated to a white heat and then beaten into a solid mass, initially with manual sledgehammers, later by mechanical drop hammers. Separate pieces were then shaped into the shank of the anchor. The flukes were prepared in the same way and welded to the arms before the latter were married to the shank. The large iron anchor ring, having been forged and shaped, would be rove through the head of the shank and welded into it. Bands to secure the two parts of the wooden stock would be prepared in a smaller forge.[244]

In the Imperial Naval Arsenal, the Ottomans kept equipment such as cordage, wire, sails and casting cannons in storage areas for prospective naval campaigns. Anchors were among this equipment. In connection with the completion of the equipment of the galleons, frigates and corvettes constructed in the naval arsenal and in Midilli, Bodrum, Limni, Rhodes, Sultaniye, Gemlik, Sinop, Eregli and Sohum, seven anchors were needed for each ship. Four would be mounted on the front parts of the ships for the usual usage on 10 December 1796. Others were kept in the stores for future use.[245]

Documents show that, in the late eighteenth century, the Ottomans purchased anchor cable, also called *gomana*, of which every galleon had to have a supply,[246] from foreigners beside domestic sources. They made a contract with a Russian merchant called Alexandre for anchor, sailcloth, cordage and some other supplies for the imperial galleons on 28 July 1796.[247] Also, on 31 May 1800, a British citizen named Thomas Thornton (Toranton in the Ottoman document), residing in Istanbul, had six new high-quality anchor cables. The Ottomans, considering it suitable for their galleons, wanted to purchase it. They reached an agreement of 4,55,5 *kantars* of anchor cable, for 50 *kuruş* per *kantar* amounting to 22,775 *kuruş*.[248]

Anchors for the ships were generally produced in anchor houses. In 1708 Ali Usta, from the Humbaracı Corps, constructed the first anchor workshop/house (*lengerhâne*), and the big anchors that had long been procured from England began to be produced there. Soon the production of anchors of 70–80 *kantars* took place in this workshop.[249] In the late eighteenth century, a new anchor house was needed. A document dated 13 September 1796 describes the *lengerhâne*'s construction. The existing *lengerhâne* had ten furnaces, which were deemed insufficient; ten more were needed. After the plan of this new construction project was presented to the Porte, an imperial edict was issued ordering that it be done. The chief architect, Ismail Efendi, examined the construction site, and a cost estimate of 12,188 *kuruş* was given. He was commissioned to undertake the project.[250]

The *lengerhâne* sometimes provided iron for the construction of equipment such as rings and nails for ships when the need arose. On 31 January 1800, the *lengerhâne*, together with some *Irâd-ı Cedîd* (a treasury established by Selim III) stores, provided 1,000 *kantars* of raw iron for the equipment of the imperial galleons. The total cost was 14,000 *kuruş*, meaning 14 *kuruş* per *kantar*, and was met by the *Siham Muacelatı* (urgent expenses treasury established for campaigns within the *İrâd-ı Cedîd* Treasury).[251]

Ine (Ayna) Island was a traditional source of iron for anchors. In 1800–01, 1,000 *kantars* of iron, at eight *kuruş* per *kantar*, were provided by this island and Samakovcuk. The cost was met by the *Siham Muacelatı*.[252] In 1802–03 a spring campaign loomed on the horizon. On inspection, it was determined that there was iron on hand for anchors and other iron equipment in the Imperial Naval Arsenal, which shows the Porte's preparedness for any emergency.[253] It is also known that the naval arsenal provided anchor iron even for *tombaz* boats (flat-bottomed river vessels without decks). In May–June 1807, 70 *tombaz* vessels being constructed at Ruscuk and Silistire needed some equipment, including anchor iron.[254]

Table 5. Some ship equipment, including anchor iron, needed for ship construction at Ruscuk and Silistire

| | Ruscuk | Silistre |
|---|---|---|
| Lenger demiri beheri 2 kantar | 35 | 35 |
| Gomana beheri 40 kulaç | 35 | 35 |
| Gomana-i ırgat beheri 120 kulac | 1 | 1 |
| Irgat maa takım | 1 | 1 |
| Makara-i pranga | 2 | 2 |
| Yarma makara | 2 | 2 |
| Alat-ı makara | 3 | 3 |
| Source: BOA. Cevdet-Bahriye, no. 2186. | | |

### *Construction of the first dry dock in the*
### *Naval Imperial Arsenal*

A dry dock is a structure that allows a ship to be repaired, fitted out or otherwise worked on when completely out of the water. It has closed sides that allow the ship to enter through a gate, which can be closed to seal it from the outside water. The structure can then be emptied of water, allowing the ship to settle on wooden blocks positioned on the floor of the dock to fit the configuration of the ship's hull. Dry docks may also be used for the construction of ships that are then launched by merely flooding the dry dock.[255] When a ship was about to enter a dock, it was disarmed and unloaded in order to reduce its weight and thus its draught.[256]

Geographical conditions are very important in the construction of dry docks. For instance, it was easy to construct and use docks in Atlantic and English Channel ports because of the strong tides, while it was difficult in the Mediterranean due to the absence of tides. Therefore, the construction of the first dry dock in the Mediterranean was of a special technical significance, leading the way for the construction of others in that area.

The need for new docks for the Ottoman navy was first voiced in the 1780s. Among the intentions of the French mission was to construct wet and dry docks within the Imperial Naval Arsenal.[257] Several negotiations were carried out between French and Ottoman authorities during the time of Grand Vizier Damad Melek Mehmed Pasha and Kaptan-ı Derya Küçük Hüseyin Pasha. It was argued that the ships careened and caulked at the European docks were more durable and could serve 40 to 45 years, while those of the Ottomans served 15 years at most. Construction of a dock was decided, but the Porte, upon learning that such as project would cost 1,000–1,500 purses of *akçe* and would take three years, rejected the proposal considering the present state of the Ottoman Treasury. However, the project came back on to the agenda of the Porte later on and was approved. Küçük Evkaf Muhasebecisi Cânib Mehmed Salih Efendi was appointed, with a salary of 750 *kuruş*, as the construction administrator (*bina emini*) to oversee the project, provide the required materials and equipment and organise the salaries of the workers.[258]

The construction of the dock was undertaken as a kind of international tender, taking into consideration the projects and methods presented by French and Swedish engineers. In 1796 French and Swedish dock engineers presented their projects to the Ottoman naval authorities consisting of the *Kaptan Pasha*, Tersâne Emini Mehmed Reşid Efendi, former Tersâne Emini Osman Efendi, Mimar Agha and some other construction experts.[259] The French plan, as mentioned in the case of Groignard, involved submerging a construction caisson after preparing the required channel by dredging and underwater blasting. The water inside the caisson would then be pumped out to allow the construction of the quay walls. A caisson of very large dimensions was required in this kind of project.

The Swedish engineers proposed driving in sheet piles in order to seal the working area and to make both excavation and construction in a dry pit. After the assessment of the two projects, the French proposal was 2.2 times more expensive than the Swedish one. Naturally, the Swedish plan seemed favourable to the Porte. The head of the Swedish engineers, RhodéÈ, ordered the digging of test pits at the shipyard in order to determine the proper place for the construction of the dry dock. The pits were 18 x 18 metres with a depth of 10.50 metres. In these pits, RhodéÈ inspected the soil strata and carried out pumping tests to check the suitability of his equipment. Understandably, he searched for a location that would allow his structure to be placed on shale bedrock.[260]

Following the assessment of the preliminary tests carried out between 7 June 1796 and 3 February 1797, construction was consigned to RhodéÈ on 2 February 1797. Within this period workbenches and pumps had been manufactured, excavation of the specified area for the dry dock completed, and a new gate, railing, and stone pavement constructed. Also, stone breaking had been carried out in the sea in front of the İncili Köşk to allow for space. For this entire work, 5,448,5 *kuruş* and 15 *paras* were spent. The construction of the dry dock started on Saturday, 4 February 1797, in a place next to the *Zâhire Ambarı* (granary) at the Imperial Naval Arsenal.[261]

As for the materials used in the construction of the dry dock, it seems that the main building elements were timber from Kidros (pine), Cide (pine), Misivri (oak), Ayholu (oak) and Iznikmid (hornbeam)[262]; stone from the quarries in Istinye (black, unhewn and rough-hewn stone blocks[263] from Balta Limani); lime mostly from Pendik; and iron. Also, *boçlana* (a type of soil) was used in the construction. This was a kind of soil thta was provided from Italy,[264] the Santron Islands and Değirmenlik in the Mediterranean.[265] Aksoy states that puzzolana mortar/soil, which was a durable material for underwater constructions, was used in the dry dock. It must have been the same material as *boçlana*. Puzzolana mortar (*puzolan harcı*) was composed of puzzolana[266] and lime. It quickly hardened under water. In fact, this material (also called 'Roman cement') had long been used widely in underwater construction before the introduction of cement,[267] especially in European hydraulic architecture during the eighteenth century.[268]

The front side of the determined construction site was cleaned via drag at the *Halic Tersanesi*. Wooden sheet piles were driven into the shore to prevent the seawater from entering the construction pit, which was dug in 37.50 m by 75.00 m and 10.50 m in depth. Water was constantly pumped out to work in dry conditions.[269]

Although at the beginning of the construction the sea front was sealed to prevent the water from coming inside, water began to seep from the sides and front into the excavated area, caused by the muddy and loose soil under the buildings used by store administrators (*ambar eminleri*) on the landfill. An imperial edict was issued ordering the demolition and rebuilding in another place of these buildings. Additionally, plans were made to build two wooden wells on the two sides of the dry dock. One of them was completed easily, while the second required careful work during the foundation excavations not to cause any damage to the nearby wall of the granary. Following the completion of the main building, a wall was built around it and new storage areas (*mahzen*) were constructed. Expenses amounted to 800,967 *kuruş* (1,617 purses of *akçe* and 467 *kuruş*), which was a far smaller figure than the estimated cost (3,000 purses of *akçe*) at the beginning of the project. The construction of the first dry dock in the Ottoman Empire started in February 1797 and was completed in May 1800.[270]

Later, a ladder was constructed in the big dry dock at the *Tersâne-i Âmire*. The cost of stone and other materials required for the construction of the ladder, amounting to 613 *kuruş*, was met by the *Tersâne-i Âmire Hazinesi*.[271]

Aksoy mentions a kind of underwater glass (*sualtı dürbünü*) that was manufactured and used by RhodéÈ for observing the construction activities under water. Rode's earlier tutelage under Thunberg, who used underwater glass and later on invented a diving tube into which a man could go and observe underwater life, supports this thesis.[272] Aksoy writes that two wells fitted with treadmills were constructed at the two sides of dry docks (including the one constructed later on in the time of Mahmud II) in the Golden Horn and that water was emptied via these wells. A type of chain pump (*sonsuz ipli kovalı tulumba*) was used in the construction of the dry docks at the Imperial Naval Arsenal, since such a device had been in use in the eighteenth-century dry docks in Europe. The use of chain pumps in the constructions of dry docks in the *Haliç Tersanesi* continued until 1856, after which time steam-driven pumps were used.[273] Correspondence between the Porte and England about the specification of a steam engine to be used in the dry dock at the Imperial Naval Arsenal in 1805 is an important indicator that at least the knowledge of a steam engine had reached the Ottoman Empire in the beginning of the nineteenth century.[274]

Regarding the physical structure of the dry dock, Toğrol and Aksoy specify that the floor slab and sidewalls of the dry dock were made of good-quality building stones from the Istinye quarries in Istanbul. This particular stone was used extensively in marine works. The thickness of the floor slab was 75 cm, mostly resting on bedrock. The sidewalls had stepped faces and vertical backs. Calculating the stability of the dry dock and the pressure acting on the walls and foundations in dry and flooded conditions reveals the distinct features of a successful design. The stresses acting on the masonry were within allowable values, and pressure distribution seems to have been nearly uniform.[275] The leading feature of the dry dock was that it was constructed with intricate stonework, without use of any mortar.[276]

The dry dock underwent some reparations and maintenance over the course of time. A document dated 1800–01 gives the details of this process, beginning with a summary of previous repairs. The outer gate of the dry dock had come to be damaged and worn, and seawater had begun to leak in. Due to damaged rocks, seawater had leaked from inside the dock as well. For its repair, quality timber, nails, lead and copper plates and other materials had been provided. Several hundred workers had been employed and the whole process had required 20–30 days. Next, the document talks about and inquires into the necessary steps for a second repair for the same problem. The document estimates that the repair would probably be expensive, considering the cost of the previous one and the uncertainty of the repair method. The real cost would appear on the construction register after the completion of the construction.

The document also describes the difficulties of the exploration and its feasibility, stating that it was still uncertain if the construction would be done like the previous one or with iron wings and lead due to the rocks, some on the sea surface and others in the sea. It is understood that there was a belief that no problem would appear with respect to the wages of divers (*sömbeki*), workers, as well as tools and equipment such as pontoons (*tombaz*) and drags (*tarak*). The workers, sellers and the payment required were to be provided by the construction administrator (*bina emini*). The supply of the required oak and hornbeam suitable for use, as stakes did not seem possible from Istanbul, would have to be provided from the countryside. The construction administrator was to pay the wages and the *Tersâne-i Âmire* was to help with the felling and transportation process.

It seems that it was intended that the construction work would be finished within the summer months, since it would be very difficult for divers to carry out their work during the winter months. The *Hububat Nazırı* (the Granary Minister), thanks to his previous experience and knowledge, was appointed to oversee the process, and a secretary was hired to keep the register of the construction. Other specialists were ordered to help him if needed. RhodéÈ, the builder of the dry dock, was also consulted during the exploration process. The estimated cost was 30,000–40,000 *akçes*.[277] Regarding the timber needed for the outer gate of the big dry dock, an urgent need appeared in the year 1806. The required timber was ordered, with specific proportions, from the Iznikmid timber superintendent, Mehmed Ağa.[278]

The dry dock underwent another reparation in 1814. Wall stones tended to set in 0,75–1,5 m towards the inside part of the dock. Besides, there was water leakage. In order to solve these problems, the section by the damaged area was dug to some extent, wooden stakes were driven in and puzzolanic mortar and rubble were poured onto the stakes. Reparation was completed covering the top with flat and wide stones.[279]

Consequently, the construction of the first dry dock (today known as *3 nolu kuruhavuz*)[280] between 1797 and 1800 was an important turning point for the Ottoman naval technology. Not only dit it become the base for the construction of various kinds of ships under the reign of Selim III, but it was also taken as a model in the construction of two later dry docks. This dry dock was later enlarged landwards in 1874–76 by Vasil Kalfa. The next dry dock (today known as *2 nolu kuruhavuz*) was completed between 1821 and 1825 by chief engineer Abdulhalim Efendi, who was a teacher in the *Muhendishane*, and Manol Kalfa, who had been employed in the construction of the first dry dock as well. Finally, the last dry dock (today known as *1 nolu kuruhavuz*) was constructed during 1857–70 by Vasil Kalfa. The constructions of the last two dry docks were carried out under the supervision of the people who had worked on the first one. During the project, reference was made to the construction registers and notebooks of the previous dry dock in order to apply the same techniques and designs. Interestingly, all three dry docks had dimensions and measurements similar to those in other parts of the world at the time.[281]

### Ottoman experience of naval gunnery in the late eighteenth century

The first time cannons were used on Ottoman ships was during the siege of Constantinople to hit the city walls from the sea.[282] Guilmartin, however, tells about a contemporary Turkish sketch preserved in Topkapı Palace showing two Ottoman siege bombards in action and he suggests that this may represent the earliest type of gun mount regularly used aboard galleys, considering the similarity to a German woodcut depicting the port of Venice and illustrating a book published in 1486. This woodcut shows a bombard, made of wrought iron or bronze cast in 'hooped' form, mounted on the bow of a galley tightly pinioned between heavy horizontal timbers lying alongside the barrel and supported by a much heavier vertical post to absorbe the recoil.[283]

If we take a look at Ottoman ships carrying cannons, irrespective of the century in which they were used, we see that among the ones powered with oars were galliot (*kalite*), brigantine (*perkende*), saika (*şayka*) with three guns, mahone (*mavna*) with 24 guns, galley (*kadırga*) with 13 guns and *baştarda* with three heavy guns and several light guns. Among sailing ships carrying guns were sloops (*şalope*) of 12 guns, brigs (*brik*), *ağribar* with over 30 guns, corvettes (*korvet*) with 20–30 guns, *barça* with over 80 guns, galleons (*kalyon*) with 60–80 guns, three-decked galleons (*üç ambarlı kalyon*) with 80–120 guns, frigates (*firkateyn*) with 30–70 guns, *kaypak/kapak* with 80–100 guns and *uskuna* with 16 guns.[284]

In the sixteenth and early seventeenth centuries, beside warships, merchant ships were observed to have guns as well. Guns required for the merchant ships owned by the state were generally provided from the *Tophâne-i Âmire*,[285] while the ones for the private non-military ships were purchased or hired in return for a certain amount of money.[286]

Considering the galleons constructed following the systematic adoption of sailing ships in 1682, we see that four out of ten galleons were 50 *zira* and had 80 bronze guns while the remaining six were 45 *zira* and had 60 guns. These sizes seem to be comparable to the ones of European ships.[287]

At the beginning of the eighteenth century, 112 guns were required for a three-decker built in 1700, and 130 guns for a big galleon *kebîr kalyon* constructed in 1701. The sizes of these guns were between three and 16 *kıyyes*. Broken guns or the ones needed to change were transferred to the *Tophâne-i Âmire* in order to be replaced with new ones. Broken ones were melted down to be cast into new guns.[288]

Looking at the first-, third-, fourth- and fifth-rate Ottoman ships between 1736 and 1739, it is seen that the *Çift Aslan*, a first-rate ship, could carry 108 guns of 8-112, 22-48, 2-24, 30-18, 28-12, 18-8 pounders. The *İki Bağçeli* and the *Büyük Gül Başlı*, two third-rate Ottoman ships, had 66 guns on board each. Sixty-six guns of the *İki Bağçeli* consisted of 4-112, 24-48, 2-18, 28-12, 8-8 pounders, while there were 28-24, 2-18, 28-12, 8-8 pounders on the *Büyük Gül Başlı*. A fourth-rate ship, the *Yaldızlı Şahin*, carried 62 guns of 26-18, 28-12, 8-8 pounders; another fourth-rate ship, the *Mavi Aslan*, had 50 guns of 22-12 and 28-8 pounders. The *Mavi Firkata*, another fifth-rate ship, could carry 36 guns of 8 and 4 pounders.[289]

Of course, these were not the only ships of the period in question. Panzac, in addition to mentioning the gun capacities of the ships between 1736 and 1739 as mentioned above, focuses on the ones operating in a more limited time period. To give the gun capacity of some other ships between 1737 and 1738, the following names can be mentioned: the *Çift Kaplan* with 102 guns, the *Sipah-ı Bahr* with 98 guns, the *Malika-i Bahr* with 98 guns, the *Yaldızlı Hurma* with 72 guns, the *Deve Kuşu* with 68 guns, the *Şadırvan Kıçlı* with 68 guns, the *İspinoz* with 68 guns, the *Küçük Gül Başlı* with 66 guns, the *Akrep Başlı* with 66 guns, the *Beyaz At* with 66 guns, the *Al-qasr* with 62 guns, the *Zülfikar* with 62 guns, the *Selvi Bağçeli* with 62 guns, the *Yaldız Bağçeli* with 58 guns, the *Ejder Başlı* with 56 guns, the *Yıldız Kıçlı* with 54 guns, the *Ay Bağçeli* with 54 guns, the *Sarı Kuşaklı* with 54 guns, the *Kırmızı Kuşaklı* with 52 guns, the *Yaldızlı Nar* with 52 guns, the *Baba Ibrahim* with 52 guns, the *La PremièËre* with 46 guns, the *La Seconde* with 46 guns, the *Küçük Şahin* with 46 guns, the *Serçe Kuşu* with 44 guns, the *Beyaz Şahin* with 38 guns, the *La Bleue* with an unknown number of guns.[290] The following table, drawn by Panzac, gives a general idea of the rates of the ships and the number of guns present on them for five different leading powers of the world between 1735 and 1740.

| Table 6. Size of navies available for the Mediterranean 1735–40 | | | | | | |
|---|---|---|---|---|---|---|
| **Rate** | **Guns** | **Ottoman** | **Venice** | **France** | **Britain** | **Spain** |
| **1st** | 90 & over | 4 | | 1 | 6 | 1 |
| **2nd** | 80–90 | | | | 10 | 2 |
| **3rd** | 65–79 | 11 | 9 | 12 | 33 | 9 |
| **4th** | 50–64 | 12 | 2 | 25 | 54 | 31 |
| **5th** | 31–46 | 6 | 2 | 8 | 17 | 2 |
| **6th** | 20–30 | | | 3 | 20 | 4 |
| *Total* | | *33* | *13* | *49* | *140* | *49* |

Source: Daniel Panzac, 'Armed peace in the Mediterranean 1736–1739: a comparative survey of the navies', The Mariner's Mirror 84/1, pp. 44–45.

According to Table 6, the Ottoman navy consisted of 33 ships: 27 ships of the line (of which four were three-deckers with 98–108 guns and 23 were two-deckers) and six ships of the fifth rank.[291]

In the second half of the eighteenth century, as the oared ship became obsolete, giving way to sailing ships such as the galleon, the three-decker, the frigate and the corvette, the number of cannons on the ships began to increase. Therefore, parallel to the growing need for ships, the manufacture and order of new cannons and ammunition increased. Ottoman documents often mention correspondence between authorities about the urgent need for the manufacture of cannons to be used on galleons and other types of ships in 1793–94.[292] It became routine for new ships to be equipped with cannons and shells cast, manufactured and processed in the shell works and the *Humbarahâne* within the *Tersâne-i Âmire*.[293]

The Ottoman authorities, including Sultan Selim III, were aware of the deficiencies of the naval ships in terms of gunnery. Selim III was so interested in contemporary war techniques and weapons that he wrote a treatise (*risâle*) on the subject. The second part of the treatise was on flares (*fişekler*) and the third part on cannons (*toplar*). It seems that the *Kaptan Pasha* checked the treatise and stated that Ottoman naval ships were deprived of these flares and cannons, and ordered the procurement of these weapons.[294]

### Types of naval cannons in the Ottoman navy

In the time of Selim III, cannons began to be cast out of iron. On 12 November 1805, the *Hasköy Tersânesi* was attached to the Imperial Naval Arsenal in order to cast naval guns.[295]

Some needs voiced by the ship captains and crew give an idea of the types of cannons used on them. In a document written by Rahtuvânî Hasan Aga, dated 17 October 1790, a quantity of cannons capable of throwing shells of seven, five and three *kıyyes* were ordered for 30 sloops, and 20 *dubas plenks* in Tuna.[296] Additionally, data exist on the use of newly invented cannons. A document from 1790 tells about newly invented *beş çakmaklı ve beş mehtaplı* (cannons with five flints and cartridges) cannons fired at Kağıthane. An imperial edict ordered these cannons mounted on the appropriate galleons and frigates. In the document, the preparation of chained cannonballs (*zincirli gülle/plankete*) was also ordered.[297] In another document, dated 1799–1800, referring to the previous year, it is said that for the requirements of galleons, two mortars, 22 in diameter (throwing a projectile of 22 pound), and four mortars of 14 in diameter, were needed. In 1799–1800, the number of English shells to be used on the galleons amounted to 300.[298]

Some cannons were used in land wars only, while others were used in naval wars and on ships. *Şâhî, cehrin, saçma/çarha, misket, eynek/enik, darbzen, prangı* (mortar), *bacaluşka* (basilisco), *kolomborno* (culverin) and *şayka* (battering gun) appear among naval cannons as well as land ones.[299] Some of these guns were already in use in navies of the fifteenth and sixteenth centuries. For instance, *şayka, baş topu* (guns fitted into the prow), *darbzen, kebîr* (big size), *sağîr* (small size) and *prangı* were among the guns used on such ships as *barça* (bargia), *ağribar, kadırga* (galley), *kalyata* (galete) and *kayıks* (caique) in 1488. The total number of guns given to these ships was 137. It is striking that 83 out of this number were for *barça* and 29 for *ağribar*, both of which were warships.[300] Also, Selman Reis' fleet in the Red Sea in 1526 had a powerful artillery of seven *bacaluşka*, 13 y*an-top* (side cannons), 20 *darbzen*, 29 *şayka*, 95 iron pieces and 97 *prangı*.[301]

The *darbzen* was a light gun with a small diameter, seven *karış* in length. It could fire small projectiles (50–100 dirhem/160 g). The weight of the gun was 56,5 kg. It was relatively quick despite its small diameter and cannonball.[302] It is reported that two huge *darbzens* firing iron cannonballs of 27 *okkas* (a measure of weigth equal to 1.288 kg) each were prepared at the *Tophâne-i Âmire* and mounted on *mauna* ships in 1517.[303] *Bacaluşka* (basilisco) was the metaphorical name given to the large cannon widely used in the Mediterranean in the sixteenth century, which witnessed extensive use of this type of gun on ships.[304] Being bigger than the *prangı*, it was a siege gun. It fired iron shots of seldom four, generally 11, 14, 16, 18 and 20 *okkas* in weight, ranging in length between 9–10 and 18–20 spans, and made of wrought iron at the beginning of the sixteenth century, but mainly of cast bronze in the wake of the reign of Suleyman the Magnificient.[305]

*Prangıs* were generally used in siege wars as both field and naval cannons. They were often mounted on small ships such as *şayka* (saika) and *firkate* (frigate), operating on rivers. The term *prangı* appears in combination with *deve prangısı* (*deve* meaning camel) in some sources. Among the military supplies provided by the *Cebehâne-i Âmire* on 21 May 1522 to a ship heading probably for Rhodes under the command of Mustafa Pasha, were 16 *deve prangısı* with gunstocks (*prangı-ı şütur ma'a kundak*).[306]

The *kolomborno*, on the other hand, had a long gunbarrel. Therefore, it was used in navies when a need for a horizontal projectile path appeared. It was usually mounted on the bow or on stern gunports. It could fire cannonballs of three, five and seven *okkas*.

*Şayka* was the name of the big boat with a flat bottom operating on the Danube and other rivers. The cannon in question took its name from the ships upon which it was mounted. The *şayka* was used both on ships and land wars during the siege of fortresses, and came in small, middle and large types. There were some with 16-*karış*-gunbarrel lengths capable of throwing cannonballs with 22 *okkas* (29 kg) in weight.

Other types of cannons formerly used in land wars were also in operation in the Ottoman navy.[307] In addition to these cannons, the *poca/boça* appears as a missile used in naval artillery in both the seventeenth and eighteenth centuries.[308]

Some others, such as the *kebir*, the *obus*[309] and the *balyemez*,[310] were also used on the galleons built at the *Tersâne-i Âmire*, Rhodes and Gemlik, Sinop, Bodrum, Kemer and the Danube. Cannons weighing between three and 44 *kıyyes* and being between eight and 16 *karış* in length were used in 1791–92. The length of the galleons to be equipped with the above-mentioned cannons was between 35 and 55 *zira*. Another important piece of information that can be deduced from an archival document is that these cannons were cast and manufactured at the Hasköy cannon foundary and the *Tophâne-i Âmire* Kârhanesi. For casting cannons, raw copper, tin and raw iron were needed. In the same year, for 81 *obus* and *balyemez* cannons, 2,320 *kantars* of raw copper (*nuhâs-ı hâm*) and 232 *kantars* of tin (*kali*) were bought, and 1,160 *kantars* of zinc (*ruy-i maye*), 120 *kantars* of which were provided from the *Tophâne-i Âmire* and 10,000 *kantars* of which from the *Tersâne-i Âmire*, and 29 *kantars* of raw iron were provided from the *Cebehâne-i Âmire* to cast cannons in the foundries for the galleons. The total cost was 29,000 *kuruş*.[311]

The Ottoman navy, and especially the galleons under construction and those whose completion was close, often demanded cannons from the *Tersâne-i Âmire/Mamûre Kârhânesi*. Sixty-eight cannons were demanded in 1797–98 for a three-decked galleon under construction at the *Tersâne-i Âmire*. Chief founder Ismail Ağa was in charge of casting these cannons. The cost of casting 68 cannons amounted to 33,440 *kuruş*. Twenty-seven thousand five hundred *kuruş* out of this amount were paid up to the above-mentioned date. The remaining 5,940 *kuruş* were paid earlier.[312]

Regarding the calibres of the cannons to be mounted on the galleons, a document of 1789–90 reports that the *Kaptan Pasha* was going to go aboard the new galleon *Bahr-i Zafer*. Therefore, it was ordered that four big cannons of 66 *vukıyyes* calibres each, which had been cast, manufactured and readied at the *Tophâne-i Amire*, be mounted on the ship.[313]

### *Projectiles*

Various shells, shots and cannonballs made of different materials were used in the cannons of Ottoman galleons. Most of them were manufactured in the shell and shot works at the arsenal. However, the basic cannon and shell factory for the Ottoman navy was at Hasköy. The Galata Tophanesi contributed to the navy as well. Some of the iron shells were cast in the foundry by the pits of the iron mine around Pravişte in Balkans. Marble shells were generally provided from the Marmara islands. The required iron for shells was supplied from the Samakov mine (in Bulgaria) as well as the Pravişte mines.[314] Marble continued to be one of the most widely used materials in projectiles. This would appear as one of the leading reasons of the failure of the Ottoman navy in wars against the British fleet in the Marmara Sea in 1806. In that war, the British fleet used iron projectiles against the Ottoman ships, while the Ottomans fired marble shells.[315]

Marble,[316] granite[317], heavy stones[318] and metal shells (*mâdeni yuvarlak*),[319] chain shots/shots joined together by an iron chain (*madenî plankete*),[320] bar shot/iron bars (two balls joined together by an iron bar), cartridge bag/grape shot (*salkım*) or canister (*sakolya/sakuleta/sakulta*), shells with five holes/carcass (*beş delik-li paçavra*)[321] and scissors of metal shells (*maden toplu mikra-zlar*)[322] were used as projectiles in the cannons of Ottoman ships. We come across almost all these types of projectiles in 1790 among the ammunition on three separate *trabago* ships led by Ülgünlü Yusuf Reis, Salih Reis and Sinan oglu Hasan Reis, as well as on a *pirigandi* called *Pirigandi-i Mahmud Pasha*, led by Ahmed Reis[323], and on a frigate called *Cabbâr-i Bahri*, led by Fettah Kapudan[324], and finally on a frigate bought from England and led by Osman

Kapudan.[325] Iron bars, and shells with five holes (*beş delikli paçavra*), shells with two bars or rings, howits/howitzer shells, grape shells, common shells and round shots also appear in the list of ammunition to be purchased from England in 1793. The list seems to have been prepared by the Ottoman authorities according to the contract signed between the two countries.[326]

These contract and list given to the British ambassador for shells, shots, mortar, mortar beds, carriages, gunpowder, tin, fire-locks, anchors and other things for the use of the artillery and arsenal, stated that these were to be of the best qualities, in accordance with the lists given by the Grand Admiral Hüseyin Pasha and the preceding Mustafa Efendi, the same being decreed by an imperial edict in the Sultan's own handwriting and ordered by a command of the Sublime Porte on 9 March 1793. On arrival of any part of the above warlike stores, the amount would be divided into six payments, the first of which would be paid on delivery of the above articles and the rest month by month, the whole in six months.[327]

In 1793 there was close interaction between Great Britain and the Porte in terms of the trade of military supplies, especially cannons to be used on land and on ships. British military goods seem to have been in great demand by the Porte.[328] A Foreign Office document by Robert Ainslie in Constantinople to the secretary of state in December 1793 gives details of the Porte's demand for shells and other military supplies. The document includes some drawings of the shells as well as their descriptions, both in Ottoman Turkish and in English. It states that '*Tersâne-i Amire trafindan verilen humbara daneleri çapıdır. İşbu daneler humbara danelerinin sath-ı zâhirîsi olub havanlarin çapı olmadığı haber verilur*', meaning 'these are the calibres of the shells given by the Ottoman arsenal, that is to say the circles are the exterior measures of the circumferences of the shells'. The description confirms that the thickness and proportions of the shells are the same as those used by the British artillery. Each circle represents the circumference of the shell, and the pencil line the diameter. The large shells were to have the same measure as in the services mentioned above, while the smaller ones, that is, all below the 8 inches are not. The fuse holes were to be the same as those English shells without projections and of the same diameter. Each shell was to correspond to the diameter marked and to the weight expressed upon each line.[329]

This close interaction between the Porte and Great Britain was still lively at the beginning of the 1800s. On 29 January 1800 the Porte, having met with such great disappointment and unfairness from Russian merchants that they would no longer procure these articles from the Black Sea, asked England for military goods and artillery in a considerable amount. A sketch of the summary of armaments drawn up by Minister of War Hacı Ibrahim Efendi shows the following equipment and their estimated value in sterling: iron shot of five different sizes, at ten piaster a *kintal*, including charges (171,000); grape shot (200,000); shells of five different sizes (45,00); pewter/if at 100 piaster per *kintal/kintals* (1,000); tin/at current price in England/cases (250); tarpauling for guns, whole pieces (2,000); paper for cartridges (1,000); muskets with bayonettes (8,000); blades for swords (6,000).[330]

The relations between the Ottomans and foreign countries in terms of the exchange of military equipment and especially projectiles can be followed through several books by Ottoman authors who were generally inspired by their contemporaries in France. Yahya Naci Efendi (d. 1824), one of the translators of the Imperial Council (*Dîvân-ı Hümâyûn*) and a teacher of the sciences and French at the Imperial School of Military Engineering (*Mühendishâne-i Berrî-i Hümâyûn*), wrote a treatise titled *Risâle-i Hikmet-i Tabiiyye* (*A Treatise on Physics*) in 1224/1809 on the motion of projectiles. The writer, who had previously studied physics in Europe, described the operational principles of artillery, such as the howitzer and gun. In addition, some physical and chemical principles were mentioned to explain the functioning of firearms. Such subjects as the motion of free-falling bodies, circular motion, weight, attraction force and impulse, the chemical composition of gunpowder and its combustion in firearms were among the most important points mentioned in the treatise. The latter was not a translation of a single book, but was prepared most likely by the study of several sources, with the author's peculiar style and emphasis. Yahya Naci Efendi's work is also important with respect to the introduction of physical and chemical terminology to the Ottoman world.[331]

Another important work, entitled *Er-Risâletü'l Berkıyye fî Âlâti'r-Ra`diye* (*A treatise of Lightning on Thunderclap Device*), was translated by Başhoca Hafız Ishak Efendi, the chief instructor at the

*Mühendishâne-i Berrî-i Hümâyûn* from Robert Fulton's *Torpedo War and Submarine Explosions* (New York, 1810). Fulton was famous for his invention of naval torpedoes and the first submarines as well as the *Clemont*, the first steam ship. Ishak Hoca[332] declared that the Black Sea and the Straits would be better defended and that there would be no need for forts if these torpedoes were adopted by the Ottomans. He described, for instance, how these weapons worked and could destroy a large sailing warship at anchor and then sail off. Ishak Hoca's book, the first Turkish translation on naval torpedoes, was a pioneering work for the development of naval technology.[333]

### Gunpowder for naval guns

As for the gunpowder required for the naval guns, an imperial edict dated 1789–90 presents several important issues. First, it points out that each naval cannon was allotted 50 cartridges (*hartuc*). Second, both black gunpowder originating in Istanbul and Gelibolu and English gunpowder were used in the Ottoman and Algerian navies. The amount of black gunpowder given to the navy is known to have been 8,440 *kantars*. The amount of English gunpowder supplied to the navy was not cited in numbers, but referred to as 'a certain amount'. Furthermore, the document mentions that the present quantity of the English gunpowder in the imperial armoury was said by the *Defterdar Efendi* (Treasurer) to be 3,880 *kantars*. The document points out that despite the good quality of the Ottoman black gunpowder, it was not of as high a quality as that of the English type (*Ingiliz perdahti*).[334]

In 1792–93, in order to store the amount of gunpowder required for the cannons on the galleons, copper pots were produced with copper of 20 *vukıyye* each, and 40 *akçes* were paid per *vukıyye*. *Hark-i nâr* (a kind of hot substance) was not included in this amount.[335] Copper for the cannons mounted on the ships came mostly from Ergani and Keban through Amasya, Sivas, Tokan, Samsun wharf and Iznikmid.[336]

Regarding the exchange of gunpowder between Ottoman and English navies, the English naval ships operating in the Mediterranean against French forces requested 500 barrels (250 *kantars* and each *kantar* for 45 *kuruş*) of good-quality Ottoman black gunpowder from the Porte in return for money. The

Ottomans, after considering that England was their ally, decided to meet the demand free of charge. It is understood that the value of the gunpowder granted to the British fleet was 12,000 *kuruş* (24–25 purses).[337]

### Secondary equipment related to naval guns

The loading, mounting, manoeuvring and limitations of recoil of the guns on the ships required some tools and materials that were crucial for the efficient use and firing of the guns. These secondary materials included cannon wagons (*top arabası*), iron rings of bolts and screws for these wagons (*ahen halka-i civata-i araba*), hooked blocks or pulleys of deck tackle to lift and locate the guns (*ahen kanca-i makara-i palanga-i top*), iron cordage for the guns (*ahen paranga-i top*), ropes, iron hooks (*ahen kanca*) and rings (*ahen halka*) to secure the guns on the broadsides, iron hooks for lifting gunports during firing (*ahen kanca-i lumbar*), cartridge bags (*hartuc kağıdı*), copper funnels (*bakır huni*), wicks (*fitil-i mısri*),[338] gun levers (*manivela-i top*), halberds (*harbe*), white felt for cannons (*beyaz top keçesi*), scoops for loading gunpowder to guns (*kepce-i top*) and cannon drill (*top burgusu*) and such to load and clean the guns.[339]

Regarding the secondary equipment, some other needs appeared from time to time. A document declared that a new sheltered space (*sundurma*) for the protection of the cannon carriages (*top arabası/kundağı*) on the imperial galleons from rain, snow and other bad weather conditions, and a manual workbench (*çark/destgâh*) for the construction and manufacture of the tenon equipment of wagon axles (*araba dingili zeban takımları*), as well as a suitable place for this purpose, were urgently needed. A French engineer, possibly Le Brun, was commissioned to construct and manufacture the above-mentioned workbench and the tenon equipment of wagon axles. In an imperial edict, the *Kaptan Pasha* ordered the *Liman Reisi* (commander of the port of Istanbul), *mimar aga* (chief architect), *usta* (foreman), *kalfa* (assistant) and other relevant personnel at the Imperial Naval Arsenal to research the feasibility and conditions of proper places for this aim. As a result of their search, the estimate cost for furnace and shed for the gunstock of cannon wagon appeared to be 5,742 *kuruş*, while the estimate cost for the workbench and an appropriate place for the construction of wagon axles was 1,098.5 *kuruş* (noting that due to its unfamiliar type, this figure could change). The total amounted to 6,346 *kuruş*.[340]

The furnace mentioned above is related to the need for the manufacture of bronze sheaves (*tunc zebanlar*) for the imperial galleons, stated earlier. In addition, four separate building projects were planned, as far as can be understood from an inspection book of 24 October 1801. The first building was a shed in which the gunstocks of cannon wagons would be stored for protection. The second one was an appropriate place for the production of wagon axles. The third one was a European type of annealing furnace (*tavlama ocağı*) with brick walls. The last was a workshop for the manufacture of workbenches and hand wheels for the production of iron pins and wagon axles with movable arms. Among the materials used in the constructions were stone, worn-out anchors, bricks, roof tiles, oak timber, iron screws, bolts and rings.[341]

### Naval artillery personnel

Each cannon on a ship was under the responsibility of a person called a *sudagabu* (gunner).[342] The number of gunners therefore matched that of the cannons on board. They were paid *rub ulufe* (a salary of one fourth) in 1795–96 and were in great demand, especially during campaigns.[343] On each galleon, there were three gunners (one of whom was the chief gunner of the deck/*güverte topçubaşısı/sertopi*) and 64 *sudagabu*. On frigates, there were two *sertopi* and 32 *sudagabu*. Among the auxiliary personnel were men who opened the gunports, directed the guns to the targets, moved the guns back and forth by means of ropes and cables, used levers and loaded the guns with gunpowder and cannonballs. When the post of chief gunner fell vacant, a *topçu kethüdası* (an official in charge of guns) was appointed to the post if he was competent. If not, a *sudagabu* who had distinguished himself with his competence and knowledge of firing guns would be preferred for the post.[344]

On some occasions, field cannoniers were employed or forced to serve on board of the ships of the Ottoman navy. Many documents note their complaints and reluctance to serve on ships. They often rebelled saying, 'We will not serve on the ships!'[345] This unwillingness can be explained by the physical difficulties and dangers of sea wars, as well as by the negative impact of being away from home for a long time on the psychology of the personnel.

When needed, foreign personnel were employed on the galleons to deal with technical problems. In a document of 1212/1797–98, the *Kaptan Pasha* complained about the carelessness in the construction of gunstocks used on the galleons, leading to premature wearing out, breaking and constant need for repair during their operation. He pointed out that the gunstocks used on European ships were carefully made with the mixture of iron and therefore were long lasting and easy to use. For this purpose, a French ironsmith named (Casey?) was employed to manufacture the iron parts of the gunstocks to be used on one- and three-decked galleons and some other ships. The Frenchman was paid 125 *kuruş* per month, starting from 1797–98.[346] The newly invented foreign cannon carriages and gunstocks were much in demand in the Ottoman realm. Already in 1793–94 the Ottomans used newly invented and constructed gunstocks and Austrian-type carriages of ironwork both on land and during naval campaigns.[347]

The Ottomans suffered from a shortage of technical personnel to carry out cannon manoeuvres in 1798–99. According to an imperial edict, a Russian translator named Fonton came to the office of the *Dîvân-ı Hümâyûn* translator and informed him that the admiral of the Russian navy, as a prospective ally of the Ottoman state, had the intention to visit the Ottoman ships in order to observe their order and that of the soldiers, and to view the manufacture and use of the cannons on ships. Upon the *Kaptan Pasha*'s order, the Ottoman authorities made the necessary preparations to show Russian officers their cannons and their use on an appropriate ship. The Russian officers were given 2,000 gold coins as a gift. It is worth noting the *Kaptan Pasha*'s words preceding the Russian visit: when asked for his opinion, he said, 'There is no one to carry out drills with cannons in our navy. Knowledgeable gunners are either in naval campaigns or in Vidin. Do not let this drill be a fiasco. Visiting the ships is enough for them. Let them finish their work before Wednesday and go. And 1,000 gold coins is a small amount, so give them 2,000 gold coins.'[348]

A Foreign Office document draws attention to the shortcomings of the Ottoman naval artillery, saying that the personnel were unaware of the true principles of gunnery and that two or more cannons of an enormous size, carrying a ball of marble of 100–200 weights, were used. The document notes that there was no uniformity of the cannons, and therefore the danger and confusion, arising from the incredible variety of artillery scattered without system on each deck, were great.[349] Thus, foreign artillery personnel were employed in the educational institutions. In 1792–93 Admiral Horatio Nelson, the famous British naval commander, recommended through the interpreter Pizani that a British artillery engineer, with proper technical knowledge in artillery and various drawings, be employed at the *Muhendishane*.[350]

To sum up, the late eighteenth century witnessed many changes in almost every aspect of naval technology. Danışman's thesis suggesting that in the second half of that century, and specifically during the reign of Selim III, the Ottomans had almost all the preconditions for industrialisation, to a great extent is valid for the shipbuilding sector of the time.[351] In this period, shipbuilding underwent a shift from a craft to a semi-scientific pursuit. The change can be called 'semi-scientific' since it did not mark a watershed in terms of the full adoption of modern naval technology. However, it was a milestone in the sense that it paved the way for the beginning of a resolute transformation in the Ottoman mentality of naval technology. In order to observe a full change in the real sense, one would have to wait until the first half of the nineteenth century.

# 3

# THE ROLE OF FOREIGN MISSIONS IN THE OTTOMAN NAVAL TRANSFORMATION

In all periods of Ottoman history, foreign missions and individuals found employment in one form or another. The *Tâife-i Efrenciyân*[1] and non-Muslim consultant physicians[2] employed in the Ottoman palace are just two examples. The unchanging factor in this policy was the Ottomans' willingness to possess knowledge of and follow developments in technology considered to be beneficial for practical purposes, rather than long-term targets. Therefore, it can be argued that the transfer of new technologies, sciences and concepts to the Ottoman Empire was to a great extent instrumental.

The Ottomans were oriented mostly toward solving immediate practical problems. The diffusion and acceptance of new knowledge were rapid as long as that knowledge could solve problems. Particularly, in such fields as military technology, firearms, mining, cartography, compasses and clock making, the Ottomans had a tendency to adopt and apply new developments efficiently without much time lapse. This adoption was realised through following technological developments by means of commissioning Ottoman ambassadors, technicians and other such travellers to observe and report what they saw abroad, and demanding technical missions from foreign countries to apply the new technology in the Ottoman lands and to educate Muslim technicians.[3]

Naval technology, as part of military and economic technologies, became a matter of great interest for the foreign missions in Istanbul, starting from the late eighteenth century. Selim III adopted a policy of transferring military and naval technologies from Europe and keeping abreast of the latest developments. Foreign powers, which fully understood the importance of this development, began to offer their services and raced to win a considerable share from this military market. The Ottoman government took this historic opportunity to follow a policy of balance despite its disadvantageous position. Thus, in many ways, Selim III, in Shaw's words, was the first ruler of an 'underdeveloped country' to manipulate and take advantage of the rivalries of the great powers to secure assistance in the development of his own country.[4]

The foreigners who came to the Ottoman Empire for work can be divided into two main categories with respect to their fields of employment and channels of procurement. Regarding the first category, they were divided into four groups composed of engineers, officials or officers teaching the art of war, workmen skilled in various branches, and physicians and surgeons. In the second category were four groups as well: those procured via the ambassadors of the foreign countries in Istanbul, those procured as a result of the attempts of the notables of state, those procured by permanent ambassadors, and finally ones who came on their own as workers without any mediator.[5]

**French missions**

From the 1780s onward, French missions began to permeate every area of Ottoman military technology. In 1784 and 1787, two French missions arrived at the Imperial Naval Arsenal in Istanbul and set to work as a result of bilateral agreements between the two countries. The approaching Russian threat and France's armament played a considerable role in the employment of French people by the Porte, considering the mutual interests of the two countries.

French engineers and draftsmen provided ship models, sought to establish an iron foundry for casting cannons, shells and bullets, and to build wet and dry docks.[6]In 1786 the number of Frenchmen employed in the arsenal increased dramatically with the addition of a large group of artisans, workmen and sailors. These men were employed most particularly at the naval arsenal.[7]

Among the Frenchmen was Laurent-Jean Francois Truguet, who was commissioned to the French embassy in Istanbul as an attaché with the specific task of preparing maps of the Marmara[8] and Black Seas. He was also the commander (with the rank of *binbaşı*/major) of the French frigate *Charleton* and taught *deniz tabyası* (naval manoeuvres) courses at the *Tersâne Mühendishânesi* in 1782 together with Tondu (Tondule)[9] .With the introduction of these two courses, the educational scope of the school was extended, as only mathematics (*hisab*), geography (*coğrafya*) and cartography (*harita*) had been taught since the opening of the school in 1776. These new courses offered by the French teachers were translated by Kirkor and Mihram Efendi into Ottoman Turkish and given to the students as textbooks. Truguet's course notes, entitled 'Traité du pilotage et de navigation' and 'Éléments de géometrie' ('Treatise on pilotage and navigation' and 'Elements of geometry') were translated into Ottoman Turkish, but not published.[10] Truguet was also famous for a book on naval manoeuvres and tactics. His *Usûlü'l-ma`arif fî vech-i tasfîf-i sefâyin-i donanma ve fenn-i tedbîr-i harekâtuhâ* (*Traité de manœuvre et de tactique pratique*) (*Treatise of Manoeuvre and Practical Tactics*), was published in 1787 by the press founded by the French ambassador, Choiseul-Gouffier.[11] The introductory pages of the book give important information about its aim.[12]

In the mid-1780s Jean-Jacques Sébastien Le Roy and Du Rest travelled to Istanbul. Of Swiss origin, Le Roy was born in Paris on 15 September 1784. As a shipbuilder in the Pyrénées, he had established a structural design enabling the easy fitting of ship masts into their proper places with the aid of a lever. Later on, he had gone to Corsica and worked in the construction of many ships at Loirent. Upon the request of Halil Hamid Pasha, the French government sent Le Roy and his assistants to Turkey. As understood from a letter (23 May 1784) written by Comte de Vergennes in Paris to St. Priest, the French ambassador to Istanbul, among the aims of his employment were the establishment of a new defence system, the training of the Ottomans in shipbuilding techniques and principles, the changing of the traditional system of shipbuilding, the re-establishment of the present Ottoman navy if possible, and its modernisation to European standards.[13]

Le Roy travelled to Istanbul in 1784 with the support of the French ambassador Comte de Choiseul-Gouffier, together with the workers of the naval arsenal in Toulon. His colleague, Du Rest, and the French team arrived in Istanbul in 1787. Among them were a caulker named Guillaume L'Abbé, a carpenter, an augerer named Michel Henri and a purser named René Peton, all from Brest; two caulkers, named Joseph-Marie Gassin and Antoine Bonveau from Toulon; and two carpenters, Antoine Olivier and Hyacinthe Gasquet.[14] Their salaries were 125 *kuruş* for Le Roy, 100 *kuruş* for Du Rest, 70 *kuruş* for Guillaume L'Abbé, 60 *kuruş* for Michel Henri and René Peton, respectively, and 50 *kuruş* for the rest.

Kaçar writes that Guillaume L'Abbé was 54 at the time. He started as an apprentice and became master in 1765. He worked for four years and three months as workshop foreman (*atölye şefi*) in Istanbul. Michel Henri, 46, started as an apprentice in 1758 and became master in 1778. He also stayed in Istanbul for four years and three months and worked under Le Roy. Peton, 61, started as an apprentice in 1741 and became assistant master in 1762.[15] Gassin, 65, started in 1733, became master in 1750, and worked in Istanbul for two years. He was regarded as incompetent and cantankerous. Olivier, 55, began his career as an apprentice in 1744, became foreman in 1779 and stayed in Istanbul for two years. Gasquet, 44, started as an apprentice in 1753, became assistant foreman in 1777, and foreman in 1779. He returned to France in June 1787, by the order of Choiseul-Gouffier. Bonveau, 42, started out as an apprentice in 1755 and became assisstant foreman in 1777 and master in 1778. He stayed on in Istanbul on the order of the ambassador, while other workers and masters returned to France in 1788.[16]

Le Roy and his colleague Du Rest were among the first French workers employed at the Imperial Arsenal. Before starting his work, Le Roy examined the arsenal and determined some needs and deficiencies. Seeing that there was no proper place dedicated to drawing, he tried to arrange a well-lit room for that purpose. The first project that he prepared was the plans and a model of a warship of 74 guns. On the arrival of the French masters and workers, the construction of the ship was started. Despite some difficulties[17] with the personnel of the arsenal and the supply of timber for ships, he managed to build several large ships.

Le Roy is also known to have made models for two sloops, one for the *Kaptan Pasha* and another for Kapudana, when a small ship was launched into the sea on 25 April 1785. These models were presented to the Porte by Choiseul-Gouffier. The total number of ships, regardless of their types and sizes, that were constructed by Le Roy and his team between 1784 and 1788 is stated to have been 112. Among the ships constructed in the period in question were the galleon *Mukaddeme-i Nusret* (*Beginning of Victory*) of 74 guns; two frigates of 12 guns; four corvettes of 14 guns (each gun of eight *parmaks* in diameter); a galliot of ten guns (eight *parmaks* in diameter) and two *mortoloz* (twelve *parmaks* in diameter); a *preme* carrying a *mortoloz* of 12 *parmaks* in diameter and ten guns (12 *parmaks* in diameter); 12 bomb vessels (bombarde) of 68 *kadems* in length and carrying a gun of 36, and a *mortoloz* of ten *parmaks* in diameter; 41 bomb vessels (bombardes) of 58 *kadems* in length, each carrying a single 24 gun; and finally 16 gunships (*top çeker*), 50 *kadems* in length and each carrying a single 24 gun on board.[18]

This team and the ones employed in the following years brought their own measuring tools and plans and sketches. They paved the way for the mutual interaction and cooperation between Ottoman and French technicians with respect to some measures of length.[19]

Due to the French–Ottoman tension in 1788–89, Le Roy was called back to France, after five years[20] in Istanbul. Considering the French quest for Black Sea naval materials and the Ottomans' strict policy preventing it, some writers tend to explain his mission in the capacity of shipbuilder as part of a French plan to encourage and assure a vigorous illicit traffic in masts from the Black Sea under the noses of the Ottomans.[21] He is reported to have considered the shape of Turkish ships' bottoms to be perfect and to have assured Eton that he took Turkish vessels as his models for the bottoms.[22]

Little is known about Du Rest, apart from the fact that he received a salary of 100 *kuruş* for his service at the Imperial Naval Arsenal, that he contracted the plague and died, after a long treatment in a hospital in Beyoğlu, on 25 September 1787, and that, following his death, the French monarchy provided financial support to his family.[23]

Toussaint Petit, like his associates Le Brun and Jean-Baptiste Benoit, was a naval architect in the second French mission. The new foundry machines were installed and put into operation under his direction and that of an unnamed German renegade.[24] During the French Napoleonic expedition to Egypt, he was imprisoned and replaced in Istanbul by Englishmen or Swedes.[25]

Alexis Guez was a master caulker and Louis Desulier was a drilling master in the same mission in 1784. During the French Napoleonic expedition to Egypt, they, too, were imprisoned and their places in Istanbul filled by Englishmen and Swedes.[26]

Jacques-Balthasard Le Brun was the most influential French engineer to serve the Ottoman Empire during the reign of Selim III. As some Ottoman documents show, the Porte determined candidates both at home and abroad. During that process, Le Brun emerged, along with his reputation at Toulon.[27] The Sultan issued an imperial edict to employ him in the construction of a 57.5-*zira* galleon.[28] On his arrival in Istanbul, Le Brun presented his official document (*kaime*) to the *Tersâne-i Âmire emini Rashid Efendi* and was employed at the naval arsenal in the capacity of shipbuilder, both in Istanbul and other places, because of his skills, experience and superiority to his colleagues.[29] The imperial edict in question warned the other officials not to fail to show their respect to him. He entered Ottoman service as a shipbuilding engineer in June 1793[30]and was granted a fixed salary, clothes, belongings and food. Meanwhile, an image of a ship was sent to Le Brun and he was ordered to draw the ship in a bigger size floating at sea and to send the drawing to the Sultan.[31]

On Küçük Hüseyin Pasha's demand, his brother Polid Brun, also an engineer, was employed at the arsenal in 1796 to help in the naval works, after being tested with the construction of a corvette.[32]

During his employment at the naval arsenal, Le Brun worked in a wide range of positions, as a shipwright, as a teacher of the science of shipbuilding at the *Hendesehâne*, as a dock engineer and as the introducer of new naval tools and equipment to the workers in the arsenal. He is also known to have provided new measures and techniques to Ottoman as well as foreign shipbuilders working at other docks or shipbuilding yards. One of his most important contributions was a new method of launching ships after their completion on the land up to their gunports and finishing the rest in the sea. Thanks to his work, the number of shipyards increased so that they were able to construct nine large ships at the same time. Two shipbuilding stocks were built at Hasköy and Ayvansaray. In the western end of the *Tersâne* site, new stone stocks replaced the old wooden ones. Additionally, small hangars were constructed at the upper end of the Golden Horn for the relatively smaller units of the navy. The construction of two new cranes with arms was completed in 1795.[33]

The various kinds of ships completed by Le Brun or with his help show his influence in a more concrete manner. The *Arslân-ı Bahrî* (a galleon of 59 *zira*, 76 guns and crew) launched in 1794–95, the *Selâbetnumâ* (a corvette of 33 *zira*, 26 guns and 150 crew) launched in 1795–96, the *Selimiye* (a galleon of 47 metres, 122 guns and 1,200 crew) launched in 1796, the *Mesken-i Gazî* (a frigate of 53 *zira*, 50 guns and 450 crew) launched in 1796–97, the *Bâdi-i Nusret* (a galleon of 47 metres/63 *zira*, 82 guns and 900 crew) launched in 1797, the *Tâvus-i Bahrî* (a galleon of 47 metres/63 *zira*, 82 guns and 900 crew) launched in 1798 and the *Bedr-i Zafer* (a frigate of 53 *zira*, 50 guns and 450 crew) launched in 1799–1800 were all built by Le Brun.[34]

Built by Le Brun and Antoin, or built by Antoin following Le Brun's instructions,[35] were the *Cengâver* (a corvette of 37 *zira*, 26 guns and 200 crew) launched in 1797–98, the *Şucâ-i Bahrî* (a corvette of 37 *zira*, 26 guns and 200 crew) launched in 1797–98,[36] the *Sâika-i bâd* (a corvette of 37 *zira*, 26 guns and 175 crew) launched in 1797–98 and the *Âteşfeşân* (a corvette of 37 *zira*, 26 guns and 175 crew) launched in 1797–98.[37]

Le Brun's Herculean performance was widely praised by foreign statesmen as well as the Porte. In a letter to the secretary of state by the British ambassador to Istanbul, he was described, despite his short time of residence (not yet two years), as 'the artist appearing not to have been employed in vain'. From the same letter, it is understood that he was expected to have laid the keel of a three-decker to be formed on the model of the *Royal Louis*.[38] Another document mentions the ceremony of launching a frigate to carry thirty 18-pounders on one deck, built after a French model by Le Brun, and indicates that laying the keel of an 84-gun ship had been undertaken by a Venetian master builder in this arsenal, where another ship to carry 74 guns was already under construction.[39] Other documents show that Le Brun and his entourage complained about the poor performance and low levels of self-sacrifice of the other French missions working in other dockyards who had higher salaries. They claimed that they deserved higher salaries than the others and demanded additional payment from the Porte in return for their efforts.[40]

Le Brun is known to have worked in casting copper nails on new models together with Dimitri[41] and in sheathing ships with copper[42] in the year 1795–96. On demand, he taught the science of shipbuilding at the *Hendesehâne* in 1796–97.[43]

As for his activities at the *Tersâne Mühendishânesi* or *Hendesehâne*, Le Brun made some proposals to the Porte in order to improve the state of the Ottoman navy and naval education. His recommendations were added to the Küçük Hüseyin Pasha *Layihası* (report). To mention some of his proposals, he first drew attention to the need for a drilling house (*talimhâne*) that would serve as a training facility. Classes would be held every day, excluding Fridays and Sundays. Training would be held in three courses: mathematics and geometry (*ilm-i rakam ve ilm-i hendese*), drawings and descriptions of ships (*resim ve gemilerin tasvîrâtı*), and application of the theoretical courses at the shipbuilding sites. The course materials of the students would be provided by the state and delivered by Le Brun, who would submit regular reports to the naval authorities on the conditions, skills, merits and capacities of the students. The aim of the education would be to train local shipbuilders and architects in order to overcome the need for foreign experts. Students would be educated to the extent that they would be able to draw plans, design and construct ships in compliance with geometrical calculations both at the naval arsenal and at other sites. They would be given a certain salary according to their success.

Le Brun's recommendations and remarks were accepted by the state and he was given full authority to implement them.[44] He, together with Honoré Benoit, remained in the service of the Ottoman navy even during the Napoleonic expedition to Egypt, when all the other French technicians in the Ottoman service were imprisoned and replaced by Englishmen and Swedes, thanks to their successful performance in creating a modern naval establishment and training a number of highly skilled naval architects to take over their work.[45] Küçük Hüseyin Pasha is said to have met with the Grand Vizier and they decided to keep him and his team in the Ottoman service.[46]

Le Brun is also known to have been commissioned by imperial edicts to build ships in the countryside regions and adjust the *endâze* (measuring device) to measure and draw the pictures of these ships in 1799–1800. When his translator was asked to inform Le Brun of this imperial edict, he said that Le Brun entrusted his daughters to the Russian embassy in Istanbul, packed his personal belongings and left Istanbul on board a Russian ship to serve Russia. He left a note advising the Porte to commission Benoit in his place for the service in question. The Ottoman government, angry with both Le Brun and the Russian government, criticised Le Brun, saying that he had been in the Ottoman service for six to seven years, paid and treated very well. They accused the admirals of the Russian ships, and Amiral Uchakov in particular, of running between the Black Sea and the Mediterranean Sea trying to entice into Russian service the skilled foreign personnel in Istanbul, irrespective of any permission from the Porte. The Ottoman government demanded that the Russian embassy respect the mutual treaty of friendship in order to avoid insurmountable consequences.

The Porte, aware of the lack of skilled engineers capable of replacing Le Brun, and that Honoré Benoit had been Le Brun's right-hand man, decided to take the necessary measures to prevent Benoit from being hired away by Russia. His salary was increased, Le Brun's former salary was added to it,[47] and he took over the course that Le Brun had taught on the science of shipbuilding at the *Hendesehâne*.[48] This sequence of events can be followed in the reports of the British Foreign Office as well. A 'most secret' document, dated 17 February 1800 and written to the secretary of state by the British ambassador, the Earl of Elgin at Istanbul, states that the shipbuilder Le Brun, whose works had been most beneficial in the arsenal, had been enticed away the previous autumn and openly received in Russia, and that this had caused continuous disappointments in all commissions for naval materials from Russia, so much so as to have obliged the government to give up any further attempts to procure them from that country.[49]

It is puzzling that an Ottoman document dated 1803–04 indicates that Le Brun was still in the Ottoman service, both as a shipbuilder in the arsenal and a teacher of the science of shipbuilding at the *Hendesehâne*.[50]

A document dated 1799–1800 shows that Benoit received 2,910 *kuruş* for his service of three months and seven days.[51] On 24 October 1800, his salary, together with that of his translator, was 2,460 *kuruş*. This amount, it was decided, would be paid from the *Irad-i Cedid Treasury* (New Treasury for New Order) and the *Seferiyye akcesi* (Temporary Treasury for Wartime Expenses).[52] Among his permenant team was his son Honoré Benoit, Kiryas (a caulker), Petri (a sail maker), Alexander (a translator) and Adriya (later on Andon/Antoine, an architect). It seems that 150 *kuruş* for his son, 150 *kuruş* for Kiryas, 140 *kuruş* for Petri, 100 *kuruş* for the translator and 150 *kuruş* for the architect were allotted.[53] Benoit took over the course that Le Brun had taught on the science of shipbuilding at the *Hendesehâne*.[54]

A foreigner named Casey (*Kisi, Keysî*) was employed as an ironsmith at a monthly salary of 125 *kuruş*, starting from the month of Şa`bân 1212/1797–98, casting cannons to be mounted on galleons as well as manufacturing iron parts for the gunstocks to be used on the galleons of one-and three-deckers and some other ships. He had been employed earlier at 250 *kuruş* in Istanbul along with 25 other Frenchmen, receiving 4,000 *kuruş* per month. When he went on leave, another worker was appointed to his post. Then he began to work at the *Tersâne-i Âmire* without a monthly salary until he was re-appointed to the above-mentioned job at 125 *kuruş* in 1797–98.[55] Due to the poor quality of the previous Ottoman cannons, he gained considerable reputation for casting cannons.[56]

The third French mission to the Ottoman Empire was composed of the engineer Pierre Ferregeau and four other people. For the constructions of a new dry dock, the Ottomans had wanted to employ the French engineer Antoine Groignard, who had constructed the dry dock at Toulon between 1774 and 1778.[57] At the end of 1795, the Ottoman government communicated this to the revolutionary French government via French consul J. B. Barthélemy. The French government sent instead of Groignard, who was quite old, the younger Ferregeau, who had been successful in the extension works of the harbour of Cherbourg and in underwater constructions. Ferregeau, unlike A. L. Barabé and A. I. Castellan in the same mission, stayed in Istanbul for nearly three years, preparing plans regarding the defense of the Bosphorus. In May 1798, he returned to Paris, together with G. A. Oliver.[58]

A British document dated 15 June 1797 on the French mission indicates that arrivals from France by land and by sea gradually formed an aggregate of more than 300 people. Among those, of particular note was a hydraulic engineer of some eminence, named Ferregeau. The same document notes that Ferregeau became popular in Istanbul with his assistance in the construction of a basin and docks for shipping upon a plan similar to those at Toulon.[59] From the same document, we also understand that the Porte preferred the project of a Swedish engineer named Rodée to that of Ferregeau.[60]

In addition to the above-mentioned information, an Ottoman document dated October 1796 reveals that *Kaptan Pasha* wrote a letter to the French government asking it to send the dock engineer Groignard to build a dry dock at the Imperial Naval Arsenal. But the French government stated that it did not know where he was. Then the Porte asked through a French trader to employ his assistant and learned that he was in Italy. The French trader recommended Groignard's son, Dushan Dumat,[61] instead of his father, saying that he was more skilled and knowledgeable than his father. Dushan Dumat came to Istanbul and waited in the trader's house for the final decision of the Porte. Meanwhile, the Porte started an inquiry and asked for information about Dushan Dumat from the French engineer Le Brun, who confirmed that he was more skilful in dock construction than his father, and the Porte decided to employ him. He was paid monthly 500 *kuruş*, like the Swedish engineer employed in the construction of the dock.[62] From another document, we learn that Dushan Dumat, after the Swedish mission's employment in the construction of the dry dock, was commissioned in March 1797 with the deepening works of the port of Rhodes. When his work turned out to be fruitless in Rhodes, he was recalled to Istanbul.[63]

Other members of the third French mission were the geodesy expert A. L. Barabé and the draftsman A. L. Castellan.[64] They returned to France in June after learning that the construction of the dry dock had been awarded to the Swedish engineers.[65]

A document dated 12 December 1796 reveals that although a French bore specialist (*oymacı*) named Joseph Benoit had been working at the *Tersâne-i Âmire* for three months, he had not been paid his agreed salary of 125 *kuruş* and was owed 375 *kuruş*. The amount in question was demanded from the authorities.[66]

A document dated 1797 states that Marko Vasalu and his four sons, Sharlo, Antuvan, Petro, and Nikola, had been working in the field of *makaracılık* (block making) at the *Tersâne-i Âmire* for more than a month and had not been paid yet. One hundred and twenty-five *kuruş* for Marko Vasalu and 30 *kuruş* each for his sons per month, amounting to 245 in total, were demanded, starting from the beginning of the month of *Cemâziye'l evvel* (May).[67]

The Frenchman Brul[68] was employed as a surgeon (*cerrah*) in the galleons of the imperial navy at five *kuruş* a day. He demanded payment of his salary (150 *kuruş*) for services rendered between May and June 1794 with a petition dated 2 July 1794. The authorities met this demand.[69] Three years later, a petition dated May 1797 recorded that Brul had continued at his post with the same amount of salary. He again requested that the authorities pay his money of the month of *Şevval* (October). [70]

One Paralé is mentioned by Shaw to have been a French officer employed to supplement the regular Ottoman staff of the naval school as a teacher of cartography (*fenn-i harita*), geography (*coğrafya*) and navigation (*seyr-i süfun*) before 1798.[71] He worked there as an assistant to Seyyid Osman Efendi until he returned to his county.[72] He was employed especially in teaching the practical side of cartography while Le Brun taught the theory.[73] He had worked in the service of the Ottoman navy as a pilot (*kılavuz*) before his employment in the naval school. He was not paid a new salary for his services in the naval school, since he already had a salary from the Ottoman navy.[74] As is understood from an undated report (*lâyiha*) by Abdülkadir Pasha, a naval captain of Selim III's period, about the Naval Engineering School (*Bahriye Mühendishânesî*), Paralé was fired from his post at the *Tersâne-i Âmire* during the naval campaign against France.[75]

A man named Penyola was a French engineer. A document of 1799–1800 mentions his name among those to be commissioned for the construction of a galleon at Gemlik. He was paid 200 *kuruş* as travel allowance. Emenili Enegli is referred to as an architect who received 100 *kuruş* in return for his services in the construction of the same galleon. A translator and an auger expert (*burgucu*), paid 50 *kuruş* each, together with a mountain architect (*dağ mimarı*), paid 100 *kuruş*, accompanied them.[76]

A Frenchman named Rikali was employed as a pilot (*kılavuz*) at a salary of 150 *kuruş* in the time of the late Kaptan-ı Derya Hüseyin Pasha. He was promoted to the post of chief pilot (*kılavuz başı*) for his skill and because he was needed at the *Tersâne-i Âmire* in the time of Kaptan-ı Derya Abdülkâdir Pasha. Records show that the 150-*kuruş* salary of one Lakos, who worked as an assistant engineer to Rhodé in the construction of the big dry dock at the *Tersâne-i Âmire*, was cut off because of his incompetence. This money, with a 25-*kuruş* deduction, was given to Rikali on 5 March 1804.[77]

In a document dated May–June 1807, one Petro is mentioned as a French whetstone master (*bileğici*), along with his guide (*kılavuz*) Igar. They are said to have received monthly 180 and 125 *kuruş*, respectively. Their salaries were provided by the *Tersâne-i Mamure Sergisi* (accounting department of the arsenal).[78] It is not known if this Petro was the same as *ayakmimarı* (base architect)-carpenter Petro, who worked with Manol Kalfa on 19 October 1801 in the construction of the dry dock in the Imperial Naval Arsenal[79] and on a three-decker[80] as well as in the repair of galleons and the gate of the dry dock in 1802–03.[81]

A man whose name is recorded as Romus was a French engineer sent to Rhodes, together with Trandafil Kalfa, to work on the deepening of the harbour in 1797–98. However, he was not employed there for a long time since he was considered to be incompetent, and was recalled to the arsenal. He received 500 *kuruş* for his service from the beginning of January 1797.[82]

Tortil was the name of a Frenchman who worked as an architect in repairing and adjusting some parts of a galleon that was completed in Bodrum and launched on 17 August 1796. He received 200 *kuruş* while Nikola, his translator, was paid 180 *kuruş* and a messenger (*tatar*) accompanying them, 100 *kuruş*.[83]

François Kauffer was an architect originally from Ponts et Chaussées de Lorraine in France who worked for M. de Choiseul. When de Choiseul left Istanbul, Kauffer entered into the pay of the Porte.[84] He worked as a draftsman (*teknik ressam*) and engineer until he was removed from his post and payment of his salary was stopped in June 1800. As a royalist, he did not want to return to his country and therefore took refuge in the Ottoman Empire. The Porte decided to keep him under service with a monthly salary of

300 *kuruş* to employ him, when needed, in drawing maps, pictures and so on.[85] He is also known to have drawn the picture of the *Mühendishâne* in 1776[86] and prepared a project for new granaries for the provision of Istanbul, winning the commission from Selim III.[87] He died of a pulmonary disease in 1802, working on plans of the Bosphorus.

These plans are the most important documents describing settlement in Istanbul and along the Bosphorus at the beginning of the nineteenth century. Kauffer applied a method known as triangulation in city planning. During his work, he used astronomer Tondu's calculations, and the French engineer Le Chevalier helped him as well. One of his Istanbul maps covers the Bosphorus up to the line of Suriçi, Pera, the Golden Horn, Ortaköy-Çengelköy and the Anatolian side up to Fenerbahçe and Çamlıca. His other map includes the Black Sea between Riva and Kilyos, and the Anatolian side up to Alemdağ and Pendik; and the line of Bakırköy, Davutpaşa and Cebeciköy on the Anatolian side. A copy of his plans was sent to Choiseul-Gouffier and the other copy kept in Istanbul. These plans were published in 1819, together with Barbié du Bocage's additions, in Melling's *Voyage pittoresque de Constantinople et des rives du Bosphore* (*Picturesque Travels in Constantinople and the Bosphorus Strait*).[88]

The engineer Antoine and general Le Baron de Juchereau de St. Denys entered the service of the Porte in 1807. De Juchereau was commissioned by a decree of Selim III to prepare a report about the fortification of the Dardanelles at the beginning of 1807. In the report, he pointed out that the passage of an enemy fleet sailing under a fair wind through the Dardanelles could not be prevented due to the absence of strong forts and fortifications. As a precaution, he suggested that such places as Kilidbahir, Kal'a-i Sultaniye and Naraburnu were the most strategically important spots along the straits and that the construction of strong forts, the digging of fortifications and placement of many guns were needed there. Furthermore, he recommended that a fleet composed of twelve ships should take up a position behind Naraburnu.[89]

### The Swedish mission

The employment of Swedish technicians and officers dates back to 1787, to the wars between Russia, Austria and the Ottoman

Empire. In the wake of these wars, the resulting treaty of alliance between Sweden and the Ottomans on 11 July 1789 paved the way for the strengthening of the technical solidarity that had already existed to some extent. The Porte, as part of its modernisation movement, was in want of technical staff to be employed in the shipbuilding works. Reisulkuttab Rashid Efendi, on orders by the Sultan, had already begun a search for shipbuilding architects and engineers through the ambassadors of the European states in Istanbul. The translator of the Swedish ambassador in Istanbul, Ignatius Mouradgea D'Ohsson, not only played an active role in providing Swedish engineers, shipbuilding architects, gun-casting experts, infantry officers and tacticians to serve in the Ottoman lands, but he also wrote some reports to the Porte about the *Nizam-i Cedid* (the New Order) and the modernisation of the Ottoman military power.[90]

Mr. Rosenblad and Mr. Ranchot, two Swedish engineers, were sent in the spring of 1790 by the Swedish government to serve under the Vizier, and returned to their countries on 25 October. A British document described this incidence: 'They returned in consequence of the bad human testified by the Turks at the unexpected defection of Sweden. It is said these gentlemen, for their greater security on the road, travelled under disguise as Prussian officers.'[91] It is understood that beside these engineers, the Porte, for some reason, also refused several other engineers.[92] In Istanbul, on 10 November 1791, there were only three Swedish engineers, who had been working there since September 1790.[93] They, too, returned to their country by sail in December 1791 after the new minister from Sweden, Mr De Asp, had an audience with the Sultan.[94]

Following the unsuccessful relations described above, the most significant Swedish mission, consisting of ten people, came to Istanbul through the mediation of Muradca, their translator, on 7 June 1795.[95] Among them were A. E. Rhodé, Fredrick Ludwig Af Klintberg, Kihlberg, Schantz, Mihrhen, Weidenhelm, Hörling, Malmen, Carlstrand, Hallen, Lijorgen, Löngren and Elmström.[96] These figures, together with others who arrived later, played considerable roles, specifically in the construction of the dry dock and some ships in the naval arsenal. After completing their work, most of them returned to Sweden.

The Swedish engineer-officer A. E. Rhodé received his education in Kariskorona under the supervision of Daniel af Thunberg, who was an expert in underwater construction,[97] and worked on several underwater projects at Carlscrona, a naval base in Sweden.[98] The Ottoman government found the dry dock construction project of the Swedish mission to be more feasible and economical than that of the French. In other words, Rodé's project was preferred to that of Ferregeau.[99] The construction of the dry dock, started in February 1797, was completed in May 1800. Within this period, new Swedish experts were employed on the project, among whom was the engineer Lakos. He became Rhodé's assistant.[100]

After the completion of the dry dock, some of the Swedish mission returned home on their own demand, and each was given 2,000 *kuruş* to cover travel expenses. Rhodé, after completing his work, stayed in Pera, where he shared his house with six people and paid 58 *kuruş* for his share. The total money for the rent was 350 *kuruş*, which was expensive for 11 May 1794.[101] He was still at charge in 1806 and died in Istanbul in 1811.[102]

Rhodé is said to have built nine shipbuilding platforms (*gemi inşa tezgahı*).[103] He is also known to have built 102 wooden workbenches (*destgâh*), a wooden wheel with clamp and some small tools in 1795–96,[104] as well as some iron tools, equipment and models during his service.[105] Among them was underwater glass (*sualtı dürbünü*) used for observing construction carried out below the surface of the water.[106] He was commissioned to construct a workshop to produce nails in October–November 1805–06. He and his translator were given a monthly salary of 750 *kuruş*.[107]

Lakos was known to have been employed in the construction of the dry dock in the capacity of assistant engineer to Rhodé and to have received 150 *kuruş*[108] per month until the end of his employment on 21 February 1804, due to reports about his incompetence and the fact that he was not needed in the arsenal any more. As mentioned above, his salary, with a 25-*kuruş* deduction, was given to Rikali, who was then appointed as chief pilot (*kılavuz başı*) in the arsenal.[109] In the removal of Lakos from his post, the meeting and the negative decisions of the *Tersâne Emini, Liman Reisi, Kaptan Pasha* and engineer Rhodé were influential.[110]

Fredrick Ludwig Af Klintberg was a shipbuilding engineer[111] who was part of the Swedish mission that arrived in Istanbul on 7

June 1795.[112] He built several ships during his service to the Ottoman state. Among these were the *Rehber-i Nusret*,[113] a corvette of 35 *zira*, copper-sheathed, carrying 26 guns and 200 crew, and built in 1796 in Rhodes; the *Kaplan-i Bahri*, a galleon of 59 *zira*, coppered, with 76 guns and 850 crew, and built in 1799–1800 in Rhodes; the *Meserret-i Bahir*, a corvette of 33 *zira*, coppered, carrying 22 guns and 150 crew, and built in 1799–1800 in Rhodes.[114] It is written that a Logarini worked as his assistant in the construction of the *Kaplan-i Bahri*. It was decided that he be paid 2,600 *kuruş* from the *Sihâm akçesi* of the *Irâd-ı Cedîd* Treasury for the months of Zilkade, Zilhicce, Muharrem and Safer of 1214/1799–1800. It was decided that his salary of the month of *Şevval*, 660 *kuruş*, which had formerly been transferred to the Furtuna Kapudan, be given by the Furtuna Kapudan to Klintberg.[115] He is also known to have built a three-decker ship in the dry dock with the assistance of the Genoese ironsmith Yakomi. In a petition, Klintberg demanded that the Porte pay his assistant's three-month unpaid salary, adding up to 240 *kuruş*.[116]

Malmen, Carlstrand and Hallen are mentioned as having been among the members of the Swedish mission under the direction of Rhodé on 7 June 1795.[117] They were employed in the construction of the dry dock at the Imperial Naval Arsenal. Carlstrand's speciality is unknown, but it is established that Hallen was a draftsman. Tezel confirms that he was the designer of the big dry dock.[118] Malmen appears to have been a *gemi topçusu* (naval gunner).[119] We know also that these three figures, together with Rhodé and their interpreter, demanded from the Porte their total salary of 1,560 *kuruş* for the month of *Ramazan* in 1212/1797–98.[120]

Little is known of the lives of Shantz, Weidenheim, Minthen, Elmström, Löngren, Leon and Bragran. They were part of the Swedish mission led by Rhodé, employed in various areas. Shantz, Weidenheim and Minthen were naval officers (*deryâ oficyali*) with monthly salaries of 350 *kuruş* each; Elmström, Löngren, Leon and Bragran were pulley/block master (*makaracı*), woodworker (*doğramacı*), ironsmith (*âhenger*) and stone cutter (*taşçı*), respectively. They received 160 *kuruş* per month.[121]

### The British mission

The first document referring to a naval technology transfer is dated 1788, just before Selim III's ascendence to the throne. This document enquires about the case of an English galleon builder sent by the English government to Istanbul as a result of an earlier agreement. An archival document states that the English ambassador was asked about the case, upon which he wrote to England to learn more about the situation. But the Ottoman government was unable to receive an answer and believed that the Spanish–English war was the reason for this delay. Meanwhile, the Porte requested two *top ve humbara dokumcu ustasi* (cannon and shell founders) from England. The English ambassador at Istanbul, while waiting for the answer from his own country and carrying out the correspondence, recommended that the Ottoman government send some skilled workers to England to observe and learn the work and the art of the masters. He estimated that they would learn the arts in question in five to six months. He also stated that he could write about this offer to England in case the Porte agreed. The Porte, not refusing the suggestion, went on asking about the promised galleon builders.[122] The results of the correspondence are unknown, but it seems that both parties were positive about military cooperation.

A letter on 22 February 1793 from Robert Ainslie, the British ambassador to Istanbul, notes that he was introduced to the *Kaptan Pasha* and requested to inspect the arsenal and point out defects and remedies. He also says that the Porte sought to establish a permanent plan and was ready to offer encouragement, being aware of their vulnerable position.[123]

An Ottoman document of 1794–95 states that the construction of a new frigate of 45.5 *zira* had been decided. For this frigate, Muradca, Swedish translator to Istanbul, set out from Bec, together with two British officers. One of them was an expert in naval affairs and the other in land military. Muradca, when asked by the Ottomans, mentioned that the naval officer was an expert in both shipbuilding (*inşâ-i sefâin*) and ship manufacturing (*imâl-i sefâin*). For a test to check his skills, he was asked to draw a picture of a model ship. He did well and was complimented by the experts. For the service of the navy built on the coast of Tuna during the campaign, two other Englishmen, who were skilled at geometry (*fenn-i hendese*) and construction, travelled to Istanbul on demand. After recovering from a disease, one of them was asked also to draw a picture of a ship, and his ship model was complimented as well. They were employed.[124]

An Englishman recorded simply as Daniel was employed in the service of the Ottoman navy in the Black Sea during the 1787–92 wars. Later on, he applied for service with the Porte with a letter of recommendation (*tavsiyyenâme*) by Yusuf Âgâh Efendi, the Porte's ambassador to London, and was employed at a salary of 400 *kuruş* on 7 March 1795, despite a written note stating that while he was cognisant of construction, he had no mastery of any science. His employment did not last long. He was removed from the post and his salary was stopped on 3 August 1795 on the grounds that he was lacking in any skills and was unsuitable for employment.[125]

We learn from a British document dated 25 June 1795, by Robert Liston, the British ambassador to Istanbul, that a naval mechanic named Richard White, lately employed in the construction of gunboats on the River Thames, also appeared in Istanbul and was taken into the service in consequence of a letter of recommendation with which he had been furnished by Yusuf Agâh Efendi, the Turkish ambassador to London. A division of gunboats, 40 in number, constructed on an improved plan and built in some of the ports of the Black Sea, had a few days earlier been brought around to the Bosphorus, and more were expected from the same quarter.[126] Another document dated 10 July 1796 states that the naval mechanic White and some royalist French figures of high rank such as the Comte de Bizemont, the Chevalier de Montclar and de Cressur had all been discharged, which was considered unjust and impolite by English authorities with respect to diplomatic courtesy. It seems that White returned home via Russia.[127]

A man named Olaf was an English dock architect (*havuz mimari*), also arrived in Istanbul by means of the *tavsiyyenâme* fom Yusuf Âgâh Efendi. However, he was not employed there, since a proper position could not be found for him. He was sent back to his country and his pre-determined salary of 500 *kuruş* was not paid in order to avoid unnecessary expenses on 22 June 1796. The employment of the Swedish dock engineer Rhodé and his team seems to have been key in this development.[128]

Shaw mentions another Englishman, Spurring,[129] without any detail in the context of the foreign technicians working in the naval arsenal. He also mentions Spurring in connection with an anonymous French document stating that he was the builder of the *Selimiye*.[130] Shaw compares this document with the one saying that

Le Brun was the builder of the *Selimiye* in Enver Ziya Karal's article.[131] Ottoman archival documents, at least the ones studied for that paper, do not mention his name. However, the British Foreign Archives cast considerable light on this controversial person, who caused temporary turmoil in diplomatic relations between the Porte and Britain as well as among British diplomats in Istanbul and England.

Spurring came to Istanbul in the winter of 1799 on the *Tigre* in the capacity of shipbuilder and was received as such by the Porte and established for a certain period at the rate of 500 piasters per month, with 140 in addition for his son. His business was to work in the Turkish dockyards and assist any British ships that might occasionally come there. His appointments and his occasion were subjected equally on all occasions to the direction of the Porte and to an intimate connection with the British embassy. Accordingly, he had apartments in the British palace and never left Istanbul upon any business except that from the *Kaptan Pasha*. In 1799 Spurring built some gunboats,[132] in which the *Kaptan Pasha* showed much interest. However, his actions and overbearing manners made him obnoxious to the *Kaptan Pasha* and he was no longer employed.

With the Earl of Elgin's mediation, Spurring again came to notice. Some arrangements were made with the *Kaptan Pasha*, and Spurring's presence was required. Elgin searched for him for two days, without being able to locate him. It turned out that he had secretly left the city on a Saturday and set out for Cyprus without letting Elgin know, placing him in a difficult position with the Porte. In his correspondence with some British bureaucrats, Elgin learned that the four British shipwrights under him had known that he had gone, but had declared that they had not been told where Spurring had gone or how long he was to be absent. Later, it emerged that Spurring had set out in the company of a group of Janissaries belonging to the Austrian internuncios. Before this, he had probably met Sir Sidney Smith and received part of his travelling equipage from him as well as letters.

On learning these facts, Elgin wrote to Mr Smith, whose answer created so much astonishment as to oblige Elgin to send a second letter.[133] From Sidney Smith's political reply, dated 17 March 1800, we learn that Spurring had taken advantage of the long stagnation of work in Istanbul to make a short excursion to rejoin his patron and commanding officer upon particular business, leaving his fore-man to execute any wishes of the *Kaptan Pasha* during his absence.[134] Unsatisfied with Smith's reply, Lord Elgin sent him another letter enquiring by whose permission Spurring had left Istanbul. Smith's answer was again diplomatic and evasive. After repeating the previous letter, he recommended that Lord Elgin ask Spurring himself or his commander at the Imperial Palace. From this reply, Lord Elgin understood that Spurring had received orders from Smith directly or indirectly.[135] In a letter dated 26 March 1800, Lord Elgin wrote to Lord Grenwille that it was no longer in his power to hold further communication with Mr Smith and he stated that the Ottoman government, in the meantime, had withdrawn the appointments of Mr Spurring.[136]

## Missions of other nations

Among the foreigners employed in the shipworks at the Imperial Naval Arsenal were two Spaniards. The first, a mechanic known as Wloa or Volla, was reported in a letter of 1794 to have been an ingenious mechanic who worked in the newly founded arms man-ufactory for a handsome salary under the supervision of Çelebi Efendi.[137] This factory at the Levend Çiftliği manufactured rifles and bullets.[138] The second Spaniard, known in the data only as Miguel, was a Spanish official who came to Istanbul with the permission of the Spanish government. He served in the Ottoman state for a salary of 500 *kuruş* paid from the beginning of January 1794. His salary did not change untill 1795–96.[139]

From Austria were Andon/Antoin of *Nemçe*, a bridge builder, and a draftsman who later converted to Islam, Mustafa, employed in Silistire on 17 October 1790 by the Porte. Both men made draw-ings and desiged the plan of a bridge in Silistire and sent it to the Porte for evaluation by the head architects. Their skills in geometry (*ilm-i hendese*) and bridge construction were much appreciated.[140]

A petition dated 1800–01 by the shipbuilding engineer Klintberg reported that Yakomi was an ironsmith (*âhenger*) of Genoise origin employed in the construction of the three-decker galleon in the Imperial Naval Arsenal producing the iron equipment (*edevat-i aheniyye*) of the aforementioned galleon.[141] He is also known to have worked in the repair of the rifles and some other iron equip-ment used on the galleons.[142] Tezel notes that Yakomi worked as a *tavşan*[143] in the construction of the big dry dock at the naval arsenal.[144] His fellow countryman Yozop, of Venician origin, worked with him as a carpenter in the construction of galleons built both at the naval arsenal and on Rhodes. He and Yakomi each were alloted an 80-*kuruş* salary on 2 June 1796. Their salaries were increased to 100 *kuruş* from May 1805.[145]

## Ottoman shipbuilders

There were also Ottoman subjects of various religions who rendered important services together with the foreigners as shipbuilders, manufacturers of new tools and equipment, carpenters, ironsmiths, repairers of the light arms, architects, augerers, drydock masons, naval surgeons and porters.

Çamlıcalı Kalfa-Mimar Kara Yorgi was among them. In 1793–94 in Kemer he built the frigate the *Gazâl-ı Bahrî* of 45 *zira*, covered with copper, with 42 guns and 375 crew. He also built a corvette named the *Mürg-i Bahrî* of 27 *zira*, covered with copper and with 22 guns and a crew of 120 in 1796–97.[146]

Petro and Manol Kalfa were employed within the entourage of a galleon engineer in the capacity of *ayak mimarı* (base architects) and carpenters in the construction of the dry dock at the naval arsenal in 1801–02.[147] They worked there from the beginning of the construction of the dry dock to its completion. They also worked in the construction of a three-decker ship.[148] Petro worked in the repair of galleons and of the gate of the dry dock in 1802–03 as well. He received a raise of 50 *kuruş*, with 15 *kuruş* in addition to his previous salary of 35 *kuruş*.[149]

On the other hand, Manol appears among the workers employed in the construction of a frigate on the island of Limni on 28 June 1800. Hristo the architect, Antuvan the mountain architect (*dağ mimarı*), Anesti the chief augerer (*burgucubaşı*) and Vasıl Kalfa were among his colleagues.[150] Manol later built, together with Osman Kalfa, the *Fethiye*, a galleon of 193 *zira* in length, 55 *zira* in width, 26 *zira* in height, 22.5 *kadem* in displacement, with 96 guns and 960 crew, in Gemlik in 1827. On this important project, he worked as an engineer with Osman Kalfa. In the year 1828, he built, together with engineer Sadık Efendi, the *Nâvek-i Bahrî*, a frigate of 42 guns in Midilli. Six years later, under his engineering and Dimitri Kalfa's architectural design, the *Teşrifiye* was constructed in Gemlik. It was a galleon 190 *zira* in length, 52 *zira* in width, 26 *zira* in height, 22 *kadem* in displacement, with 96 guns and a crew of 960.[151]

In the following years, Manol remained active. He worked in the construction of a dry dock (today known as the Number Two dry-dock, *kuruhavuz*) together with the chief engineer, Abdulhalim Efendi, who was a teacher at the *Muhendishâne*. They completed the dry dock between the years 1821 and 1825. There is no doubt that his previous experiences in the reign of Selim III played an important role in his later services.[152]

Nikoli Kalfa was chief augerer and chief architect, as understood from a document dated 5 November 1802. He had worked at the naval arsenal for 40–50 years as a deputy of the chief architect and also worked as a chief augerer (*burgucubaşı*) in the construction of naval ships, and second of a three-decker ship and an imperial frigate.[153]

Following the death of İsmail Kalfa, the First Architect of the Imperial Naval Arsenal (*Tersâne-i Âmire Başmîmârı*), he was appointed chief architect and given all the salary and other allowances of the previous chief architect. In turn, his post of *bur-gucubaşılık* and other allowances were given to Anastas Kalfa. As for the salary and other allowances, it is recorded that he, as the chief architect of a galleon (*sermîmâr-ı kalyon*), received a 6,000-*kuruş* monthly salary, two *kıyyes* of butter (*revgân*) and four loaves of bread (*nân-ı azîz*) a day from the superintendent of the naval arsenal (*Tersâne-i Âmire Emini*) and two *kıyyes* of mutton (*kuşt-ı ğanem*) a day from the chief butcher (*kassabbaşı*).[154]

Anastas Kalfa, or Anesti the chief augerer (*burgucubaşı*), appears among the workers employed in the construction of a frigate in Limni on 28 June 1800, along with Manol, Hristo the architect, Antuvan the mountain architect (*dağ mimarı*) and Vasil Kalfa who would build a dry dock between 1857 and 1870, and work in the enlargement landwards of the dry dock that was con-structed in 1874–76 during the reign of Selim III.[155] In October–November 1802 he worked as an augerer at the Imperial Naval Arsenal. Later on, he was given the income of the post of *burgucubaşı* and the other allotments of Nikoli Kalfa. Anastas Kalfa's salary and allotments in turn were given to Todori, the sec-ond augerer (*burgucu-i sânî*) and, as a result of sequential promoting, he received Anastas Kalfa's salary. Petro, the chief porter, worked in this capacity at the naval arsenal for 30–40 years. Citing his long-term service, he demanded from the authorities a document indicating his exemption from the poll tax, which was levied on non-Muslims (*cizye*), and his right to a daily allotment of two loaves of bread from the bakery at the *tersâne zindanı* (prison).[156]

A document of 1795–96 describes one Dimitri Kalfa as a *zimmi* (non-Muslim Ottoman subject) citizen working as an *ayak mimari* in the Imperial Naval Arsenal. He was employed as a *burgucubaşı* during the construction of an imperial frigate of 55 *zira* at Ereğli in the Black Sea,[157] together with Tanaş the engineer, Isterbo/Isteryo the architect second in chief, Yani the mountain engineer and Dimitri the chief augerer in 1800–01.[158]

In 1834, Dimitri was employed as an architect in the construction of the *Teşrifiye* in Gemlik. In this project he accompanied Manol Kalfa, who was the engineer of the galleon.[159]

Mimar Papaço (Joseppo) Kalfa was the builder of a 51-*zira* galleon, the *Hilâl-i Zafer*, in Bodrum in 1790, which was clad with copper, carried 66 cannons and had a crew capacity of 650.[160]

Nevsim Kalfa is known to have built the *Ejder-i Bahrî*, a 57-*zira* galleon in Gemlik in 1793–94. This galleon had a capacity of 74 guns and a crew of 800. In 1797–98 he built another galleon, the *Beşâretnümâ*, of 59 *zira*, clad in copper, with a capacity of 76 guns and a crew of 850 men.[161]

Nikolay/Nikoli Kalfa was a shipbuilder who worked especially in Sinop and Bodrum. Among the ships that he built were the *Feyz-i Hüdâ*, a galleon of 55 *zira*, coppered and with 72 guns and 650 crew, built in 1789–90 in Sinop; the *Fâtih-i Bahrî*, a galleon of 47 *zira*, coppered, with 60 guns and a crew of 550, built in 1791–92 in Sinop; the *Pertev-i Nusret*, a 53-*zira* galleon, coppered, with 68 guns and a crew of 700, built in 1793–94 in Sinop; the *Şehbâz-ı Bahrî*, a 57-*zira* galleon, coppered, with 74 guns and a crew of 850, and built in 1793–94 in Bodrum; and the *Heybet Endâz*, a 51-*zira* galleon, coppered, with 74 guns and a crew of 850, built in 1796–97 in Bodrum.[162]

In a document dated 1791–92, the superintendent of the *Tersâne-i Âmire* complained about the chief carpenter, Hristo, who was employed in the *paşa gemisi* (a paşa ship), and a *zimmi* carpenter named Mavri, employed in the *kapudâne* (a naval rank) ship. He described their laziness, bad manners and provocation of the workers at the arsenal.[163]

Filip (Philip) Kalfa was the builder of the 51-*zira* galleon *Şevket-nümâ*, which was copper-clad, had 50 guns and a crew of 450 men, and was built in 1796 on Lemnos/Limni.[164]

Trandafil Kalfa was employed in the capacity of dry-dock mason in the construction of the dry dock in the arsenal, and later on, worked with the French engineer Romus in the deepening works of the harbour of Rhodes in 1797–98. During his work in Rhodes, he dealt with the removal of a rock in the sea and he received 80 *kuruş* per month. The five other masons with him received 40 *kuruş* each.[165]

The names Masoraki and Arbili are mentioned in connection with staff in a hospital, the building of which near the large dry dock at the *Tersâne-i Âmire* was declared in the resolutions of the *Bahriye Kânunnâmesi* (Naval Regulations) of February 1805. The hospital was to treat patients around the clock. The law also declared that the *Bahriye Nazırı* (Naval Minister) was responsible for commissioning physicians and surgeons for the naval ships contingent upon need. Masoraki, a physician who had been promoted to chief physician (*hekimbaşı*), and Arbili, a surgeon, who had been appointed to the post of chief surgeon (*cerrahbaşı*) in this hospital, each received 250 *kuruş* a month. Seven students earning 40 *kuruş* each and servants earning 30 *kuruş* were among other staff.[166] A *tıbhâne* (medical school) was annexed to the earlier hospital on 9 January 1806. From this date on, candidates seeking to become surgeons and physicians began to be educated there, not only for the Imperial Naval Arsenal and Navy, but also for institutions throughout the country.[167]

In addition to the foreign missions and non-Muslim Ottoman subjects, there were Muslim shipbuilders and other craftsmen involved in work for the navy. These shipbuilders had a long tradition in shipbuilding and naval construction. They helped the foreign missions to organise personnel, procured the required raw materials, carried out the construction projects, and taught navigation and shipbuilding courses at the naval school. They combined old and new techniques to create a new synthesis in naval shipbuilding to be transferred to the following generations. Unfortunately, full accounts of their activities and the division of labour they undertook are unavailable. Nevertheless, an examination of the available sources allows the formation of a general idea of the kinds of work in which these men were engaged.

Ismail Kalfa/Halîfe was the chief architect of the Imperial Naval Arsenal and builder of the galleons *Bahr-ı Zafer* and *Âsâr-ı Nusret*[168] at the *Tersâne-i Âmire* in 1789–90 and 1793, respectively.[169] He must have died towards the end of the year 1802, since we learn from a document dated 5 Kasım 1802 that Nikoli Kalfa (the second architect in the naval arsenal) was appointed chief architect in the place of Ismail Kalfa, and that Ismail Kalfa's salary and other allowances had been transferred to Nikoli Kalfa. Additionally, it can be judged from the same document that Ismail Kalfa must have held the post of chief architect in the arsenal for a long time, since Nikoli had been the second architect for 40–50 years.[170] Another document of 8 July 1767 sheds light on the beginning of Ismail Efendi's role as chief architect. When Mustafa Halife was the chief architect, Ismail Halîfe was the second *halife*. Therefore, Ismail Efendi must have been appointed to the post of chief architect after 1767.[171]

Ismail Efendi had such duties as monitoring the procurement of shipbuilding materials and tools and the shipbuliding process, working in cooperation with the other authorities at the arsenal to make decisions about the employment of Otttoman and foreign architects, and informing his superiors about the progress of construction projects.[172]

Hammâmîzâde Ahmed was the builder of a 37-*zira* corvette, the *Ferahnümâ*, which was clad in copper and carried a crew of 150 and 24 guns. It was built at Silistire in 1792–93. Gülşen Bey built the galleon *Kilidü'l Bahir*, a 59-*zira* with 24 guns, at Sohom.[173] He also oversaw the construction of a 60-*zira* frigate at Sohum during 1797.[174]

A Numan Bey built a corvette at Kalas and at the *Tersâne-i Âmire* of 37 *zira*, copper-sheathed, with ten guns and 150 crew.[175] He also built a 51.5-*zira* galleon in Gemlik in 1795. For this galleon, 2,100 *kantars* of raw iron were used.[176] He is also reported to have built some other galleons, in 1798 and 1804 in Gemlik, and to have sent them to the *Tersâne-i Âmire* for rigging and fitting out.[177]

Another shipbuilder, whose name is recorded as Konyalı Ebubekir, built a galleon of 51 *zira* in Midilli in 1791.[178]

Captain Ahmed Hoca learned the science of shipbuilding (*fenn-i inşâ-i süfun*) from the French shipbuilder Le Roy, the engineer of the galleon *Mukaddime-i Nusret*,[179] and became an assistant (*şakird*) to the Swedish engineer Rhodé. He constructed the galleon *Zîver-i Bahrî* in Midilli in 1796[180] on his own.[181] A picture of this ship was shown in Mahmud Raif Efendi's book.[182] Rhodé recognised Ahmed Hoca's abilities, and naval authorities appointed him chief master supervisor (*baş halife*) to the Naval Engineering School on 26 January 1797. After his appointment to this post, his former rank of captain, with a salary of 86.5 *kuruş*, was removed and his pay was increased to 100 *kuruş* a month.[183] In an imperial edict of 1803–04, his name was mentioned among the masters and engineers who had taught the science of shipbuilding at the *Hendesehâne* and then were commissioned and assigned to the construction of imperial ships in the provinces and presently were employed at the Imperial Arsenal. In the document, Ahmed Hoca appears as a captain and the first master supervisor (*halife-i evvel*). At this post, he received a monthly salary of 100 *kuruş*, 30 *kıyyes* of *erz* (rice), 15 *kıyyes* of *revğân-ı sâde* (butter), 45 *kıyyes* of *lahm-ı ğanem* (mutton) and 210 loaves of *nân-ı aziz* (bread).[184] He passed away in 1838 as one of the senior instructors of the *Mühendishâne*. His position was filled by the second *halîfe*, Mehmed Ali Efendi, who later was replaced by Ahmed Hoca's son, Mehmed Fâzil Efendi.[185]

Seyyid (*Büyük*)[186] Mustafa Hoca/Molla Mustafa became chief *kalfa* (assisstant foreman) under Le Brun. During his work under Le Brun, he learned shipbuilding using geometrical techniques (*nisbet-i hendesiyye üzre sefâin inşasını tahsîl*). Then naval authorities, in order to test his abilities, asked him to draw a picture of a frigate. He drew it and presented it to Sultan Selim. Four other people were also asked to draw similar pictures. All the pictures, including that drawn by Mustafa Hoca, were appreciated by the Sultan and they were awarded 720 *kuruş* (*atiyye*) in total.[187] In 1796 he constructed the 41-*zira* frigate *Bûlheves* at Kalas.[188]

Mustafa Hoca was appointed as an instructor (second *kalfa*) with a salary of 80 *kuruş* at the *Mühendishâne-i Berrî-i Hümâyûn* in 1797.[189] He seems to have worked in his capacity as commissioned shipbuilding engineer/shipwright in the construction of the cutwater (*talimar*) of the bow, the caulking and the building of the stern and the upper part of the stern of a galleon being constructed on 3 September 1797 in Kal'a-i Sultâniye in the Dardanelles Strait. He was given, probably by Le Brun, some measuring equipment (*endâzeler*) with which to work. After the completion of the required parts, launching was undertaken by other architects.

The government notables gave considerable importance to Mustafa Hoca. The document related to his employment in the above-mentioned work also indicates that Küçük Hüseyin Pasha insistently requested the *Kal'a-i Sultâniye Nâzırı*, the superintendent of the naval activities in Kal'a-i Sultâniye, not to fail in showing the required respect to Seyyid Mustafa and in making him feel comfortable in terms of accomodation, travel allowance and foodstuff.[190]

His name is mentioned in the same imperial edict of 1803–04 among the teachers. In the document, Mustafa Hâce appears as the second master supervisor (*halîfe-i sâni*), with a monthly salary of 83 *kuruş*, 20 *kıyyes* of *erz* (rice), ten *kıyyes* of *revğân-ı sâde* (butter), 30 *kıyyes* of *lahm-ı ğanem* (mutton), and 120 loaves of *nân-ı aziz* (bread).[191] Later, Seyyid Mustafa served under Mahmut II as well. Leaving his post at the *Mühendishâne* in 1813, he was appointed chief architect of shipbuilding with a 300-*kuruş* salary, two *vakıyyes* of meat, two and a half *vakıyyes* of olive oil and six loaves of bread from the *Tersâne-i Âmire Zindanı Fırını*. He replaced the *Tersâne-i Âmire Başmimarı*, Nikoli Halîfe, who had been removed from his post due to incompetence.[192] With the official title '*Ser Mimâr-ı Hâssa* (Chief Royal Architect)', he participated in the foundation ceremony of the dry dock at the naval arsenal on 27 November 1823, together with Grand Vizier Silahdar Ali Pasha, Şehremini Hayrullah Efendi, Tersâne Emini Ataullah Efendi, Teşrîfâtî Süleyman Necîb Efendi and other notables. He stayed in this position for 11 years before he was removed from it on 15 November 1824. Afterwards, he seems to have fallen into bad straits, and a 250-*kuruş* pension was allotted to him.[193]

Among the Muslim shipwrights were a number of men of foreign birth who had converted to Islam as well. One such shipbuilder was the engineer Selim, also known as Mühendis Selim Ağa, Selim Efendi, İngiliz Selim, Baily and Bailey. He is reported to have left his country because of his anger with a relative over a matter of dignity (*şeref meselesi*) [194] and embraced Islam. This young English engineer took the name Selim and entered the service of the Porte in 1792, with a salary of 30 *kuruş*.[195]

He worked in the capacity of assistant to the director of the works, Küçük Râşid Efendi, who was a man of ability and a favourite of the late Reis Efendi. Selim Efendi had the charge of the restoration of the fort of Bender. During his stay in that district, he was ordered to reconnoitre the greatest part both of the Dniestr and the Danube, and on his return reported the expediency of fortifying the positions of Akkerman, on the Dniestr, approximately ten leagues below Bender, Kilia, situated near the northermost mouth of the Danube, which was said to have the deepest water for navigation. His plans for these places were then taken under the consideration of the military committee of the supreme council, of which Çelebi Efendi was a leading official.[196]

Together with Hüseyin Rıfkı Tamani (*second halîfe* then), Selim Efendi translated a treatise entitled 'Usûl-i Hendese' ('Method of Geometry') on 27 October 1797.[197] He also, supposedly, helped Hüseyin Rıfkı Efendi translate Euclid.[198]

Selim Efendi is recorded as having been discussed to accompany the Otoman army in its defence of Egypt under the command of Grand Vizier Yusuf Ziya Pasha in the aftermath of the French attack in 1799. Having declined to join the campaign, his monthly salary of 100 *kuruş* was stopped. He was soon reemployed by the state with the salary of 100 *kuruş* to prepare maps, to translate English, French and Italian books related to geometry, the construction and siege of forts, temporary-trenches digging, the construction of bridges and an *Atlas-ı Kebîr* (world atlas), as well as to explain how to draw instruments in books and how to apply all this theoretical knowledge in practice.[199]

He was appointed fifth assisstant, or *kalfa* (until then, there had been four caliphs), to the *Muhendishâne-i Berrî-i Hümâyun*, with the recommendation of the instructor at the *Mühendishâne*, Abdurrahman Efendi, and given *berat* (written permission) on 12 August 1801. His salary was first increased to an annual 600 *kuruş* and later on to 750 *kuruş*, paid from the *cânib-i mîrî* (state treasury). Meanwhile, he continued his services at the Imperial Naval Arsenal and at Beykoz. He seems to have invented and constructed some wheels (*çarh*) and been involved in similar works.[200]

Selim Efendi is perhaps best known for his efforts to fly trial balloons, the first attempt to utilise such technology for military purposes in the Ottoman Empire. Such balloons were used when conditions made it impossible to send messages to or to correspond with allies outside of a fort besieged by the enemy. In the autumn of 1801, Selim Efendi filled a balloon with hot air and carried out several unmanned flights. He presented his invention to Sultan Selim III and it was welcomed. In his first trial, his balloon came back to earth in a field beyond Çorlu. When the owner of the field took this strange object to the local judge (*kadi*), the news reached Istanbul. In Selim Efendi's second trial, he attached a human form made of wood. The wooden man made it as far as Bozhâne, when the balloon became hung up on the wall of a fort.

In the third trial, a balloon made of red fabric was flown. Letters bearing the message 'If this balloon reaches any of you under your administration, let the Sublime Porte/Istanbul know about it, adressed to the *kadı*s and *nâib*s (aides)' were put inside the balloon. This trial was successful. Sakız Naibi Efendi saw it off Marmara and took it to Istanbul. Selim Efendi was awarded by the Sultan and appointed to the *Mühendishâne*.

Selim Efendi launched another trial in front of the Yalı Köşkü during the ceremonies marking the saving of Egypt on 26 October 1801. At the time, Selim Efendi was a *halîfe* at the *Hendesehâne* and in charge of manufacturing fireworks (*havâî fişek*) at the arsenal.[201]

In 1803–04 he presented a petition demanding that his salary of seven months (from the beginning of *Rebiulahir* to the end of the month *Şevval*), which amounted to 1,190 *kuruş* (170 *kuruş* monthly), be paid in return for his various services. The government assessed his petition and agreed to pay him the sum. He served the Imperial Army during the campaign in Egypt and drew maps for various purposes. He worked in the service of the Porte on 1800–01 and his salary was increased by an additional 70 *kuruş* beginning from May–June 1802. Furthermore, in 1803–04 he was commissioned to travel to England by Kaptan Hüseyin Pasha and again during the administration of the governor of the Imperial Naval Arsenal, Aziz Efendi, to learn the construction and manufacture of a newly invented fire pump (*ateş tulumbası*) for the gates of the large dry dock at the arsenal.[202]

His name (as Baily) is mentioned in the correspondence dated 2–11 December 1805, in connection with the Ottoman request for a steam engine from England, between the British mission at Istanbul and the British government in England. He was described as a renegade Englishman with a sufficient knowledge of mathematics and mechanics to pass for a good mechanical engineer among the Turks, and as very much in their confidence.[203]

After the deposition of Selim III in the aftermath of the Kabakçı Rebellion, Selim's salary was stopped, in spite of his 15 years of service and his title, *Hassa Silahşörlüğü* (a rank for palace officers in charge of weapons), which he had been awarded not long before. Since he depended on this salary, he soon fell into bad straits. His later applications for the allotment of a salary were ignored by the authorities, which suggested he wait until the appearance of a suitable position.[204] Some writers suggest that he left the country as a result of bad treatment,[205] while others think that he might have been killed by rebellious Janissaries following the Kabakçı Rebellion.[206]

From Austria (*Nemçe*) was a convert known by the name of Mustafa. He was employed by the Porte as a draftsman, along with the bridge builder Andon/Antoin, in Silistire on 17 January 1790. They worked in drafting pictures of and designing the plan of a bridge.[207]

In addition to the names mentioned above were those of other naval architects such as Ismail, Çakır Ali, Fidanoglu Mehmet, Kalaslı Ali, of whom little is known beyond their names.[208] A document dated October–November 1802 states the names of some Muslim architects in the Imperial Naval Arsenal and their other allotments. Among these names were Gümüşhaneli Hacı Mustafa, who received a 1,800-*kuruş* monthly salary, 1 *kıyye* of butter (*revğân-ı zeyt*) and two loaves of bread (*nân-ı azîz*) a day from the superintendent of the naval arsenal, and 0.5 *kıyye* of mutton (*kuşt-ı ğanem*) a day from the chief butcher (*kassabbaşı*); Ali Halîfe, who received a 1,800-*kuruş* monthly salary and 1 *kıyye* of butter, two loaves of bread and 0.5 *kıyye* of mutton a day; Mustafa, with a monthly salary of 1,800 *kuruş* and 1 *kıyye* of butter, two loaves of bread and two *kıyyes* of mutton a day; Samatyalı Oğlu Mustafa Halife, with a monthly salary of 1,800 *kuruş* and 1 *kıyye* of butter, two loaves of bread and two *kıyyes* of mutton a day; Karayaki, with a 1,200-*kuruş* monthly salary and 0.5 *kıyye* of butter, two loaves of bread and 0.5 *kıyye* of mutton a day; and finally Ali, a recently hired architect who was given a salary of 720 *kuruş* along with 1 loaf of bread and 0.5 *kıyye* of mutton a day.[209]

An imperial edict (*Hatt-ı Hümâyûn*) gave information about the personnel at the *Hendesehâne* of the Imperial Arsenal of 1803–04 in three parts. In the first part were given the names, salaries and victuals of the masters and engineers who had previously taught the science of shipbuilding at the *Hendesehâne* and then were commissioned and assigned to the construction of the imperial ships in the provinces and presently employed at the arsenal. Beside Ahmed Hâce, captain and the first master supervisor/*halife-i evvel*, and Mustafa Hâce, second master supervisor/*halife-i sâni*, both of whom were discussed above, other personnel included Hafız Hâce, Ali Hâce, Muhammed Hâce, Mimar Manol Kalfa (mentioned above), Costa, Küçük Mustafa Hâce, Giridî Ahmed Hâce, Tahir Hâce, İstanbullu Abdullah Hâce and Mimar Tanaş Kalfa.[210] Each received a salary of 25 *kuruş*.

The second part included the names, salaries and victuals of the masters (*üstâd*) and their students (şakirdân) dealing with cartography and geography at the *Hendesehâne*. Among the names were Osman Efendi, the first instructor/*hâce-i evvel*, and Ahmed Hâce, the first master/*halife-i evvel*, receiving a monthly salary of 60 *kuruş* along with 20 *kıyyes* of rice, ten *kıyyes* of butter, 30 *kıyyes* of mutton and 120 loaves of bread. Others were Hafızzâde Eşref Hâce, Çavuşbaşızâde Halil Hâce, Gemiağasızâde Ahmed Hâce, Miftahağasızâde Cafer Hâce, Kasımpaşa'lı Süleyman Hâce, Yeniçeşmeli Hâfız Râşid Hâce, Kolancı zâde Muhammed Hâce, Atıyye Kapudanzâde İsmail Hâce, Tophaneli Seyyid Muhammed Hâce, Ali Kapudanzâde Muhammed Hâce, Kerânecizâde İsmail Hâce, Kabataşlı Hâfız Arif Hâce, Pasha Kapudanzâde Mustafa Hâce, Flemenk Kapudanzâde Salih Hâce, Hacı Osmanzâde Ali Hâce, Tophaneli Ahmed Hâce and Hâce Efendizâde Şakir Hâce, receiving 15 *kuruş* each.

The third part of the document gave the names of the *mülazım şakirds* (teaching assisstants) at the *Hendesehâne*: İbrahim Kapudanzâde Selim Hâce, Asitaneli Salih Hâce and Riyâle Beyzâde Salih Hâce. Also mentioned is a *Mimâr-ı Sütûn*, with a salary of 2,100 *kuruş*, who was in charge of selecting and classifying the various kinds of posts.[211]

The names of other men working in secondary jobs in the naval arsenal were Mutemed Said Ağa (paymaster), Kâtib Mehmed Emin Efendi, Mahzenci Dede Mustafa (store keeper), Divanhâne Çavuşu Mustafa (officer in charge of the Divanhâne, the official residence of the *Kaptan Pasha*s), Tosyalı Mehmed, Gebzeli Mehmed Kaptan,

Seyyid Ahmed, Ser-hammâl Cezal (chief porter), Hacı Süleyman (foundryman or *dökmeci*), Lağımcıbaşı Lütfullah (sapper), Hasan, Dolab Reisi Mehmed (officer in charge of the use of the treadmill), Ibrahim Çavuş and Taşçı kalfası Tahir (stonemason).[212]

It is also important to stress that a fertile setting for these activities had been prepared by the administrative and naval reorganisations and regulations issued between November 1804 and May 1805. The post of minister of naval affairs (*Umûr-i Bahriye Nezareti*) replaced the post of chief of the arsenal (*Tersâne Emâneti*). All the duties, responsibilities, division of labour, salaries, rations, ranks, signs, uniforms and retirement issues of the personnel of the arsenal, navy and naval school were determined and organised in detail by this institution.[213] One of the most important novelties of the regulations was the establishment of an independent treasury (*Tersâne Hazinesi*) peculiar to the navy and administered by the minister of the navy (*Bahriye Naziri*).[214]

4

# THE NAVAL SHIPS OPERATING DURING THE REIGN OF SELIM III

The linguistic and literary assessment of ship names has received little attention from historians and other academics.[1] However, their importance cannot be ignored, considering the close relationships between Ottoman ships and the names attributed to them.

Every ship, irrespective of its being naval or mercantile, must bear some kind of distinguishing label for identification, reference and communication. This rule was valid for Ottoman ships as well. However, Ottoman ships were not given individual names during the period of galleys, up to the eighteenth century, but were called by the names of their commanders, such as 'Hasan Reis' galley', or 'Ahmet Reis' galliot'. Of course, there were some exceptions to the general trend. Two ships of the *baştarda* type (an old war galley of intermediate size) were named the *Yeşil Melek* (Green Angle) and the *Sultan*. The first was used during Süleyman I's Rhodes campaign in 1522, and the second during his Malta campaign in 1565.

Ottoman ships began to be given proper names in the second half of the seventeenth century. This period was also marked by the transition to the galleon-type sailing ship. The previous ship naming tradition continued for some time. Only the triple-decked galleons belonging to naval commanders such as the Kapudân-ı Deryâ, Kapudâne, Patrona and Riyâle were named.[2]

Ottoman galleons were named in various ways. Occasionally, they were named after the person or people who financed their construction. The *Uzunçarşı*, for instance, the first big galleon supposedly built for the Ottoman navy and the keel of which was put on the stocks in the Imperial Naval Arsenal in 1648, was given this name because it had been financed by the tradesmen of Uzunçarşı during the Crete campaign.[3]

At the beginning of the eighteenth century, the most striking physical features of a ship, such as its colour, stern, bow, hull shape and figurehead, came to be influential in its naming. Close examination of the ship names sheds considerable light on the shapes and technical features of the ships and allows for the establishment of a visual gallery of ships. In this context, such names as the *Ejderbaşlı* (Dragon-figureheaded), the *Fırkateyn-i Kaplan Başlı* (Frigate with Tiger-Figurehead), the *Yılanbaşlı* (Snake-figureheaded), the *Akrepbaşlı* (Scorpion-figureheaded), the *Gülbaşlı* (Rose-figureheaded), the *Küçük Gülbaşlı* (Small Rose-figureheaded), the *Bayaz Atbaşlı* (White Horse-figureheaded), the *Siyah Atbaşlı* (Black Horse-figureheaded), the *Al Atbaşlı* (Red Horse-figureheaded), the *Karnı Atbaşlı* (Having the Belly of a Horse Figurehead), the *Esterkıçlı* (Mule-Sterned), the *Şadırvankıçlı* (Fountain-sterned), the *Çifte Ceylankıçlı* (Double Gazelle-sterned), the *Zülfükarkıçlı* (Having the Stern of Ali's Double-Headed Sword called Zülfikâr), the *Yaldızlı Narkıçlı* (Having a Pomegranate Gilded-stern), the *Yaldızlı Batkıçlı* (Having a Gilded, Narrow Stern), the *Güneşkıçlı* (Sun-sterned), the *Kadırgakıçlı* (Galley-sterned), the *Servibahçeli* (Having a Garden of Cypress), the *Kuşbahçeli* (Having an Aviary), the *Kırmızıkuşaklı* (Red-belted), the *Yeşilkuşaklı* (Green-belted), the *Mavi Arslanbaşlı* (Blue Lion-figureheaded), the *Siyah Arslanbaşlı* (Black Lion-figureheaded), the *Maviboyalı* (Painted Blue), the *Yaldızlı Hurma* (Gilted Date) and the *Çifteçaprazlı* (Double Transversed) were just a few of the names to appear in 1716–17.[4]

Between 1736 and 1739, most of these ships were still in use, along with some additional ones. New names were the *Çift Aslan* (Double Lion), the *Büyük Gülbaşlı* (Big Rose-figureheaded), the *İki Bağçeli* (Double-gardened), the *Yaldızlı Şâhin* (Gilded Falcon), the *Mavi Arslan* (Blue Lion) and the *Mavi Firkata* (Blue Frigate).[5] Between 1737 and 1738, among other ship names seen were the

*Çift Kaplan* (Double Tiger), the *Sipâh-ı Bahr* (Army of the Sea), the *Mâlika-i Bahr* (Owner of the Sea), the *Deve Kuşu* (Ostrich), the *İspinoz* (Chaffinch), the *Beyaz At* (White Horse), the *Al-qasr* (the Palace), the *Zülfikar* (Double-headed Sword of Ali), the *Yaldız Bağçeli* (Having a Gilded Garden), the *Yıldız Kıçlı* (Star-sterned), the *Ay Bağçeli* (Moon-sardened), the *Sarı Kuşaklı* (Yellow-belted), the *Yaldızlı Nar* (Gilded Pomegranate), the *Baba Ibrahim* (Ibrahim the Father), the *La PremièÉre*, the *La Seconde*, the *Küçük Şahin* (Young/Small Falcon), the *Serçe Kuşu* (Sparrow), the *Beyaz Şahin* (White Falcon) and the *La Bleue*.[6] This practice of naming boats after their appearance continued into later periods. The *Tek Direkli Uskuna* (Single-masted Uskuna), operating in 1791, is a good example of shape-based naming.[7]

From the mid-eighteenth century onwards, combined heroic (*hamasi*) and epic names began to prevail. The attempts at establishing a new Ottoman navy in the aftermath of the Çeşme Incident in 1770 and with Selim III's ascendance to the throne, two decades later, accelerated this change, as did the long Russo–Ottoman wars. The *Niheng-i Bahrî* (Crocodile of the Sea), the *Şehbâz-ı Bahri* (Sea Falcon/Braveheart of the Sea), the *Râd-ı Bahrî* (the Braveman/Generous Man of the Sea), the *Burc-ı Zafer* (Tower/Fortress of Victory), the *Peleng-i Bahrî* (Sea Tiger), the *Nasr-ı Cenk* (Victory of War), the *Serheng-i Nusret* (Warrior for Victory), the *Peyk-i Nusret* (Harbinger of Victory), the *Mukaddeme-i Nusret/Mukaddeme-i Zafer* (Beginning of Victory), the *Necm-i Zafer* (Star of Victory), the *Seyyâd-ı Bahrî* (Hunter of the Sea), the *Berîd-i Fütuh* (Courier of Conquests), the *Nesîm-i Zafer* (Breeze of Victory), the *Hilâl-ı Zafer* (Crescent of Victory), the *Fâtih-i Bahrî* (Conqueror of the Sea), the *Mesken-i Gâzi* (Residence of the Victorious Fighter for the Islamic Faith), the *Peyk-i Zafer* (Harbinger of Victory), the *Kâid-i Zafer* (Leader of Victory), the *Reber-i Nusret* (Guide to Victory), the *Küh-ı Revân* (Agile/Flowing Mountain), the *Hüsn-i Guzât* (Beauty of Holy Warriors), *Nüvîd-i Fütuh* (Glad Tidings of Victories), the *Bahr-i Zafer* (Sea of Victory), the *Hilâl-ı Zafer* (Crescent of Victory), the *Âsâr-ı Nusret* (Signs of Victory), the *Pertev-i Nusret* (Beam of Victory), the *Ejder-i Bahrî* (Dragon of the Sea), the *Hümây-ı Zafer* (Phoenix of Victory), the *Arslan-ı Bahrî* (Lion of the Sea), the *Salâbetnümâ* (Showing Power/Firmness), the *Şiâr-ı Nusret* (Hallmark of Victory), the *Heybetendâz* (Awe-

/Majesty-inspiring), the *Şehper-i Zafer* (Great Wing of Victory), the *Şevketnümâ* (Showing Majesty), the *Bûlheves* (Very Enthusiastic), the *Zaferküşâ* (Bringing victory), the *Cenk-Âver* (Brave Fighter), the *Bâdi-i Nusret* (Sailing Ship of Victory), the *Tîz Hareket* (Swift Moving), the *Kaplan-ı Bahrî* (Tiger of the Sea), the *Seddü'l Bahir* (Barrier of the Sea), the *Bedr-i Zafer* (Full Moon of Victory), the *Civân-ı Bahrî* (Handsome Young Man of the Sea), the *Bed'-i Nusret* (Beginning of Victory), the *Beşîr-i Zafer* (Harbinger of Victory), the *Husn-i Gazât* (Beauty of Victories), the *Bidâyetü'l Fütûh* (Beginning of the Conquests), the *Mukaddime-i Nusret/Mukaddime-i Zafer* (Beginning of Victory), the *Tılsım-ı Zafer* (Talisman of Victory), the *Şihâb-ı Sâkib* (Shooting Star), the *Burc-ı Zafer* (Tower/Fortress of Victory), the *Has Gazât* (Unique Holy Wars), the *Bâis-i Nusret* (Reason for Victory), the *Nusret-Nümâ* (Showing Victory), the *Pulâd-ı Bahrî* (Steel/Sword/Mace of the Sea), the *Menba-ı Nusret* (Source of Victory), the *Kilidü'l Bahir/ Kilidü'l Bahrî* (Lock of the Sea), the *Şehîd-i Zafer* (Martyr of Victory), the *Îed-i Nusret* (Feast of Victory), the *Zü'l Ukâb* (Owner of an Eagle) and the *Cabbâr-ı Bahrî* (Orion/the Grand Sovereign of the Sea) were some examples of compound heroic names.

The most striking aspect of these heroic names is the use of such motifs as wild animals, hunters, fortresses and mountains as deterrents to other navies and encouragement to the Ottoman warriors. Common features that they associate are power, self-confidence, agility, glory and glad tidings of victory. Another motif is the role of leading warriors to victory in holy war against the infidels.

An important point to note is the similarities between ship names in different countries. Similar ship names, for instance, in England go back to the reigns of Henry VII and Henry VIII, when fighting ships appeared as a type separate and distinct from merchant ships armed with cannons. The *Regent,* the *Lion,* the *Dragon,* the *Greyhound* (1545, and another ship of the same name in 1712), the *Bonaventure,* the *Mary Rose* and the *Sovereign of the Seas* (1637, and later on *Royal Sovereign* in 1660) are ship names that survived into the twentieth century. However, most Elizabethan ships bore warlike names such as the *Victory* (1765), the *Triumph,* the *Repulse,* the *Revenge* (1577), the *Defiance*[8] and, later on, the *Valiant* (1759), the *Inflexible* (1776), the *Thunderer,*[9] as well as some compound names such as the *Dreadnought,* the *Vanguard,* the *Swiftsure* and the *Warspite*.[10] Some French ships such as the *La Gloire* (1707), the *Terrible* (1739), the *Panthèĕre* (1744), the *Invincible* (1744), the *Le Protecteur* (1755) and the *Superbe* (1785),[11] and ships from the United States such as the *Rattlesnake* (1781), the *Wasp* (1794) and the *Revenge* (1805)[12] can be put in this category.

In the Ottoman Empire in the same period, names such as the *Zîver-i Bahrî* (Ornament of the Sea), the *Tâvus-ı Bahrî* (Peacock of the Sea), the *Ankâ-yı Bahrî* (Phoenix of the Sea), the *Mürg-i Bahrî* (Bird of the Sea), the *Serçe* (Sparrow), the *Devekuşu* (Ostrich), the *Gazâl-ı Bahrî* (Gazelle of the Sea), the *Ceyrân-ı Bahrî* (Gazelle of the Sea) and the *Hûri-yi Bahrî* (Houri of the Sea) were common. The use of the names of some birds and of gazelle can be explained through their aesthetic and cultural associations. Additionally, the legendary bird, the phoenix, refers to the tale '*Simurg*' ('The Thirty Birds') by Feridüddin Attar. On the other hand, the houri, the angel-like female creature of Paradise, appears as one of the divine rewards for sailors who died in holy war against the infidels and therefore had the right to enter Paradise as well as to enjoy pleasure, good service and comfort.

The introduction of names from Greek and Latin mythology, reflecting the classical flavours of the age, began to be felt in every walk of English life from the mid-eighteenth century onwards. The names of gods, goddesses, nymphs, princes, kings, heroes and monsters of mythology became favourable for ships. Examples are the *Jupiter*, the *Agamemnon*, the *Bellerophon*, the *Minotaur*, the *Minerva*, the *Dido* and the *Arethusa*.[13]

In the Ottoman Empire, the *Ferahnümâ* (Showing Happiness and Relief), the *Küşâde Baht* (Having Good Fortune), the *Nîreng-i Bahrî* (Magic of the Sea), the *Birr-i Bahrî* (Goodness of the Sea), the *Meserret-i Bahrî* (Joy of the Sea), the *Beşâretnümâ* (Showing Glad Tidings), the *Meşreb-i Bahrî* (Spring of the Sea), the *Secâ-ı Bahrî* (Nature/Disposition of the Sea), the *Sâika-ı Bâd* (Drive of Wind), the *Seyyâh-ı Bahrî* (Traveller of the Sea) and the *Bahr-ı Amîk* (Deep Sea) were also among names used for ships.[14] Here the common elements were happines for and glad tidings of a future victory as well as harmony with the sea.

Another striking point is the preference for names of wild animals, such as the lion, tiger, snake, scorpion, crocodile, eagle, falcon and the legendary dragon, in order to emphasize the terrifying and dashing quality of the ships. The horse and mule, on the other hand, symbolise the lasting character of the navy. The main aim in using such names was double-sided: to encourage the Ottoman crew and warriors, and to terrorise the enemy psychologically before and during a battle. Similar names were used for Western vessels. In the first three quarters of the eighteenth century, English ships had names such as the *Leopard*, the *Dragon*, the *Antelope*, the *Eagle*, the *Panther*, the *Kingfisher*, and the *Swallow*. In the late eighteenth century, some other names, for example the *Elephant*, were added.[15]

Names bearing religious associations or representing the wishes for God's victory or help were also common. Various attributes and names of God, some in Arabic and some in Persian, were used in these name combinations. Among the examples were the *Nâsır-ı Bahir* (Helper of the Sailors), the *Feyz-i Hüdâ* (Bounty of God), the *Mazhar-ı Tevfik* (Worthy of Heavenly Aid), the *Fethü'l Fettâh* (Victory of the Great Victor/God), the *Nusret-i Yezdân* (Victory of God), the *Avn-i İlahî* (Aid of God), the *İnâyet-i Hakk* (Aid of God), the *Dâd-ı Hakk* (Justice of God), the *Kerem-i Bârî* (Generosity of God), the *Hıfz-ı Hüdâ* (Protection of God) and the *Hüdâverdi* (Favour/Blessing of God).[16]

In England, the use of names of religious significance for ships dates back to the time of Henry V. Among them, vessels with names such as the *Jesu*, the *Holigost*, the *Grace Dieu* and the *Trinity Royal* were much in the limelight. A century later, these names appeared coupled with a ruler's name, that of Henry VIII: the *Trinity Henry*, the *Henry Grace a Dieu* or the *Great Harry*.[17]

Sometimes the cannons, weapons, firepower on board or associated attributes of a ship determined the name. During the reign of Ahmed III, a type of galleon called *üç kantarlı kalyon* (a galleon with cannons firing cannonballs of three *kantars*) appeared in 1721 and in 1726. This name stemmed from its guns, since it carried a cannon firing cannonballs of three *kantars* in weigth.[18] In 1753 and 1758, two new *üç kantarlı kalyon* were constructed. Names directly related to firing power were the *Berk-i Hâtıf* (Dazzling Lightning), the *Berk-i Bahrî* (Lightning of the Sea), the *Şihâb-ı Bahrî* (Flame/Shining Star of the Sea), the *Sâikâ-ı Tîr* (Thunderbolt/Driver of the Arrow), the *Âteşfeşân* (Sparking Fire), the *Şihâb-ı Sâkıb* (Shooting Star), the *Ra'd-ı Bahrî* (Lightning of the

Sea) and the *Tılsım-ı Bahrî* (Talisman of the Sea).[19] Here again the purpose was to strike fear into the hearts of the enemy as well as to embolden the Ottoman sailors.

Similar names can be seen in almost all the navies of the world. Among the English bomb vessels of the eighteenth century were the *Terrible*, the *Basilisk*, the *Carcass*, the *Furnace*, the *Lighting*, the *Thunder*, the *Comet*, the *Firedrake*, the *Mortar*, the *Serpent*, the *Terror*, the *Granado*, the *Volcano*, the *Etna*, the *Infernal*, the *Meteor*, the *Devastation*, the *Hound*, the *Falcon*, the *Bulldog*, the *Fury*, the *Kingfisher* and the *Racehorse*.[20]

From the time of Selim III onwards, ships began to be named after Ottoman Sultans, for example the *Selimiye*, the *Mansuriye*, the *Mesudiye* and the *Mahmudiye*. Although Tezel claims that in the time of sailing ships none of the naval ships were named after *Kaptan Pasha*s, other commanders or the places/wars where glorious victories were won,[21] some foreign sources mention names that were probably those of ship commanders. Six frigates — *Hüseyin*, *Abbas*, *Zeynel*, *Süleyman*, *Kerim* and *Ahmed* — and five corvettes — *Mustafa*, *Hüseyin*, *Ali Bey*, *Mehmed* and *Hâlit Bey* — were a few ships mentioned by a foreign source to be operating in 1801.[22] The names of the sunken or scrapped ships were given to newly constructed ones to carry on the old names.[23]

Therefore, it is common for an archival researcher studying ship names to come across similar names in different time periods, which is often a difficult issue to clarify.

Some ships, such as the *Fethiye*, the *İskenderiyye*, the *Fırkateyn-i Cedîd-i Gümrü* and the *Tûnus*, bore the names of the places in which they had been built, while others were related to the function and duty of the ships, such as the *Sefîne-i Mektup* (Mail Ship) and the *Fırkateyn-i Aktarma* (Frigate of Transfer and Transport).[24] Geographical names were much more common in the European navies. In the first half of the eighteenth century, names such as the *Edinburgh*, the *Glasgow* and the *Union* were common in England.[25]

Although it is difficult to say that all Ottoman warships had proper names,[26] it is understood that naming ships was a kind of tradition, especially in the late eighteenth century. Vasıf Efendi confirms that it was a tradition for newly constructed galleons to be given new names.[27] An imperial edict of 1794–95 decreed that naval ships constructed earlier or later with no names had to be given proper names. In the same document, the Sultan ordered the *Tersâne-i Âmire Emiri* to write down on a paper the ship names[28] that he considered to be proper for the above-mentioned ships and to submit them to him along with the notebooks of the ships prepared by the *Kaptan Pasha*s. The Sultan, as understood from the postscript note (written by him), then let the other authorities (the Kaptan Pasha or the *Tersâne-i Âmire Reisi*) choose a name for each ship. However, as can be deduced from the process, the Sultan seems to have had the final say in the naming of the ships.[29]

The names determined by the Sultan or people authorised by him were given to the ships during launching ceremonies attended by all of the leading statesmen, such as the *Sadrazam* (Grand Vizier), the *Şeyhülislam* (top religious authority), the *Kaptan Pasha* (Grand Admiral), as well as arsenal workers and onlookers. The launching ceremony, as in the case of the one marking the setting up of the sternpost at the beginning of the construction,[30] was organised on a date deemed auspicious (*vakt-i muhtar*/chosen time) by the chief astronomer (*Müneccimbaşı*).[31] The Sultan's attendance at ship-launching ceremonies was obligatory by a law dating back to the reign of Süleyman the Lawgiver and maintained by Selim II and Murad III.[32] Before the Sultan's arrival at the ceremony, his throne was decorated with precious cloths,[33] and written invitations (*tezkire*) were sent to the above-mentioned statesmen. Separate marquees were set up, one for each statesman. Gift cloths, which were called *âvize/askı*, were draped on the hulls of the ships for exhibit. These cloths were divided between the ship's engineer, architect, foreman and workers. Animals were sacrificed and prayers[34] were recited by the Şeyhülislam just before launching. The same day, the Sultan presented *samur kürkler*(sable furs), caftans and *hilats* (robes of honour) as gifts to all the participants, from the Grand Vizier to all the personnel working at the *Divanhâne*[35] and the Imperial Arsenal. The ship, after being launched into the sea, was towed into position beneath a crane (*macuna*) —called a *Darağacı* (gallows)— for rigging out.[36]

### Types of Ottoman naval ships constructed in the
### last quarter of the eighteenth century

In the time of Selim III, all naval ships were counted and classified according to their sizes, which was an important step towards the standardisation and development of the Ottoman navy.[37] In this context, some types of sailing ships began to draw the attention of the naval circles in the late eighteenth century. The construction of such galleon-type ships as the *kapak/kaypak/kapak açar kalyon* (two-decked galleons), the *üç ambarlı* (thriple-decked galleon), the *şehtiye*, the frigate, the corvette, the gunboat, the brig and the fire ship was accelerated. The *Tersâne-i Âmire*, Gemlik, Sultaniye, Midilli, Bodrum, Rhodes, Sinop and Sohum were generally the building sites of these sailing vessels.[38]

Von Pivka says that in the year 1790 the Turkish fleet consisted of 30 ships of the line with 50–74 guns, 50 frigates with ten to 50 guns, and 100 galliots. The total cannon numbered 3,000 and there were 50,000 seamen, mainly Greeks from the Aegean Sea. In a report written in 1706 by the French ambassador in Istanbul to Napoleon Bonaparte, the Ottoman naval force is said to have been composed of 27 triple-deckers and 20 frigates. It also was described as the most beautiful fleet in Europe.[39]

This positive description of the Ottoman navy is echoed in a report from St. Vincent to Berkeley. The report, written on the *Royal George* on 28 July 1800, read, 'I could not have conceived it possible that this squadron (channel fleet of Great Britain) should have been in so many instances worse arranged and economized than the ships of Spain or Russia; I do assure you the armed vessels of the Porte, Tunis, Tripoli and Algiers are so clean in every part that the officers of many of the ships of this fleet ought to blush at the comparison.'[40]

Coming to the year 1807, when the naval activities of Selim III began to offer positive outcomes, it is seen that except for a few classical galleys scattered here and there, they had almost completely disappeared. In the reports and observations, they do not appear on the tables and lists concerning the Ottoman navy. In this context, the following table is noteworthy.[41]

| Table 7. Turkish force at Istanbul (1807) | | | |
|---|---|---|---|
| **Place** | **Line-of-the-battle (three-deckers)** | **Frigates** | **Corvettes** |
| At the arsenal fitting | 3 | 5 | 4 |
| At the anchorage near the Saraglio point | 3 | 5 | 7 |
| At Büyükdere | 2 | 0 | 2 |
| At the arsenal | One three-decker ship apparently nearly ready | | |
| Dardanelles | 1 | 2 | 3 |
| Source: PRO. FO 78/55 (27 January 1807), p. 122. | | | |

The data in Table 7 was a part of a report prepared by Captain Capel. The most striking point here is the appearance of new ship types and the disappearance of the old oared vessels. Line-of-the-battle ships, frigates and corvettes appear to be the leading types of naval ships promoted by the Porte. The general trend in both foreign and local interpretations and observations about the time in question seems to have been positive. The modernisation efforts and their immediate consequences seem to have played an important role in this respect.

Having mentioned the rise of some types of naval ships and their numerical analysis, the discussion will now turn to the main properties and specifications of the vessels.

### *Üç Ambarlı Kalyon (three-deckers)*

Three-decked galleons, one of the largest types of galleons, began to be constructed for use in the Ottoman navy from 1093/1682 onwards. This class of ship had guns on each deck. Its length ranged from 59 to 65 *zira*. The number of guns, excluding the upper deck, was 110–120, and the number of men on board was 800–1,000. The construction of a three-decker galleon was seen under the reign of Mustafa II (1695–1703), but the programme was scrapped because of lack of use. Later, in the time of Ahmed III, new three-decker galleons were built.[42] There were guns on each of the three decks of the ship as well as on the upper deck. The second deck after the upper deck was called the *palavra*, followed by the middle deck, and last the gun deck (*top ambari*).[43] The construction of three-decker galleons increased during the reign of Selim III. The three-decker *Selimiye* is one of the best examples of this type in the late eighteenth century.

The number of line-of-the-battle ships (including three-decker galleons) was 24 on 22 April 1784[44] and 26 on 25 April 1787, excluding the six still on the stocks.[45] Foreign sources state that in 1790 the Ottoman fleet had 30 ships of the line, with 50–74 guns. The number of three-decker galleons is given as 27 in the French ambassador's report written to Napoleon Bonaparte in 1796.[46] It seems that the construction of these types of ships continued in the following years. As a result of administrative regulations issued in 1804, the crew of the triple-decked galleons and their number were governed by a set of rules.

The total number of crew was 370, including two *reis-i evvel* (executive officers), two *sertopî* (artillery chiefs), one *başhoca* (chief scribe and instructor), two *reis-i sânî* (executive assistants), two *bâdbânî-i evvel* (chief sailmakers), two *bâdbânî-i anbar* (sailmakers in charge of stores), two *sertopî-i güverte* (artillery chiefs on the upper deck), one *hoca-i çorba* (official in charge of provisions), one *hoca-i jurnal* (scribe in charge of keeping the logbook), two *reis-i sâlis* (executive assistants), two *ser-oda* (chief officers in charge of rooms), four *ser-aylak* (heads of the temporary seamen hired for six moths), six *çavuşân* (officers responsible for security), two *vekilharç* (ship stewards), 150 *gabyâr* (officers in charge of monitoring a ship's rigging), 40 *rubu'lu reisler* (officers responsible for masts), two *ser-dümen* (chief helmsmen), two *cebeci-başı* (chief officers responsible for ammunitions), 150 *sodagabo* (artillery men), two *ağa-yı kalyon* (officers responsible for the sailors on a galleon), two *anbarî* (persons in charge of stores), seven *ser-marangozân* (chief carpenters), one *ser-kalafatcıyân* (chief caulker), 12 *marangozân* (carpenters) and seven *kalafatcıyân* (caulkers). During naval campaigns, seven other posts were added to this number: one *kethüdâ-yı dümen* (helmsman), one *kethüdâ-yı cebehâne* (officer in charge of ammunition), one *çavuş-ı kandil* (officer in charge of lighting candles), one *varilci* (person in charge of barrels), one *imam* (religious leader), one *aşcı* (cook) and one *söˆmbeki* (diver).[47] This list of personnel shows that the triple-decked galleon was a huge platform with an extensive division of labour.

The following years witnessed the construction of more of this type of ship. The construction of a triple-decked ship was almost completed in Istanbul on 27 January 1807, which shows the extension of the process and the importance attributed to this type of ship by the Ottoman authorities.[48]

### *Kapak/Kaypak/Kapak Açar/Kapak Kaldırır Kalyon* (*double deckers*)

The double decker man-of-war with 80 to 110 guns and with two gun decks below the spardeck was known as a *kapak/kaypak/kapak açar/kapak kaldırır kalyon*. On the third-rate *kapaks*, the number of guns was 60–80 with a crew of 600–800. There were 800–1,000 warriors on board, together with the crew.[49]

Records show that a certain amount of specific kinds of timber were ordered from Numan Bey in Iznikmid for a *kapak kaldırır* galleon of 63 *zira*, with 80 guns, as well as a corvette of 36,5 *zira*, with 26 guns, both under construction at the *Tersâne-i Âmire* on 21 March 1797.[50]

According to the administrative regulations in 1804, the number of crew on a galleon was 242 including two *reis-i evvel*, two *sertopî*, one *başhoca*, two *reis-i sânî*, one *bâdbânî-i evvel*, two *bâdbânî-i anbar*, one *sertopî-i güverte*, one *hoca-i çorba*, one *hoca-i jurnal*, two *reis-i sâlis*, two *ser-oda*, two *ser-aylak*, four *çavuşân*, one *vekilharç*, 100 *gabyâr*, 30 *rubu'lu reisler*, two *ser-dümen*, two *cebeci-başı*, 64 *sodagabo*, one *ağa-yı kalyon*, two *anbarî*, one *sermarangoz*, one *ser-kalafatcıyân*, ten *marangozân* and five *kalafatcıyân*.[51]

Captain Capel's report on the Ottoman force at Constantinople and its environs on 27 January 1807 states that three ships of the line were at the arsenal for fitting, another three at the anchorage near the Seraglio point, two at Büyükdere and one at the Dardanelles.[52] Here the document uses the word 'line', which most probably refers to ships other than triple-decker galleons, frigates and corvettes, since the same documents mention these last three types separately. Therefore, it is likely that it refers to double-decker galleons, though 'line of the battle' generally refers to wooden warships with two or three decks.[53]

### Firkateyn (frigates)

The word 'frigate' appears to have emerged in the Mediterranean and came to be used rather loosely for any swift ship of some force until the eighteenth century, at which time they came under the strict rating system of the British Royal Navy as fifth-rates. The main function of frigates was to keep well out of fighting range, but have the enemy under constant observation. They were the eyes and ears of the fleet, repeating signals and carrying despatches. During a fleet action, they assissted disabled ships and took possession of captured enemies. Sometimes they were sent to attack enemy commerce or to protect their own, to hunt down privateers or pirates, or to take part in the conquest of a colony.[54] Almost all frigates were built entirely of oak, with masts and spars of pine. These ships were fit to stay at sea in any weather and could carry six months' worth of provisions.[55]

As for Ottoman frigates, they emerged in the late eighteenth century in parallel to the developments in the maritime world. On 26 March 1783 there were ten frigates at the Imperial Arsenal, carrying cannons of three-, six- and nine-pound balls.[56] According to the table taken from M. Bonneval's report dated 22 April 1784, the total number of frigates at the time was 15. Their gun capacity was 30–50. As for their construction sites and gun capacity, out of seven frigates constructed in Istanbul, one had 50 guns, two had 40 guns, two had 36 guns, one had 32 guns and one had 30 guns. A frigate constructed at Midilli had 30 guns, one built at Brest had 36 and one built in England had 40.[57]

To the 15 frigates of 22 April 1784 were added nine more on 25 April 1787. Out of these 24 frigates, 14 had 32–40 guns, while the other ten had 24–30 guns. Two frigates of 40 guns each were on the stocks at the time. Regarding the locations of these 24 frigates, five of them were in the Mediterranean Sea, eight in the Black Sea and 11 at Istanbul.[58]

In the squadron prepared in the arsenal on 22 March 1789 for a naval campaign in the Black Sea against Russia, there were five frigates: one with 50, three with 40 and seven with 28–36 guns. Besides these five frigates in the squadron, there were an estimated 23 frigates at the arsenal as well.[59]

From a list of the warships prepared by Karal, a general idea of the specifications of the 14 Ottoman frigates constructed under the reign of Selim III (1789–1807) can be obtained. These frigates had a length of 37–53 *zira* in general. Their number of gun ranged from 32 to 50. The number of men on board ranged from 200 to 400, depending on the size of the frigate. The *Tersâne-i Âmire*, Rhodes, Kemer, Limni, Kalas, Sinop and Ereğli[60] were the main construction sites for this type of vessel. Four were built in Rhodes, two in Limni, two at the *Tersâne-i Âmire*, two in Ereğli, one in Sinop and one in Kalas between 1789 and 1807.[61] These frigates were not the only ones operating at the time in the Ottoman navy. Frigates of 30, 31 and 53 *zira*, which do not appear in Karal's table, were encountered during the research for this study. They may be thought to have been given as presents or bought from abroad or captured in naval campaigns. Ahmed Cevdet gives the name of 22 frigates among the other warships at the *Tersâne-i Âmire* in 1801–02.[62] The number of frigates seems to have fluctuated, since it is given as 50 with ten to 50 guns in the year 1790,[63] but as 20 in a French report dated 1796.[64]

Administrative regulations in 1804 set the number and duties of the crew of frigates. The total number of crew was to amount to 163 and consist of one *reis-i evvel*, one *sertopî*, one *başhoca*, one *reis-i sânî*, one *bâdbânî-i evvel*, one *reis-i sâlis*, one *ser-oda*, one *ser-aylak*, two *çavuşân*, one *vekilharç*, 75 *gabyâr*, 20 *rubu'lu reisler*, one *ser-dümen*, one *cebeci-başı*, 40 *sodagabo*, one *ağa-yı kalyon*, one *anbarî*, eight *marangozân* and five *kalafatcıyân*.[65]

In Captain Capel's report, five frigates were at the arsenal for fitting, another five at the anchorage near the Seraglio point and two at the Dardanelles.[66]

### *Korvet (corvettes)*

The corvette was a three-masted man-of-war, 33–39 *zira* in length with 20–30 guns on the upper deck.[67] Karal's table shows that 11 Ottoman corvettes constructed under the reign of Selim III each had a length of 27–37 *zira*. Their gun capacity ranged from ten to 26. Crew numbered 120–200, depending on the size of the vessel. The *Tersâne-i Âmire*, Rhodes, Silistire and Kalas were the main construction sites for corvettes. Between 1789 and 1807, seven were built at the *Tersâne-i Âmire*, two in Rhodes, one in Kalas and one at an unknown site. When we add the two corvettes (both 31 *zira*, one with 22 and the other with 24 guns) sent by the Sultan of Morocco and one purchased from France during the Corfu campaign (43 *zira*, 40 guns, 250 men), this number increases to 14.[68]

As far as the 1804 regulations are concerned, the total number of crew on corvettes or small frigates was to be 112. The crew consisted of a *reis-i evvel*, a *sertopî*, a *başhoca*, a *reis-i sânî*, a *bâdbânî-i evvel*, a *reis-i sâlis*, a *ser-oda*, a *ser-aylak*, two *çavuşân*, a *vekilharç*, a *gabyâr*, 15 *rubu'lu reisler*, a *ser-dümen*, a *cebeci-başı*, 22 *sodagabo*, an *ağa-yı kalyon*, an *anbarî*, six *marangozân*, and four *kalafatcıyân*.[69]

Captain Capel reports that on 27 January 1807 four corvettes were at the arsenal for fitting, another seven at the anchorage near the Seraglio point, two at Büyükdere and three at the Dardanelles.[70]

### *Şehtiye /Şitye*

The *şehtiye* (a Turkish word in origin)came in two types: small ones of 23–27 *zira* and larger ones of 29–35 *zira*. They had generally two masts, but some large ones could have three. The total personnel, including officers (*zâbitân ve gedikli*) and other crew, were approximately 200 in the late eighteenth century.[71]

In an imperial decree, or *hüküm*, to Osman, the *Âyân* (local notable) of Varna, dated 17 October 1803, we can see the construction of *şehtiyes* together with *kalyon kıçlı üç direkli* (three-masted and galleon sterned vessel), *pergandi* or *pergende*, *çekleve* and *çenber* that were previously left for a period of time for the construction of smaller ships, such as *çekdirme* (a small oared vessel) and *beş çifte*. The reason behind this attitude is reported to have been the lack of larger ships with the capacity to carry heavier loads.[72]

### *Şalope/Şalopa/Şalupe (sloops)*

Sloops — small sailing ships of war without a hold — were generally two-masted and 27 *zira* in length. The two masts were rigged with plain sails called *sübye*. In 1815 a sloop carried 12 guns and its personnel consisted of a *reis*, a *bâdbânî*, a *hoca-i emanet* (assistant scribe), a *çavuş*, a *klavuz* (pilot), a *humbaracı halifesi* (an officer responsible for cannonballs), four *humbaracı* (bombardiers), one *topçubaşı* (chief artillery man) and six *sodagabu*, which amount to 62.[73]

The Imperial Naval Arsenal in Istanbul,[74] Biga Gümrüğü,[75] Galatz,[76] Sinop[77] and Idra[78] were important construction sites for sloops. The Porte occasionally had recourse to the purchase of American-[79] and British-built[80] sloops. The iron required for the *planketes* (chain shots) for the equipment of new sloops was generally provided from the *Tersâne-i Âmire*.[81]

The number of sloops appears as 40 in a document dated 25 April 1787, ten of which had 16–20 guns, and 30 eight to 12 guns. In terms of the geographical distribution of these 40 ships, 20 of them were in the Mediterranean, four in the Black Sea and 16 at Istanbul.[82] According to a report by Mahmud Raif Efendi, several hangars and sheds (*göz*) had been built at the entrance of Kağıthâne, and over 50 sloops were put into them.[83] Considering their superiority in number over the other kinds of ships of the time, it is reasonable to assume that they made up an important part of the Ottoman navy in the late eighteenth century.

In many places, sloops are mentioned in connection with naval campaigns. Sloops of war are recorded as having been employed at Büyükdere,[84] in Egypt,[85] in the Black Sea,[86] in Galatz,[87] the Dardanelles,[88] Varna, the Danube and so on. Five sloops appear among a list of ships prepared for a naval campaign to Varna on 22 March 1789 in order to harry the ice-bound Russian fleet in the Boristhenes.[89] On 17 October 1790 there were 60 sloops employed in the Danube navy. A certain number of guns firing cannonballs of three, five and seven *kıyyes* were ordered from Istanbul.[90]

Sloops seem to have been used in such works as drawing off enemy ships,[91] cruising for the defence of the Ottoman coasts and the islands in the Archipelago[92] and accompanying training ships. In 1790–91 two sloops were ordered to rig out and equip for that last purpose. Two ships were prepared for training. As was the tradition, red flags were hung from the stern of one of the ships. In order to differentiate between the ships, a white flag was flown from the middle mast and a small white flag from the first mast on the other training ship, which was carrying Swedish officers. The training process was to start the following Wednesday at 1.30 p.m.[93]

Records show sloops to be rigged out and repaired depending on the employment period. Among the 17 ships at the Imperial Naval Arsenal to be rigged out were two sloops of 19 *zira*. Furthermore, among 24 ships to be fully repaired, caulked and greased were 14 sloops of 22–23 *zira*.[94] Sloops, like other ships, faced harsh weather conditions. For instance, a sloop of war was run aground on the Black Sea coast between Amasra and Sinop on 10 November 1787, although all hands and the artillery were saved.[95] In another storm that raged for 72 hours from Thursday 2 April 1801, two sloops heading for Dimyat sunk and many other ships, such as the *Selimiye*, the *Tâvus-i Bahrî*, the *Ceyran-i Bahri*, the *Şehîd-i Zafer* and a galleon carrying British Admiral Keys, were damaged.[96]

### *Ateş Gemisi/Kayığı (fire ships)*

A fireship was a vessel of the same size and general lines as a sloop, but fitted with an extra 'fire deck' to take combustibles and fireworks, and extra features to encourage the rapid spread of flames such as downward-opening ports and special chimneys. Merchant ships and warships could be converted into fire ships.[97]

Generally classified as sailing ships because they had sails in addition to oars, they were used for setting enemy ships on fire during sea battles. Loaded with barrels full of explosives and inflammable materials, the ships were sent towards enemy ships, especially at night or in foggy weather. When they approached the enemy ships, the crew of the fire ships, who were experienced sailors, would set the explosives and other materials on fire by lighting their fuses, jump down from the portholes in the stern of the ship into the sea and swim to their other ships or escape in life boats before the fireship rammed into the target. Ramming the enemy with a ship full of explosives could set the enemy ship on fire and sometimes destroy a whole fleet. Fire ships, since they were extremely difficult to stop once they were launched at a target, could only be blocked by fast vessels sent in time to meet them and tow them off track by hooks.[98] Fire ships were used at the battle of Çeşme by the Russian fleet against the densely crowded Ottoman fleet and played an important role in its destruction.[99]

As for the use of this type of ship in the Ottoman navy, foreign documents report that French architects introduced fire ships to the Ottoman navy. Four were ready in February 1788 in the Imperial Arsenal.[100] An Ottoman document refers to the French role as well: the vizier is encouraged to do his utmost to send certain materials and to have French engineers arrange fire ships and feluccas.[101] Vessels previously built for other purposes were sometimes converted into fire ships.[102]

### *Uskuna (Schooner)* and **Kırlangıç**

An *uskuna* was a two-masted sailing ship, 27 *zira* in length. The first mast (*pruva direği*) was square-rigged (*kabasorta donanımlı*) and the second one (*grandi direği*) was single-rigged (*sübye donanımlı*). In 1831 a typical *uskuna* had 16 guns and 90 men on board.[103]

As for the *kırlangıç*, it was an oared ship used for duties such as war or coast guarding, or trade. A number of these were constructed in Sinop in 1789–90.[104] A new type of *kırlangıç* (*kırlangıç-ı kebîr-i new îcad*) was produced that would carry a 100-man crew in 1790–91.[105]

### *Trabago (trabacco)*

A *trabago* (trabacco) was a type of vessel used in the Adriatic Sea. The name appeared in the second half of the eighteenth century. Fifteen ships of this kind are mentioned in connection with a plan for naval construction in 1768.[106] An Ottoman document dated 1790–91 mentions two *trabagos* whose bottoms were ready and whose construction would be launched starting first with the stern-post part at the *Tersâne-i Âmire*.[107] An edict dated 23 March 1791 ordered that *trabago* ships should be constructed at the *Tersâne-i Âmire* and guns mounted. The document tells of the demand for casting of 50 *obüs* and *sürat* guns for the *trabago* and some other ships at the *Tophâne-i Âmire*. It also states that 72 *kantars* of *kali-yi İngilizî* (British tin) were required for casting these guns.[108]

### *Bomb ketches/bomb vessels*

It is generally accepted that bomb ketches were invented by the French in the late seventeenth century, particularly for shore bombardment with heavy mortars, and that they were first used by Du Quesne against Algiers in 1682. A bomb ketch was designated to enable a pair of heavy mortars to be located on an uncluttered deck forward of the main mast. Mortars were firmly secured to absorb the recoil. Bomb ketches carried a single anchor, onto the cable of which another rope was clapped in order to enable the mortar shells to be accurately aimed. The entire vessel could be pointed at the target by means of heaving and veering these and setting steadying sails. Range was achieved by the size of the charge while the timing of the explosion was calculated by the length of the fuse. The forward-standing rigging was made of chain to avoid damage.[109]

As for the bomb ketches used in the Ottoman navy, the table showing the state of the Ottoman navy on 25 April 1787 indicates that there were eight bomb ketches — two in Mediterranean and four at the Imperial Naval Arsenal.[110] This number seems to have increased with new additions in the following years.[111]

We see bomb ketches employed in some missions in the Archipelago, Egypt and Morea,[112] Büyükdere,[113] Ockachov,[114] the Black Sea,[115] the Dardanelles[116] as well as at the Imperial Naval Arsenal on various dates.[117]

It is understood that two French shipbuilders, Le Roi and Dureste, were commissioned to build some ships, including two large bomb ketches.[118]

Bomb ketches seem to have been used in such works as searching and drawing off enemy ships attacking Ottoman merchant ships.[119] They often accompanied and escorted these ships in order to protect the merchandise on the ships from enemy attacks. For instance, a detachment of the Ottoman fleet returned from Egypt, after remaining at anchor in the Propontis with a great deal of merchandises and property, entered the Imperial Arsenal on 13 December 1786. In this detachment was a bomb ketch.[120]

In some cases, different names appeared for bomb vessels in the late eighteenth century under the reign of Selim III, such as *korvet-i bomba* (bomb corvette)[121] and *fırkateyn-i bomba* (bomb frigate).[122]

### *Gunboats*

Ottoman gunboats appear to have been employed in many naval campaigns, drawing off enemy ships, escorting and protecting merchant ships, cruising the coasts in locations such as the Dardanelles,[123] Büyükdere,[124] Ockachov,[125] Crimea,[126] the Black Sea,[127] Varna[128] and Kilburun.[129] This type of boat was usually constructed according to French plans, as in the case of four gunboats constructed at the Naval Arsenal in July 1784.[130] A document dated 10 October 1785 about the newly constructed harbour for gunboats and galleys with a complete battery in the bay of Buyukliman, indicates that it was completed under the direction of French engineers.[131] In the following years, some engineers from other countries built gunboats, as did the Englishman Spurring, who built some in 1799.[132]

The number of gunboats shown in a chart on the state of the Ottoman navy on 25 April 1787 was 21: 11 in the Black Sea, eight in Istanbul and two in the Mediterranean. These gunboats carried a 24-pounder and a mortar of 10 inches each, and most of them had been constructed by French engineers at the Imperial Arsenal.[133] In the following years, the number of gunboats and their gun capacity increased with new additions in the face of new threats.[134] There were, for instance, 12 new gunboats constructed at Sinop, each carrying a 36-pounder and a mortar of 10.5 inches, in May 1788.[135] The number of gunboats was estimated to be 40[136] in 1789, 30–40 in March 1791[137] and 40 at the arsenal in June 1795.[138]

### Şebek (xebec/chebec/zebec)

The *şebek* was a three-masted ship much used by the corsairs of North Africa to patrol their coasts and raid enemy merchant vessels with considerable success. Later on, the navies of France, Spain and Britain adopted this type of ships by copying, capturing and purchasing. *Şebeks* were of several types. Some were large enough to mount up to 40 guns, like frigates, while others served as cargo vessels with lengths up to 40 metres. Although the *şebek* was characterised by oars and oar-benches, its great reputation was for its qualities as a sailing vessel, usually lateen-rigged in full, but often, after about 1750, incorporating square rig. The *şebek* was also famous for its manoeuvrability.[139] It was also regarded as a type of caravella with a narrow and long stern, and generally used in the Mediterranean.[140]

A British document mentions two Algerian *şebeks* — one with 36 guns, the other with 20 — that chased a Russian ship into Modon in September 1782.[141]

*State Papers* reported that between 1785 and 1789 there were about nine new *şebeks* a year.[142] These ships accompanied the other Ottoman ships of war, as in the case of two Ottoman ships of war at Büyükdere in June 1783.[143] In 1789 they joined a fleet and sailed out of Istanbul.[144] In September 1789, three *şebeks*, carrying 24 guns each, sent as a present to the Sultan by the emperor of Morocco, arrived at Istanbul. They were fine vessels, well outfitted and carrying a treasure amounting to 3 million piasters, sent as a subsidy to the Porte. Additionally, about the same date, four Algerian *şebeks* arrived at the Dardanelles accompanying a Russian prize (a captured Russian ship), also destined to reinforce the Ottoman navy.[145]

Documents also mention that in April 1790 a squadron of 14 frigates and *şebeks*, with two ships of the line intended for the Archipelago, was delayed waiting for crew to arrive from the Mediterranean.[146]

To sum up, all the documents and sources show that *şebeks* were mostly of Algerian origin, and were an important part of the Ottoman navy before and after the late eighteenth century.

### Pergandi/ Pergende (Brigantin)

An imperial decree reinstituted a kind of boat called a *pergandi*, which had been abandoned for a period of time in favour of smaller ships, such as the *çekdirme ve beş çifte*. Ships with bigger freight capacity were in greater need; the *pergandi* was brought back to fill this need. The construction of ships with capacities of less than 50,000 *kiles*[147] of load came to an end.[148]

### Karavel/Karavela/Karavila/Karavana (caravel)

The caravel, or *caravella, karavel, karavela, karavila* or *karavana*,[149] was closely linked to the Portuguese and Spanish explorations that spearheaded the opening of a sea route to the East Indies and the conquest of the New World. Both Colombus and Vasco da Gama took caravels on their voyages.[150] From the mid-fifteenth century on, these ships gained popularity across Atlantic Europe and the Mediterranean as small- to medium-size cargo carriers, warships, patrol or despatch boats, and corsair vessels. From the 1430s to the 1530s was the European century for the caravel.[151] This type of ship had a blunt, transom-built stern with a large rudder and was caravel-built, that is constructed with planks joined edge to edge, rather than overlapping as in the norhern style. Both square- and lateen-rigged sails were used on the caravels.

In the late fifteenth century they became vessels much feared on the seas, thanks to an invention by Portugal King John II (1481–1495), who discovered the effectiveness of mounting great guns in small caravels, which had greater manoeuvrability than other ship types. A few small caravels with big guns could force many larger ships to surrender.[152] As for Ottoman caravels, they were not a common type of ship and generally are described as a type of galleon. In the reign of Süleyman the Lawgiver, galleons like Venetian caravels were built, but later were abandoned because of their inpractibility in the absence of wind.[153] They were originally employed to protect convoys and later came to be used as transporters or corsairs, cruising against adversary ships.[154] The Ottoman caravels in the later periods were said to have been generally 40 *zira* or more in length and had 500 *levend*s (sailors employed during sea campaigns) and 500 sailors on board.[155] Caravels served both as warships and freighters.[156] In June 1785 there were two Ottoman caravels at Büyükdere to proceed into the Black Sea as part of a naval campaign.[157] In January 1786 a large Ottoman caravel is known to have sailed out of the Istanbul Arsenal for Cazdakli on the Black Sea coast to load a cargo of planks, ready there for the use of the arsenal.[158] Again, regarding its cargo function, it is known as an Ottoman squadron composed of 16 two-deckers and 12 frigates, exclusive of about 20 sloops, bomb ketches and other small craft destined for the Archipelago, departed for the Dardanelles in consequence of the intelligence that Sig Qulielmo, with two large frigates and three sloops, was off Rhodes, into which they had chased a large Ottoman caravel richly loaded from Alexandria and destined for Istanbul on 22 May 1791.[159]

### Ships constructed and repaired in the reign of Selim III

Having discussed at length the types of ships dominant during the reign of Selim III, now a closer look will be taken at them, as much as the data at hand allow. The ships mentioned here are not necessarily the ones constructed or repaired in Selim's reign. To pose a background to this specific period, we consider it to be beneficial to include some ships constructed and repaired as an extension of the modernisation current in the aftermath of Çeşme. The lists of ships prepared by Ahmed Cevdet and Karal are accepted as a starting point, and many other names found in local and foreign archival documents as well as the chronicles of the period enrich the material available. Another point to make is the difficulty in presenting a standard description of the ships, since the same data for all the ships mentioned here are not always available. Therefore, some ships are examined in more detail while others are given only a few sentences. Finally, the lack or insufficiency of the pictures or drawings of the ships in archival documents and even in some secondary sources is another drawback for the student of naval technology. Therefore, we must be content with presenting what visual data are available.

The *Bahr-i Zafer* was a galleon of 55 *zira*, covered with copper, with 72 guns and 750 men aboard, constructed at the Imperial Naval Arsenal by Ismail Kalfa, who had also been a chief architect in the reign of Abdulhamid I. All but its gun deck was finished when Selim III ascended the throne, after which it was completed and launched in 1789–90.[160] A document from 1789–90 reveals that four large cannons of 66 diameters each (throwing a projectile of 66 pounds) were produced at the Imperial Cannon Foundry (Tophâne-i âmire) and ready to mount on this new galleon, which the Kaptan Pasha would command.[161]

Uzunçarşılı, referring to a certain naval document, reports that there were 59 *aylakçı* (temporary sailors recruited for six months) serving on the *Bahr-i Zafer* in 1790.[162] Some of its equipment underwent repair and maintenance in 1793–94, when its hoses became worn out. The *Tersâne-i Âmire Tulumbacıbaşısı* (the chief official in charge of pumps at the Imperial Naval Arsenal) installed two new ones.[163]

Shaw writes that when the *Bahr-i Zafer* was launched in 1794, it boasted a new provisioning system that provided the cooks with wood, salt and oil sufficient for the entire voyage at the expense of the Treasury, the first of its kind to be installed on a ship of the line.[164] Tezel notes that this provisioning system was applied not only to the *Bahr-i Zafer* but also to the *Humây-i Zafer* at the same time, in 1793–94.[165] Gencer supports Tezel with a quote by Halil Efendi and says that there was a kitchen system on most of the naval ships in 1794, which provided not only regular nourishment for the crew, but also eliminated the clutter and disorder preventing cannons from efficient firing due to the haphazardness of private stoves.[166]

In early 1800–01 *Bahr-i Zafer* cast anchor in the Bosphorus Strait (*Bahr-i Sefid Bogazi*) under the command of Mustafa Kapudan from Eyup. It is understood from the correspondence between the *Tersâne Emiri* and Mustafa Kaptan that the galleon in question had been taking in one *karış* of water per hour for five days and had had a difficult time. He was asked to come to the *Tersâne* as soon as possible, by a caique on 11 January 1801.[167] The *Bahr-i Zafer* was still in use at the Imperial Naval Arsenal in 1801–02.[168]

The *Feyz-i Hüdâ* was a galleon of 55 *zira*,[169] covered with copper, with 72 guns and 650 men aboard. Like the *Bahr-i Zafer*, its construction started in the time of Abdulhamid I and was completed under Selim III, in 1789–90, by Nikoli Kalfa in Sinop.[170] A British Foreign Office document reports that some ships of the line built in Sinop were launched on 22 July 1789.[171] It is probable that the *Feyz-i Hudâ* was one of them. In 1790–91 the foretopmast (*trinkete sutunu*) of the *Patrona-i humayun kalyon-ı Feyz-i Hüdâ* (the vice-admiral's flagship) accidentally fell into the water and was in difficult straits thereafter.[172]

The *Feyz-i Hüdâ* is qualified as a *Patrona-i Humayun*, the vice-admiral's flagship, in a document dated 1793–94. Its hoses had become worn out and two new ones were mounted in 1793–94 by the chief official in charge of supply and delivery of the pumps and related equipment at the naval arsenal.[173] A document dated 3 September 1800 mentions that the *Feyz-i Hüdâ*, prepared and equipped in Beşiktaş, needed a crew of 150 men. The required crew were hired from among volunteers and the total payment for the crew increased to 12,000 *kuruş*.[174] The *Feyz-i Hüdâ* being in use at the naval arsenal in 1801–02[175] appears with 72 guns among the ships ready at Marmara in 1806[176] during battles against the British fleet, and also among the list of the auxiliary fleet of the navy at the *Tersâne-i Âmire* in 1810.[177]

The *Hilâl-i Zafer* was a galleon of 51 *zira*, covered with copper, with 66 guns and a crew of 650. Its construction started in Halicarnassus/Bodrum in the time of Abdulhamid I. After spending seven years on the stocks, it was completed in 1790–91 by Papacho Kalfa. Although it was reported to be in bad condition and left for scrap[178] in 1791–92, its name appeared on a list of the ships to be repaired and rigged.[179]

Another document of 1790–91 describes a galleon, without giving its name, under construction at Halicarnassus/Bodrum under the supervision of Süleyman Bey. The document notes the cost and some of the materials required. Süleyman Bey was ordered to finish the construction by early spring. Five thousand *kuruş* from the Imperial Treasury, 20,000 *kuruş* from the *Menteşe Mütesellimi* (governor of the district of Menteşe), 800 *kantars* of raw iron, 35,000 *kuruş* from the *Aydın Muhassılı* (district administrator) and Çavuşzâde, the *Menteşe Mütesellimi*, and 50,000 *kuruş* from Egypt were among the material and monetary sources dedicated to the construction of this galleon.[180] Considering the names and places, it seems plausible that this galleon was the *Hilâl-i Zafer*.

In another document, an unnamed galleon of 51 *zira* was noted as under renovation through the agency of Kapucubaşı Mir Süleyman at Halicarnassus/Bodrum on 2 June 1792. Ninety thousand one hundred and fifty-four *kuruş* from the Imperial Treasury and 2,150 *kantars* of raw iron and other equipment had been used up to that time. Süleyman was asked about the construction process and was urged to complete the ship at the earliest possible date.[181] It is most probable that this galleon was the *Hilâl-i Zafer* and that Mir Süleyman was not the builder but the person responsible for supervising the work.

The *Kepçe Kıçlı Kalyon*, a 53-*zira* vessel, was under construction in January–Febrary 1792 at the *Tersâne-i Âmire* in Istanbul. The quality timber required for the construction of the galleon was provided from İznikmid by İznikmid Emini Ali Ağa at a price of 30,000 *kuruş*, out of which 17,500 *kuruş* had been paid up to the abovementioned date. More timber (*kemerelik lata-i kebîr-i çam, pıraçol-ı kebîr-i meşe*) was demanded as soon as possible for the completion and launching of the galleon. Fifteen thousand *kuruş* were needed for the felling and transportation of this timber.[182]

The *Fâtih-i Bahrî*, a galleon of 47 *zira*, coppered, with 60 guns and a crew of 550 men, was constructed in 1791–92[183] by Nikoli Usta in Sinop.[184] However, it must have been in use earlier, since it appeared in 1790–91 in the Straits under the command of Riyâle-i Cezayir Yakup Kapudân when its main topmast (*gabya çubukları*) fell and the foretopmast (*trinkete*) and mizzen topmast (*mizana sutunları*) were crippled.[185]

It is understood that its hose became worn out; a new one was mounted in 1793–94 by the chief official in charge of pumps at the Imperial Naval Arsenal (*Tersane-i Âmire tulumbacıbaşısı*).[186] In 1799–1800, while returning from a mission along with some other ships on the Egyptian coast, the ship was caught in a storm near Gelibolu and ran aground.[187]

The *İnâyet-i Hak* is mentioned in a document dated 1793–94 as a *Riyâle-i Hümayun* (rear admiral's flagship) whose hoses had become worn out. Two new ones were installed in 1793–94 by the chief official in charge of supply and delivery of the pumps and related equipment at the naval arsenal.[188]

The *Ferahnümâ* was a corvette of 37 *zira*, covered with copper, with 24 guns and a crew of 150 men, constructed in 1792–93 by Hammâmizâde Ahmed in Silistire during the office of former Grand Vizier Yusuf Pasha. Later on, it was sent to the Imperial Naval Arsenal to be scrapped because of its unsuitability for employment.[189] This ship, however, was most likely rebuilt, since it appears as a brig on the list of the auxiliary fleet of the navy at the *Tersâne-i Âmire* in 1810.[190]

The *Âsâr-ı Nusret* was a 55-*zira* galleon, with 74 guns and a crew of 800, constructed in 1792–1793[191] by Ismail Kalfa[192] (the chief architect) at the naval arsenal.[193] Sultan Selim III attended its launching ceremony.[194] It was sheathed with copper in 1795.[195]

The *Âsâr-ı Nusret* is referred to as a *Kapudâne-i Hümayun* (imperial admiral's flagship) in a document dated 1793–94. Its hoses had become worn out and two new ones were mounted in 1793–94 by the *Tersâne-i Âmire tulumbacıbaşısı* at the naval arsenal.[196] The *Âsâr-ı Nusret* being in use there in 1801–02[197] played an active role during battles against the British fleet in the Marmara Sea, with 74 guns in 1806. It defended itself for half an hour against an 84-gunned British galleon and then ran aground. Refusing to abandon their vessel, the sailors went on firing their guns. A British ship directed itself towards the *Âsâr-ı Nusret* and destroyed it completely.[198] It is possible that this ship was repaired or rebuilt later on, since its name appears on a list of the auxiliary fleet of the navy at the *Tersâne-i Âmire* in 1810.[199]

The *Pertev-i Nusret* was a galleon of 53 *zira*, with 68 guns and a crew of 700, constructed in 1793–94 by Nikoli Kalfa[200] in Sinop.[201] The application of the copper sheathing to the *Pertev-i Nusret* was completed in 1795.[202] Altıkulaçzâde Hüseyin, the Kastamonu *Mütesellimi* (Governor), was ordered to construct the galleon along with another one of 51 *zira* in Sinop. For the construction of the two galleons, 40,000 *kuruş* and 1,200 *vukıyye*s of raw iron were spent up to 2 June 1792.[203] Before that date, on 6 November 1791 Altıkulaçzâde had demanded iron materials such as shrouds, rudders, rings and a *çene* (a slightly round place at the connection of stem and keel). In addition, he demanded pipe and copper tools.[204] Altıkulaçzâde demanded more materials, workers and money in the following months. The authorities, after advising him on the procurement of the required materials, ordered him to finish the 53-*zira* galleon, of which only one-third had been completed, as well as the galleon of 51 *zira* (the careen of which was far from completed) as soon as possible.[205] No further information is available about the *Pertev-i Nusret*, except that it was in use at the Imperial Naval Arsenal in 1801–02[206] and on the list of the auxiliary fleet of the navy in 1810.[207]

The *Ejder-i Bahrî* was a 57-*zira* galleon, with 74 guns and a crew of 850, constructed in 1793–94[208] by Nevsim Kalfa using Le Brun's measurements in Gemlik.[209] It was not sheathed with copper until 1796–97, on order of the *Kaptan Pasha*. The ship needed lead plates of 32 and 33 *vukıyye*s but there were none left in the *mahzen-i surb*. It was decided to supply 100 large lead plates (*tahta kurşun*) of 32 and 33 *vukıyyes* each through the chief lead supplier, *Hassa Kurşuncubaşı*.[210] The vessel was present at the Imperial Naval Arsenal in 1801–02[211] and later appeared as a 74-gun ship among ships in the Marmara Sea[212] in the battles against the British fleet in 1806 and on the list of naval ships at the Imperial Arsenal in 1810.[213]

The *Şehbâz-ı Bahrî* was a galleon of 57 *zira*, with 74 guns and a crew of 850, constructed in 1793–94 by Nikoli Kalfa, using Le Brun's measurements in Bodrum.[214] It was covered with copper in 1795.[215] Tezel claims that this ship was constructed in Rhodes along with the galleons *Hıfz-i Hüdâ* and *Tevfikullah* in 1798.[216] It appears on the list of the ships to be caulked, pressed and greased in 1791–92.[217] It is known to have been still in use at the Imperial Naval Arsenal in 1801–02.[218] It participated in battles against the British fleet, appearing on the lists with 74 guns among the ships ready in the Marmara Sea in 1806[219] and among the list of the auxiliary fleet of the navy at the *Tersâne-i Âmire* in 1810.[220]

The *Hümây-ı Zafer* was a frigate of 53 *zira*, with 50 guns and a crew of 450 men, constructed in 1793–94 by Dimitri (second architect) at the Imperial Naval Arsenal.[221] It was coverd with copper in 1794.[222] Along with the galleon *Bahr-i Zafer*, it adopted new provisioning and kitchen systems in 1793. This system supplied the cooks of the ships with wood, salt and oil in sufficient quantities for the entire voyage at the expense of the Treasury.[223] The hose of the *Hümây-ı Zafer* became worn out and a new one was mounted in 1793–94.[224] The *Hümây-ı Zafer* was still in use in 1801–02[225] and among the list of the auxiliary fleet of the navy at the *Tersâne-i Âmire* in 1810.[226]

The *Şiâr-ı Nusret* (a frigate of 51 *zira*, 50 guns and a crew of 450 men) and the *Nesîm-i Zafer* (a frigate of 47 *zira*, 40 guns and a crew of 375 men) were both constructed in 1793–94 by Antuvan Kalfa (Antoin) on the island of Rhodes.[227] They were both sheathed with wood. Both were in use at the Imperial Naval Arsenal in 1801–02,[228] and the *Şiâr-ı Nusret* was on the list of the auxiliary fleet of the navy at the *Tersâne-i Âmire* in 1810.[229] Regarding the *Nesîm-i Zafer*, we learn that its hose became worn out and was replaced in 1793–94.[230]

The *Gazâl-ı Bahrî*, a frigate of 45 *zira*, was covered with copper, carried 42 guns and had a crew of 375. It was constructed in

1793–94 by Kara Yorgi Kalfa in Kemer.[231] It was still in use at the Imperial Naval Arsenal in 1801–02.[232]

All that is known of the *Zafer-i Hümâyûn* is that it was a galleon-type ship constructed at the *Tersâne-i Âmire* in 1793–94 and launched the same year.[233]

More is known about the *Arslân-ı Bahrî*, a 59-*zira* galleon covered with copper, with 76 guns and a crew of 850 men. Being constructed in 1794–95 by the French shipbuilder Le Brun at the Imperial Naval Arsenal,[234] it was among the ships to receive copper sheathing in 1795.[235] An Ottoman document dated 12 October 1795 lists the *Arslan-ı Bahrî* of the *Kaptan Pasha* and other galleons and flagships whose signs, sword and regiment flags, and colours were to be renewed, repaired and dyed. The document gives all of the expenses in total without special reference to each ship. The expenses of dye, tailors and silk thread added up to 1,339 *kuruş*.[236] Another Ottoman document detailing the repair of the kitchen ovens of the *Rehber-i Nusret* and the *Necm-i Zafer* refers to the *Arslân-ı Bahrî* as well. It says, in a small note, that the price of the iron sheets produced formerly for the galleon *Arslân-ı Bahrî*, which had been boarded by the *Kaptan Pasha*, would be applied to the above-mentioned ships.[237] The *Arslân-ı Bahri* was still in use at the naval arsenal in 1801–02.[238] During battles against the British fleet in the Marmara Sea, it was inactive with 76 guns in 1806[239] and also on the list of the navy in 1810.[240]

Little is known about the *Salâbetnümâ*, a corvette of 33 *zira* covered with copper, with 26 guns and a crew of 150 men, except that it was built in 1795–96 by Le Brun at the Imperial Naval Arsenal[241] and that it was still in use at the arsenal in 1801–02.[242] It was also the case of the *Küşâde Baht*, a frigate of 37 *zira*, covered with copper, with 38 guns and a crew of 300 men. It was constructed at the Imperial Naval Arsenal at an unknown date. However, it is established that it was captured by enemy forces and after some time returned to Istanbul under the name of the *Golermo* en route to the Black Sea. It was not allowed to sail to the Black Sea and was bought by the Porte. In 1795–96 it was commissioned to Corfu.[243]

The *Zîver-i Bahrî* was built by engineer Ahmet Hoca Kaptan, a student of Le Roy's[244], in Midilli[245] in 1796–97.[246] Of 53 *zira*, the ship was covered with copper, carried 68 guns and had a crew of

700. The *Zîver-i Bahrî* was still in use at the Imperial Naval Arsenal in 1801–02.[247] It seems inactive with 68 guns during the battles against the British fleet in the Marmara Sea in 1806[248] and is on the list of the auxiliary fleet of the navy in 1810.[249] A picture of this ship appeared in Mahmud Raif Efendi's book, where it was shown carrying 70 guns. Its length is given as 59.5 French *pic*.[250]

The *Selimiye* was a three-decked galleon of 62 *zira*, covered with copper, with (62-110-122-132) guns and 1,200 men aboard. It was built in 1796 by Le Brun at the Imperial Naval Arsenal, according to French models.[251] Sultan ordered its construction on 18 October 1794, and two years later it was completed. In the beginning, it was planned to be of 67 *zira*, six-storeyed and triple-decked.[252] Although its construction did not begin immediately, its keel was to have been laid on the model of the *Royal Louis*[253] shortly after that date.[254]

The timber for masts and yards required for the *Selimiye* were demanded from Hasan Çelebizade Seyyid Halil Ağa, a notable from Kidros, and a certain İbrahim Ağa in his retinue. An architect furnished with the necessary measuring equipment was to be sent from the *Tersâne-i Âmire* to accompany them. They were warned to be meticulous in searching for the proper trees in Kidros, Cide and surrounding places, in felling them according to the pre-determined measures and diameters, and in transferring them to the *Tersâne-i Âmire* in safety. A document dated 18 October 1796 reports that a galleon of three decks (referring to *Selimiye* without giving its name) was under construction at the *Tersâne-i Âmire*. When it neared completion, large masts and yards in specific diameters and sizes would be needed. Since those on hand in the *Tersâne-i Âmire* were not of high enough quality to equip a ship like the *Selimiye*, 40 new great masts (each 40 *zira* in length, a down edge of ten to 11 *karış* and an upper edge of six–seven *karış*), ten large masts (each 34 *zira* in length and with a down edge of 89 *karış* and an upper edge of five–six *karış*) and another ten masts (each 32 *zira* in length and with a down edge of 7,5–8 *karış* and an upper edge of five–six *karış*), amounting to 60 in total, were required.[255]

There is disagreement over the identity of the builder of the *Selimiye* and the number of guns it carried. Shaw refers to an anonymous French document saying that the Englishman Spurring was the builder,[256] and he compares this information with some suggesting that Le Brun built it.[257] However, no sound evidence was found in the course of the research for this book showing that anyone (including Spurring) other than Le Brun constructed this ship.

Regarding the guns of the *Selimiye*, various figures are given. Unlike the figure mentioned in Karal's article (62 guns), 122 at its launch in 1796 is given by Goodwin,[258] and 132 in letters from the Earl of Elgin to the secretary of state on 6 November 1799[259] and 21 April 1800.[260] It is also said to have had 110 guns aboard during the war waged against France in Egypt on 26 March 1801,[261] and 62 guns in 1806.[262]

It is reported that on 13 April 1801, a 72-hour storm damaged the *Selimiye* and a number of other ships, breaking two rudder tillers.[263] However, the *Selimiye* appears at the Imperial Naval Arsenal in 1801–02[264] and among the fleet with its 62 guns during the wars with the British fleet in 1806.[265] It also appears as a triple-decker galleon in 1810 on the list of the navy.[266]

On the other hand, Tezel describes a certain *Selimiye* galleon of 128 guns and with crew of 1,280, constructed in 1808 by Monsieur Löˆbral (an engineer) and Monsieur Benoit (an architect). He says that its length was 147 *kadem*, its beam 50 *kadem*, its height 25 *kadem* and its deplacement 23.5 *kadem*.[267] Most probably, the *Selimiye* described by Tezel is a different ship bearing the same name.

The *Heybetendâz* was a galleon (*patrone-i humayun*) of 59 *zira* covered with copper, with 76 guns and 850 men aboard. It was constructed in 1796 by Nikoli Kalfa, using Le Brun's measures, in Bodrum.[268] The *Heybetendâz* of 74 guns was in use in 1801–02[269], inactive during wars with the British fleet in 1806[270] and on the list of the auxiliary fleet of the navy in 1810.[271]

In *Çeşmî-zâde Tarihi*, under the section '*zikr-i nuzûl-i kalyon der-Tersâne-i âmire*' ('about the launch of the galleon at the Imperial Arsenal'), the *Mesken-i Gâzî* appears as a galleon launched to sea on 6 April 1766 with the attendance of the Sultan and Kaptan-ı Derya Mehmed Pasha.[272] This name was later given to a frigate in the time of Selim III, which was 53 *zira*, covered with copper, carrying 50 guns and 450 men. It was built in 1796 by the French shipbuilder Le Brun at the Istanbul Arsenal.[273] The *Mesken-*

*i Gâzî* was in use in 1801–02.[274] It is reported that on 21 February 1802, some large mirror glasses were required for its equipment, at a cost of 379 *kuruş* and 16 *para*.[275] During the battle against the British fleet in 1806, it was blown up, together with the frigate *Nesîm-i Futûh*. At the time, it had 38 guns aboard.[276] It also appears among the list of the ships in 1810.[277] It must have been repaired or rebuilt.

The *Şehper-i Zafer* was a frigate of 53 *zira*, covered with copper, armed with 50 guns, and with 450 men aboard. It was constructed in 1796[278] by the architect Antuvan (Antoin?) on Rhodes, using Le Brun's measures. It was among the Corfu navy and then was commissioned to join the Ancona (an Adriatic port and capital of the Marche region of central Italy) siege. It sailed to Trieste in the winter and was still there in 1796.[279] This vessel was still in use at the Imperial Naval Arsenal in 1801–02.[280]

Filip (Philip) Kalfa built the frigate *Şevketnümâ* in 1796 on the island of Lemnos/Limni.[281] It was 51 *zira* in length, covered with copper, with 50 guns and 450 men aboard. When the frigate underwent a crash and sunk in the following years, its equipment was rescued and transferred to the Imperial Naval Arsenal via another galleon, the *Beşâretnümâ*. As far as is known, the *Şevketnümâ* was composed of three parts: an upper deck (*birinci ambar*), a main deck (*palavra*) and the bilge (*sintine*). Among the mast equipment were the royal mast (*kontra babafingo*), the topmast (*gabya çubuğu*), the yard (*seren*), the main mast (*ana direk*), the boom (*bumba*) and the bowsprit (*cıvadıra*).[282] The *Şevketnümâ* was still in use at the naval arsenal in 1801–02.[283] It was probably repaired or rebuilt later on.

The *Bûlheves*, a frigate of 41 *zira*, covered with copper, filled out with 40 guns and a crew of 275, was constructed in 1796 by Mustafa Molla (Büyük Seyyid Mustafa of the Mühendishâne instructors and chief assistant to Le Brun) in Kalas. It was among the ships of the Corfu navy and then was commissioned to the Ancona siege and sailed to Trieste in the winter and was still there in 1796.[284] This vessel seems in use at the Imperial Naval Arsenal in 1801–02.[285] It also appears among the list of the auxiliary fleet of the navy at the *Tersâne-i Âmire* in 1810.[286] A picture of this frigate is shown in Mahmud Raif Efendi's book, where it appears to have 48 guns and to be 49,5 French *pic* in length.[287]

The *Zaferküşâ*, a corvette of 37 *zira*, covered with copper, with 26 guns and 200 men aboard, was constructed in 1796 by Le Brun at the Imperial Naval Arsenal.[288] It was in use there in 1801–02,[289] participated with 34 guns to the wars with the British fleet in 1806 in the Marmara Sea[290] and appeared on the list of the auxiliary fleet of the navy at the *Tersâne-i Âmire* in 1810.[291]

A Swedish shipbuilder by the name of Klintberg built a 35-*zira* corvette, the *Rehber-i Nusret*, on Rhodes in 1796. It was clad in copper, had 26 guns and 200 men aboard.[292] This corvette had been planned as a corsair ship. Murâbitzâde Hasan Kapudân, the governor of Rhodes (*Rodos mutasarrıfı*), was in charge of the administration of the construction of this vessel. All the cost of the necessary materials and equipment were met by the state. The corvette cost 23,308 *kuruş* in total.[293]

The *Rehber-i Nusret* appears both as a galleon and a corvette along with a ship called the *Necm-i Zafer*, the kitchen ovens of which needed repair on 22 July 1797. The ovens were renewed by the *Liman Reisi* (the commander of the Port of Istanbul). The required iron sheet (*âhen sac*) and some iron equipment were purchased. All the expenses, including workmanship, amounted to 903.5 *kuruş* and ten *para*.[294] It was still in use at the naval arsenal in 1801–03.[295]

Little is known of the *Necm-i Zafer*. It appears both as a galleon and a corvette. Because its name is mentioned together with the *Rehber-i Nusret*, with which it underwent the same repair process, it might be judged to have had similar features.[296]

The *Mürg-i Bahrî* was a corvette of 27 *zira* covered with copper, with 22 guns and a crew of 120. It was constructed in 1796 by Çamlıcalı Kalfa Kara Yorgi, at an undisclosed site. It sailed to Alexandria in the company of merchant ships in 1796[297] and was still in use at the Imperial Naval Arsenal in 1801–02.[298]

There was another ship with the same name, of the *şehtiye* type, 33 *zira* in length. It appears among the ships at the Imperial Naval Arsenal for rigging out in 1791–92.[299] The total personnel consisted of a *kaptan* (captain), *reis-i evvel* (first commander), *reis-i sânî* (second commander), *reis-i sâlis* (third commander), four other *reis*, a *bâdbânî* (man in charge of rising or lowering the sails), an *ağa*, a *hoca* (kâtip/scribe), two *çavuş*, a *vekiliharç* (a kind of majordomo or butler), a *topçubaşı* (chief gunner), ten *topçukethüdası* (gun officers), 12 *topçu* (gunners), a *serhazine* (chief treasurer), a *serdümen* (chief helmsman), a *dümen kethüdası* (a helmsman), an *aylak başı* (chief temporaray mariner with a certain salary), five *aylakçı*, 18 *aylakçı* of Greek origin, eight *aylakçı* of Armenian origin, a *kandil çavuşu* (officer in charge of oil lamps), a *klavuz* (guide), a *sermarangoz* (chief carpenter), a *serkalafat* (chief caulker), three *kalafatçı* (caulkers) and a *varilci* (man in charge of barrels).[300]

The *Tevfîk-i Hüdâ* was a galleon commissioned to İznikmid to transport timber in 1796. The transport of timber was generally carried out by a type of sailing ship called a *çekeleve*,[301] but because of the urgent need for a large quantity of timber for the construction of a three-decked frigate before the approaching winter, the *Tevfîk-i Hüdâ* was assigned this task. [302]

The *Rûzgâr-ı Bahrî* was a corvette of 22 guns, with a crew of 120, built in 1796 (the construction site is unknown). Its name does not appear in Cevdet Pasha's or Karal's lists, only in Tezel's list of ships constructed between 1789 and 1799.[303] Unlike Tezel, Güleryüz writes that it was 37 *zira* and with ten guns and a crew of 150.[304]

A corvette of 37 *zira*, covered with copper, with 26 guns and 200 men aboard, the *Cenk-Âver* was constructed in 1797–98 by Le Brun, together with Antuvan at the Imperial Naval Arsenal.[305] It was still in use at the arsenal in 1801–02.[306]

Another corvette of 37 *zira* built by Le Brun and Antoin in the same year was the *Secâ-ı Bahrî*. It also carried 26 guns and a crew of 200. It was sheathed with copper as well.[307] It was still in use at the arsenal in 1801–02.[308]

In 1798–99 Le Brun and Antuvan built the *Sâika-bâr/Sâika-ı Bâd* at the Imperial Naval Arsenal. It, too, was 37 *zira* in length, covered with copper, with 26 guns and 175 men aboard.[309] The *Sâika-bâr/Sâika-ı dâd* was still in use at the arsenal in 1801–02.[310] During the battles against the British fleet in the Marmara Sea in 1806, it was active with 24 guns,[311] and on the list of naval ships in 1810.[312]

The *Âteşfeşân* was another corvette of 37 *zira*, covered with copper, with 26 guns and a crew of 175, constructed in 1798–99 by Le Brun and Antuvan at the Imperial Naval Arsenal.[313] It was still in use in 1801–02[314] and on the list of the auxiliary fleet of the navy at the *Tersâne-i Âmire* in 1810.[315]

The *Beşâretnümâ* was a galleon (*Riyâle-i Hümâyûn,* the rear admiral's flagship) of 59 *zira,* covered with copper, with 76 guns and 850 men aboard, built in 1797–98 by Nevsim Kalfa, using Le Brun's measures, at Gemlik.[316] It was still in use at the arsenal in 1801–02.[317]

The *Bâdi-i Nusret,* a galleon of 63 *zira,* covered with copper, with 82 guns and 900 men aboard, was built in 1797–98 by Le Brun and Antoin at the Imperial Naval Arsenal.[318] In the same year, for the equipment of this three-decker, various blocks (*makara*) with Santo sheaves were purchased from the Galata traders through Idris Pasha. The price paid for the blocks was 283 *kuruş.*[319] This vessel was still in use at the arsenal in 1801–02.[320]

The *Seyyâd-ı Bahrî* was a galleon of 59 *zira* covered with copper, with 74 guns and 850 men aboard, constructed in 1797–98 by the Venitian Joseph Kalfa, using Le Brun's measures, at Kal'a-i Sultâniye in the Dardanelles.[321] During the battles with the British fleet, it was active with 74 guns.[322] It is listed as a galleon of *Riyâle-i Hümâyûn* (the rear admiral's flagship) in 1810.[323]

Dimitri (second architect) built the *Şâhin-i Deryâ,* a frigate of 53 *zira,* covered with copper, with 50 guns and 450 men aboard, in 1797–98, using Le Brun's measures, in the Black Sea Ereğlisi dockyard.[324] In 1797 it was recorded that this vessel was a galleon of 53.5 *zira* and that its hull had cost 48,529 *kuruş.*[325] It was still in use at the Imperial Naval Arsenal in 1801–02.[326]

The *Hediyyetü'l Mülûk* was a frigate of 39 *zira* covered with copper, carrying 46 guns and a crew of 200, constructed by Mustafa (the second assistant to Le Brun at the arsenal) in Sinop in 1797–98 and then was commissioned to Corfu.[327] A picture of the corvette can be found in Mahmud Raif Efendi's book, where Mustafa appears as 'Çavuşoğlu Mustafa' and where the numbers given for the length (36,5 French *pic*) and for the guns (24) differ from those given above.[328]

The *Tîz Hareket* was a frigate that at one time was under the command of the Grand Vizier. Of 38 *zira,* it was covered with copper, with 32 guns and 200 men aboard. It was constructed in 1797–98 by Antuvan (Antoin) Kalfa, who used Le Brun's measurements, on Rhodes.[329] A document of 1803–04 states that this frigate would be ready to set off from Samsun wharf in two to three days, loaded with raw copper, bound for the Imperial Naval Arsenal. In the same document, a firman orders that the crew of the ship be paid as soon as the ship arrived at Istanbul. The salary in question, when calculated together with that of the *Bahr-i Amîk* crew coming from Canik with a load of 850 pieces of *karaağaç* (elm) timber, added up to 19,488 *kuruş*.[330] The *Tîz Hareket* appears on the list of the navy at the *Tersâne-i Âmire* in 1810, charged with timber transportation.[331]

A copper-hulled galleon (*Kapudâne-i Hümayun*) of 63 *zira*, the *Tâvus-ı Bahrî* had 82 guns and 900 men aboard and was constructed in 1798–99 by Le Brun at the Imperial Naval Arsenal.[332] It was launched on 22 December 1798.[333] A document of 13 April 1801 mentions that, as a result of a severe storm that lasted two hours, the *Tâvus-ı Bahrî*, on which the Kapudâne was present, was damaged significantly. The rudder was ripped off when the bearing pintles were lost.[334] The vessel was still in use at the naval arsenal in 1801–02.[335] In the 1806 Marmara battles against the British fleet, it was inactive with 82 guns.[336] It also appeared on the list of the auxiliary fleet of the navy at the *Tersâne-i Âmire* in 1810.[337]

The *Kaplân-ı Bahrî*, a galleon of 59 *zira* covered with copper, with 76 guns and 850 men aboard, was built in 1799–1800 by the Swedish shipbuilder Klintberg on the island of Rhodes.[338] A document by the Chief of the Imperial Naval Arsenal (*Tersâne-i Amire Reisi*) of 1800–01 states that the *Kaplân-ı Bahrî* and another vessel named the *Seddülbahir* were to be covered with copper. As there was not enough of the material in the *mahzen-i sürb*, it was decided that 10,000 *vukıyye*s of raw copper, valued at 6,666.5 *kuruş*, would be transferred from the *Darphâne-i-Âmire*.[339] The *Kaplân-ı Bahrî* was still in use at the arsenal in 1801–02.[340]

Launched to sea in 1799, the *Seddülbahir* was a new galleon of 59.5 *zira*, covered with copper, with 76 guns and a crew of 850, completed[341] by Benuva (Benois) at the Imperial Naval Arsenal.[342] As discussed above, like the *Kaplân-ı Bahrî*, the *Seddülbahir* was covered with copper provided from both the *mahzen-i sürb* and the *Darphâne-i Âmire* between 1799 and 1801.[343] Thirty bronze guns, 13 *karış* in diameter and 14 *kıyye*s in weigth, were cast for the *Seddülbahir*, since there were no guns of the required measures available at the *Tersâne-i Âmire*. At the same time, 250 bronze guns were cast for other ships. Among these ships were a frigate of 54 *zira* and two galleons under construction on Rhodes and in

Sohum.[344] The *Seddülbahir* was still in use at the naval arsenal in 1801–02.[345] In 1806 it was inactive against the British navy with 76 guns.[346]

A frigate of 53 *zira*,[347] covered with copper, with 50 guns and a crew of 450, was built in the Eregli dockyard in 1799–1800 by Dimitri Kalfa (second architect), using Le Brun's measurements.[348] Named the *Bedr-i Zafer* it was still in use at the Naval Arsenal in 1801–02.[349]

Of the *Civân-ı Bahrî*, a frigate of 53 *zira*, covered with copper, with 50 guns and 450 men aboard, all that is known is that it was built in 1799–1800 by Benuva (Benois) on the island of Lemnos/Limni.[350] Likewise, of the *Meserret-i Bahrî*, all that is known is that it was a corvette of 33 *zira*, covered with copper, with 22 guns and 150 men aboard, constructed on Rhodes in 1799–1800 by the Swedish shipbuilder Klintberg. It was commissioned to transport the Ottoman soldiers on Rhodes.[351]

Gülşen Bey built the *Kilidü'l Bahir/Kilidü'l Bahrî* in Sohum, at an undisclosed date. The galleon had a length of 59 *zira* and carried 24 guns. Covered with copper, it was furnished with war equipment.[352] The *Kilidü'l Bahir* was still in use at the Imperial Naval Arsenal in 1801–02[353] and served during the battles against the British with 74 guns.[354] It is also listed among the auxiliary fleet of the navy at the *Tersâne-i Âmire* in 1810.[355]

The construction date, site and builder of the *Ceyân-ı Bahrî* are unknown. However, a document of 13 April 1801 reports that as a result of a severe storm that lasted two hours, the *Ceyrân-ı Bahri*, on which Giridî Hüseyin Kapudan was travelling, had been damaged considerably and its rudders lost.[356] Its name is also mentioned among the ships at the Imperial Naval Arsenal in 1801–02.[357]

The *Bed'-i Nusret* was a galleon of 45 *zira*, the construction of which was ordered by imperial edict at the naval arsenal before 1784–85. It was launched to sea, along with a recitation of the Qur'anic verse *bismillahi mecrâhâ ve mursâhâ*[358] on Thursday, 24 *Receb* 1199/1784–85 in a ceremony attended by the Sultan Abdulhamid I, the Grand Vizier, the *Şeyhülislam* and Gazi Hasan Pasha, the *Kaptan Pasha*. During the ceremony, sable furs, caftans and robes of honour were presented to the people of the Imperial Naval Arsenal.[359] The *Bed'-i Nusret* is known to have operated during the reign of Selim III. In a document dated 1790–91, it appears as a galleon under the command of el-Hac Süleyman Kaptan, *Cezayir kapudanesi* (full admiral of Algeria), requiring equipage, crew and provisions at Büyükdere.[360]

This vessel is also mentioned in a document dated 1793–94. Its hose had become worn out and the *Tersâne-i Âmire tulumbacıbaşısı* at the naval arsenal installed a new one in 1793–94.[361] No further information about it is available other than this galleon was still in use at the arsenal in 1801–02.[362]

The specifications of the galleon *Hüdâverdi* are unknown. A document indicates that it was at anchor off Daragaci at the Imperial Naval Arsenal in 1790–91. The same document reports fire smoke billowing from the stern of the galleon, caused by the care-lessness of the crew. It is understood that the fire was put out and that the necessary measures were taken.[363]

The *Seyyâh-ı Bahrî* was a frigate commanded by Omer Kapudan in 1790–91. All that is known beyond this is that, in the same year, there was a mutiny on board. Many crew were killed, and the safe of the ship was forced open and the money inside stolen.[364] Even less is known of the *Kerem-i Barî*. A document dated 1790–91 states that it was a galleon under the command of Hasan Kapudan, *Cezayir Kapudanesi*, and was to be equipped, manned and vict-ualled at Büyükdere.[365]

From a document dated 1790–91, we learn that the *Hıfz-ı Hüdâ* was a galleon-type ship in the straits under the command of el-hâc Ibrahim Kapudân, *Kapudâne-i Tunus* (full admiral of Tunus), and that its bowsprit, cutwater and lion figurehead had fallen, requir-ing it to be equipped, manned and victualled at Büyükdere. [366] Tezel says it was constructed at Rhodes, along with the galleons *Şahbâz-ı Bahrî* and *Tevfikullah*, in 1798.[367]

The *Nuvîd-i Fütûh* was a galleon under the command of Hasan Bey Kapudân. A document from 1789–90 states that it was to be equipped, manned and victualled at Büyükdere. From the same document it is learned that a galleon named the *Pulâd-ı Bahrî* was under the command of Ülgünlü Idris Kapudân, and was also to be equipped, manned and victualled at Büyükdere.[368] This vessel appears in 1791–92 as a frigate of 53 *zira* within the list of the ships that were to be caulked, pressed and greased.[369] Tezel says it was constructed on the island of Lemnos/Limni in 1798,[370] together with three other galleons: the *Şehbâz-i Bahri*, the *Tevfikullah* and the *Hıfz-ı Hüdâ*.[371] The *Pulâd-ı Bahrî* was still in use at the Imperial Naval Arsenal in 1801–02.[372]

The *Serheng-i Nusret*, according to the document dated 1790–91, was a frigate under the command of Süleyman Kapudân of Algeria/Karabağ, and was to be equipped, manned and victualled at Büyükdere, as was the *Beşîr-i Zafer*, a frigate under the command of Tunuslu Ali Kapudân.[373] The *Beşîr-i Zafer* is mentioned in a document dated 1793–94 because its hose became worn out and was replaced by the *tulumbacıbaşı* of the Imperial Naval Arsenal in 1793–94.[374]

The *Hüsn-i Gazât* was a type of ship known as a *şehtiye*, according to a document dated 1790–91. Under the command of Ülgünlü el-hâc Ibrâhim Kapudan, it was to be equipped, manned and victualled at Büyükdere. The same document reports on a frigate by the name of *Bidâyetü'l Fütûh* under the command of Abdulvehhâb Kapudân. It was also to take on supplies and men at Büyükdere.[375]

The *Tılsım-ı Bahrî* and the *Şihâb-ı Sâkıb* were bomb frigates of 30 *zira* each on the list of the ships that were going to be repaired and rigged out in 1791–92 at the Imperial Naval Arsenal. One of them, the *Burc-ı Zafer*, was a galleon of 43 *zira*, to be caulked, pressed and greased.[376] This vessel was still in use at the naval arsenal in 1801–02[377] and appeared passive with 24 guns in the Marmara Sea against the British in 1806.[378] It was also on the list of the auxiliary fleet of the navy at the *Tersâne-i Âmire* in 1810.[379]

One document mentions three ships that were to be repaired in 1791–92, the *Has Gazât*, a *şehtiye* of 33 *zira*; the *Bâis-i Nusret*, a frigate of 45 *zira*; and the *Peyk-i Nusret*, a frigate of 30 *zira*.[380] This last vessel is also mentioned in a document dated 25 September 1796, written to Süleyman Ağa, the chief officer in charge of providing bread for imperial galleons (*kalyonlar ser-habbâzı*). It states that the daily allotment of bread for the *gedikliyân* (sailors) and *zabitân* (officers) of this frigate, commanded by (Trablisî) Hasan Kapudân, was 64 in total.[381]

The *Nusret-nümâ*, a frigate of 35 *zira*, was also on the list of the ships to be caulked, pressed and greased in 1791–92.[382] Noyan gives 1746 as its construction date.[383]

The *Berk* was a galleon constructed on the island of Rhodes in 1801–02. Ten thousand *vukıyyes* of raw copper were ordered for both *Berk* and a corvette launched to sea. 6,566.5 *kuruş* were paid for the copper, which was provided from the Imperial Mint as *seferiyye akçesi* (temporary wartime treasury for urgent needs).[384]

The *Bahr-i Amîk* was commissioned in 1803–04 to take 850 pieces of *karaağaç* (elm) timber from Canik to the Imperial Naval Arsenal. The salaries to be paid for its crew, together with those of the men on the frigate *Tiz Hareket*, added up to 19,488 *kuruş*.[385]385 BOA. CB, no. 1897.

It was still in use at the Arsenal in 1801–02[386]386 Cevdet: *Târih-i Cevdet*, vols 7–8, pp. 349–51.

and it was on the list of the navy at the *Tersâne-i Âmire* in 1810 engaged in timber transportation.[387]

Ahmed Cevdet lists the *Fethiye*, the *Ankâ-yı Bahrî*, the *Menbâ-ı Nusret*, the *Tûnus* (Tunisia), the *Hûri-yi Bahrî*, the *İskenderiyye*, the *Meşreb-i Bahrî*, the *Îœd-i Nusret*, the *Zü'l Ukâb* and the *Hâlit Bey Korveti* as in use at the Imperial Naval Arsenal in 1801–02.[388]

Out of these ships, triple-decked *Fethiye* was built on a large dry dock and launched in 1801.[389] During the battles with the British fleet in 1806, it took part with 84 guns.[390] It also appears, along with the *İskenderiyye*, on the list of the auxiliary fleet of the navy at the *Tersâne-i Âmire* in 1810.[391]

A document dated 13 April 1801 mentions that as a result of a severe storm that lasted two hours, the frigate *Şehîd-i Zafer*, on which Girîdî Salih Kapudan was travelling, had been disabled, with its rudders lost.[392]

The date and place of construction of the *Cabbâr-ı Bahrî* are unknown. However, it is understood to have been in use before 1790–91. According to a register book dated 6 July 1791, it was a frigate under Fettah Kapudan. In the register book, detailed information is presented about its inventory, including riggings, gunnery, spare equipment and materials, and also about the conditions of these materials in question, their number, if they were usable or broken, or had been fallen into the sea or not. Among the items were various types of guns, cannon wagons, cords for securing guns, shells, lanterns, compasses, pulleys and blocks, sheaves, pumps, hourglasses, water barrels with iron rings, sledgehammers, various types of bolts and nails, various chains, straw carpets, chisels, cauldrons for cooking, boats and various kinds of ropes and sails, mostly in the colour green.[393]The *Ukkâb-ı Bahrî* appears in the records as a galleon under the command of Cezayli Karabıçak Ali Kapudân, to be equipped, manned and victualled at Büyükdere in 1790–91.[394] Another document, dated 29 September 1792, gives more information about its specifications. It was a galleon of 45 *zira* built by Ismail Ağa at Midilli. The same document mentions another galleon of 51 *zira* built by Bekir Ağa of Kalona at Midilli. When this galleon's timber and structure fell into bad condition in two to three years, it was converted into a galleon of 45 *zira*, like the *Ukkâb-ı Bahrî*. So the conversion of the 51-*zira* galleon into a 45-*zira* one was given to Ismail Aga, considering his experience.[395] We learn that its hose became worn out and a new one was installed in 1793–94 by the *Tersâne-i Âmire tulumbacıbaşısı* at the Imperial Naval Arsenal.[396]

The *Mukaddime-i Nusret/Mukaddime-i Zafer*, as reported in the document of 18 March 1801, was a galleon of 59.5 *zira*, built in 1786–87[397] by the French shipbuilder Le Roi[398] at the Imperial Naval Arsenal.[399] Another document, dated 1790–91, states that it was a galleon, a *Kapudâne-i Hümayun*, and that outside the straits on the Anatolian side its captain Seyyid Ali was wounded.[400] Uzunçarşılı, referring to a certain naval document, says that there were 43 *aylakci* (temporary mariners recruited during the campaigns for six months at a time) serving on the *Mukaddime-i Nusret* in 1790.[401]

It is understood from another document, dated 1796–97, that the French builder of the *Mukaddime-i Nusret* taught shipbuilding to Ahmed Hâce, who later was the builder of a galleon in Midilli.[402] The *Mukaddime-i Nusret* later became disabled and, following inspections by Hüseyin Pasha, was ordered to be removed from use on 28 March 1801 by Canib Mehmet Efendi.[403]

Little is known about the galleon *Fethü'l- Fettâh*, except that it was stubby and high, and its interior too narrow. It had a crew of 700 men in 1790. The *Tevfîk-i İlâhî* was a galleon with 450 men on board also in the year 1790. Like the *Fethü'l-Fettâh*, it was stubby and with a narrow interior.[404]

The beginning date of the construction of the galleon *Mes'ûdiye* is not known for sure, but it appears in the sources to have operated in the straits under the command of Kaşoğlu Ahmed Kapudan. Its main yard (*mayıstra sütunu*) fell in 1790.[405] However, it is estimated that it was completed in 1799–1800 at the Imperial Naval

Arsenal.[406] It was a three-decker with 118 guns and 1180 men, 191 *kadem* in length, 50 *kadem* in beam, 25 *kadem* in height and 13 *kadem* in displacement. Its engineer was Mr Benoit and its architect Andreya.[407] The *Mes'ûdiye* appears in Cevdet Pasha's list of 1801–02 as well.[408] It was careened along with other unnamed ships at the large dry dock in 1803. Two hundred *kantars* of lead were requested for the equipment and fitting out of the ships, including the *Mes'ûdiye*. After the 140 *kantars* of lead (costing 3,542 *kuruş*) given in the previous year, this time 150 *kantars* of lead (*kurşun*) at 23 *paras* per *kantar* (total 3,795 *kuruş*) were given to these ships.[409] During the battles with the British fleet in 1806, this vessel appears with 84 guns.[410] It was also on the list of naval ships in 1810.[411]

The *Mansûriye* is another ship about which very little is known. In Cevdet Pasha's account, it is stated that the *Mansûriye* was in use at the Imperial Naval Arsenal in 1801–02.[412]

Somewhat more is known about the *Tevfîk-nümâ*, a galleon constructed on Rhodes in 1803 and sent to the *Tersâne-i Âmire*. It is understood that its picture was drawn and presented to the Sultan. Although he stated that the picture seemed to have been drawn without geometrical measures and riggings, he ordered that a gift be given to the artist who drew it. It was decided that the picture in question would be kept at the *Tersâne-i Âmire*. The engineer of the galleon was then given several presents in order to encourage others.[413] During the battle against the British fleet in 1806, this vessel participated with 84 guns.[414]

The *Âyet-i Hayır*, the *Süreyyâ* and the *İkbâl-bâr* were among the Ottoman fleet ready at Marmara for the battle against the British fleet in 1806, with their 40, 36 and 34 guns respectively. The frigate *Âyet-i Hayır* played an active role in the war and engaged in a fierce struggle with British galleons of 84 guns. In the face of British superior gunfire, it had to head for the European side of the Marmara Sea. When a British frigate was sent to catch it, rather than surrender their vessel, the crew on the *Âyet-i Hayır* blew up it.[415] The frigate *Süreyya* appears on the list of the auxiliary fleet of the navy at the *Tersâne-i Âmire* in 1810.[416] It is not known what happened to the *İkbâl-bâr*.

The *Fırkateyn-i Kaplan Başlı* was among the ships ready to be rigged in 1791–92 at the Imperial Naval Arsenal. It was 31 *zira* and in want of timber.[417] It was employed in 1793 to transfer timber for a galleon almost completed in Sinop.[418]

The *Fırkatey-i Cedîd-i Gümrü* is mentioned as a 45-*zira* frigate in a list of ships to be caulked, pressed and greased at the naval arsenal in 1791–92. Additionally, there were ten sloops of 22 and 24 *zira*, as well as one *şehtiye* and one mail ship.[419] Among the small and big ships ready to be rigged in 1791–92 at the arsenal were three *sefine-i mektup* (mail ships), each of 25 *zira*; two *firkateyn-i aktarma* (river ships),[420] each of 30 *zira*; two *şalope* (sloop), each of 19 *zira*; and one single-masted *uskuna* (a type of sailing ship, typically with 16 guns and 90 men).

In addition to these ships, there were others, the names of which are unknown. Among them were two galleons constructed in Bodrum, one of 63 *zira* built in 1803 and the other of 55.5 zira in 1806. In Gemlik, a frigate of 51 *zira* in 1790, a galleon of 55 *zira* in 1792, a galleon of 59 *zira* in 1800 and finally a galleon of 59 *zira* in 1803 were constructed. In Limni, two frigates were built in 1798 and 1803. As for Midilli, three galleons, one of 45.5 *zira*, the second of 51 *zira* (by Konyalı Ebubekir) and the last of 53,5 *zira*, were built in 1790, 1791 and 1794 respectively.[421] A frigate was built in Silistire in 1791 and another was under construction in 1794 in the same place. Also, a frigate of 45.5 *zira* was under construction at the Biga Kemeri (around the Dardanelles) by Hacı Emir Mehmed Ağa in the same year.

A galleon of 56,5 *zira* was under construction in Çanakkale/the Dardanelles by İznikli Osman Bey in 1793. The architect of this galleon was Yozep, and its augerer was Yorgaki.[422] A galleon of 47.5 *zira* was built in Rhodes in 1790. Some frigates and galleons were also built in 1791 and 1803 in Sinop, a galleon in 1795 and two new ones in 1800 in Sohum. Beside the big ships constructed in the above-mentioned arsenals, small-size river ships such as sloops, houseboats (*duba*)[423] and caiques were built for the Tuna fleet in 1790.[424]

Although its name and construction date are unknown for certain, a corvette of 31.5 *zira* was built in Kalas by İnegö^llü Numan Bey. Upon his death before its completion, some shipbuilders were sent to the construction site from the *Tersâne-i Âmire*. The length of the corvette was extended by six *zira*. When completed, it was transferred to the *Tersâne* and used in timber transportation.[425]

Information about the construction of a corvette in Midilli is available from summary notes written by el-Hâc İsmail Ağa (the governor of Midilli) and a *dergâh-i âlî kapucubaşı*[426] (leader of the palace servants), to the *Defterdar Efendi* (Treasurer of the Imperial Treasury) on 11 August 1798. No information is given about its size, artillery or crew capacity, although the document does say that a corvette, the construction, launching and rigging out of which had been ordered by an imperial edict, had been completed at Midilli within about 11 months. After that, it was delivered by el-Hac Mustafa Kapudan's men at the *Tersâne-i Âmire*. The pine timber of *koguşluk* type was provided from Midilli and the Kazdağı regions for the vessel. The document complained that the Central Treasury had sent no money and all the expenses had been met by getting into debt the surrounding villages.[427]

### Ships purchased from foreign countries and traders

In addition to the ships constructed in the Ottoman shipyards, some vessels were sent by the rulers of the other states as gifts on occasions such as the ascendancy of a new sultan to the throne, and other times they were purchased from foreign states or traders. It is important to remember that all these kinds of ships may well have constituted opportunities for the Ottomans for technology transfer over time.

In a letter to Anthony Hayes on 12 January 1778, Robert Ainslie states that Throsten Christians, Nils Johnson, Peter Sunbar, Bewn Ulsen and Jens Williamson (the one a Dane and the other four Swedish seamen) navigated out of the Port of London to Istanbul, on board an English ship, which was then sold there.[428]

It is also reported that in 1784 a light frigate was purchased by the Vizier from a Mr Humphry, an English merchant lately appointed agent of the court of Denmark. This vessel, formerly called the *Lord Thurlow*, was an armed ship, previously a Compos French frigate fitted out at London, but lately from Smyrna (Izmir), loaded with approximately 400 iron cannons, 200 barrels of gunpowder, with some large cable, and cordage. That ship was purchased by the Porte, together with all of its equipment and armaments. It probably was intended as a present for the Algerians or Tunisians.[429]

As understood from Robert Ainslie's letter of 9 October 1784 to the Marquis of Carmarthen, England had three ships for sale in

Istanbul: two capable of mounting 50 guns each, and the third mounting 26.[430] On 10 November 1784, there were five stout English armed ships, mounting 30–50 guns, all for sale, although only two of them (a Spanish prize and an old Indiaman) were purchased by the Imperial Arsenal.[431] Tezel reports that two frigates were bought from England in 1785. One was named the *Mazhar-ı Saadet* and the other the *Dâd-ı Hakk* (Justice of God).[432] The *Mazhar-ı Saadet* is mentioned in a document of 1793–94. It is understood that its hose became worn out and the *Tersâne-i Âmire tulumbacıbaşısı* at the naval arsenal mounted a new one in 1793–94.[433] The *Dâd-ı Hakk* is described in a document dated 1791–92 as an 'English frigate' of 43 *zira* on the list of the ships to be caulked, pressed and greased.[434]

It is evident from a British document that a sloop with 26 guns had just been purchased from the Imperialists (probably the French) at the Imperial Arsenal.[435] Another letter (1 May 1788) to the Marquis of Carmarten by Robert Ainslie refers to a frigate of 36 guns, which formerly was a French corvette and lately renamed the *Phoenix*, sold by the commander Captain St. Barbe to the Porte.[436]

On 1 March 1789, the Porte purchased three armed ships brought out on speculation by British merchants, for the sum of 22,000 pounds. Two of them were French frigates captured during the last war; the third was formerly the *Camilla Sloop*, reformed from the British navy.[437] In the following days (around 15 March 1789), the Porte purchased two more foreign vessels, one a large Swedish ship to serve as a transport, the other a very handsome American-built sloop of war brought out by English merchants, being the fourth now sold by them to the Porte.[438]

An imperial edict dated 1789–90 reports that the Ottomans had previously bought an English frigate to use in their navy. There were 46 guns on the ship, but the Ottomans authorities, after testing the guns, decided that they were not useful to the navy and declined to buy them.[439]

Karal mentions a corvette called the *Nimet-i Hüdâ* (copper-sheathed, 43 *zira*, with 40 guns and 250 crew capacity) among the ships bought from France during the conquest of Corfu. He says that it was in bad condition.[440] However, Güleryüz suggests that this ship was a frigate built in 1792 and captured from the Russian navy.[441]

Gencer, judging from an archival document,[442] claims that the Ottoman state started negotiations with Holland (Flemenk) to buy six warships from that country via its ambassador in 1790–91. It was the first time that the Ottoman state had moved to buy warships from a foreign country. Negotiations began with traders from Holland, who said that they could supply new and sound ships of 60–70 guns, five of which had never sailed out of their harbour, and one of 60 guns, which had sailed once out of the harbour. In addition to these ships, there were five others that were difficult to sail out because they needed repairs and they would not be ready to head for the Porte for a long time.[443] Unfortunately, nothing else is known about how these negotiations developed.

Another document, dated 15 January 1791, reports that a frigate had been bought from England or English merchants. It is understood that this frigate was under the command of Osman Kapudân at the time. The document gives detailed lists about the riggings, gunnery and spare equipment and materials on board.[444]

On some occasions the Ottomans ordered ships from foreign countries. In the spring of 1790, the Ottomans planned to purchase three galleons from England and three from Holland, together with their equipment and rigging. For this aim, official petitions were written to the ambassadors of these countries.[445]

A British Foreign Office document of 1793 reports that two French ships, formerly used as merchant ships, especially in trade with Izmir (Smyrna), had been sold to the Ottomans, and now sailed under their flag.[446]

In a *takrir* (official petition) dated March 1793, the Porte requested some galleons and frigates from the British authorities through the British ambassador. First of all, the Porte wanted to buy a test frigate of 47.5–50 *zira* in length, younger than three years, constructed according to the drawings and measures (*arşın hesabı*) used at the Imperial Naval Arsenal, copper-sheathed, fully equipped, with 14–15 cannons on board. If there were no ships at hand of these specifications, the Porte said that it would purchase one of the ships at hand that did. This ship needed to be at least 45 *arşın* (according to the measures used at the arsenal), copper-sheathed, at most three years old, and resembling the drawings given to the ambassador by the Porte. When the frigate reached Istanbul, its cost would be negotiated and fixed in a meeting between the Ottoman authorities and the British ambassador. In case such a ship was not available, the Porte would ask the British government via the British ambassador to give a certain time period for the construction and rigging out of such a ship.

After receiving an answer, the process would start. A galleon might also be constructed instead of the frigate, depending on the negotiations. Twenty-five thousand *kuruş* were paid to the British ambassador for the test frigate. The British ambassador stated that he had received the money and would try his best to provide the aforementioned ships as soon as possible. He also pointed out, in a letter dated 15 March 1793, written in French, that he would refund the money in case he was unable to provide the ships.[447] The result of the correspondence is unknown. However, later developments showed that the relationship regarding the purchase of ships between the two countries continued.

It seems that in the following years the Porte occasionally ordered other ships from foreign powers. A document dated 25 February 1803 indicates that Reis Efendi, through the British ambassador, requested that England sell the Sultan two ships of war of 18–30 guns, or allow two ships of that force to be purchased from British subjects, for the purpose of employing them in the Red Sea.[448]

Apart from naval ships, merchant ships were also purchased from foreign traders in Selim III's period, to be used to transport goods and personnel in the Mediterranean and Black Seas. Therefore, the number of merchant ships increased as well.[449]

### Ships received as presents or captured at war

Karal writes that the emperor of Morocco, Mevlânâ Muhammed, sent two corvettes to Sultan Selim III as a present in 1789. One was of 31 *zira* with 24 guns, the other 31 *zira* with 22 guns.[450] The number of ships must have been higher, considering an imperial edict reporting that *four* ships and 1,000 *kantars* of gunpowder had been sent to the Imperial Naval Arsenal by the emperor of Morocco during 1789. The same emperor also freed some slaves to work at the arsenal, and sent a certain amount of money for the poor in Mecca and Medina (*Harameyn*). In carrying out these actions, the emperor used his commander, Tahir bin Abdulhak, and some *Atabegs* (local commanders).[451]

A British letter by Robert Ainslie to the secretary of state mentions the presents and says that three xebecs, each carrying 24 guns, sent as a present to the Sultan by the emperor of Morocco, had arrived there on 9 September 1789. It states that they were really fine vessels, well fitted up, and on one of them was the greatest part of the treasure, amounting to three million piasters, given as a subsidy to this court. Four Algerian xebecs likewise arrived at the Dardanelles accompanying a Russian prize also destined to reinforce the Ottoman navy.[452]

Another document reports on new bar shot/chain shot (*planketa*) and metal cannons (*maden topları*) ordered to be prepared at the casting foundaries at the Imperial Naval Arsenal for equipping the frigates received from Morocco.[453]

Another letter to the secretary of state, this time by Arbuthnot, reported that the *Justice*, a French frigate, had been handed over as prize to the Ottomans by the English at the evacuation of Egypt and that the *Kaptan Pasha* had embarked on this frigate then.[454454] PRO. FO 78/50 (26 June 1806)

This information is validated by some other sources along with additions. Clowes mentions a ship named the *Justice*, of 48 guns (he gives the figure 40 at one point, which should be the correct one), as having been given to the Ottomans along with the *Causse*, with 64 guns, and a former Venetian 26-gun frigate.[455] Anderson states that the *Montaue*, with 30 guns, was the third frigate handed over to the Porte.[456] William James adds the *Heliopolis*, stating that it was probably a former Ottoman corvette restored to the Kaptan Pasha.[457] Additional ship names and explanations are given in the *Keith Papers*. The commander of the British Mediterranean fleet, George Keith Elphinstone, in a letter dated 30 November 1801, to Foundroyant, Valette to the Navy Board, gives the names and the valuation of the French ships found in the harbour of Alexandria when it surrendered. He distinguishes the ones taken by the British from those delivered to the Porte.[458]

| Table 8. Captured French ships in the harbour of Alexandria in 1801. | |
| --- | --- |
| Commissioned in His Majesty's service | |
| Egyptienne | £23,663-0-0 |
| Regénérée, now Alexandria | £16,771-13-6 |
| Ships Delivered to the Turks | |
| Justice | £17,095-2-2 |
| Mantou | £9,607-1-0 |
| Hatul Bey (Halil Bey?) | £2,365-10-6 |
| Morngo Balerie | £2,593-12-8 |
| Salâbetnümâ | £4,465-19-3 |
| Source: Lloyd, Christopher (ed.), The Keith Papers, vol. 2, 1950, pp. 358–59. | |

In the second part of the table, the *Hatul Bey* and the *Salâbetnümâ* seem to be out of context, since they have Turkish names. In fact, no other sources mention them as French ships being captured. As discussed above, the *Salâbetnümâ* was actually constructed in 1795–96 at the Imperial Naval Arsenal,[459] and it was still in use there in 1801–02. So it was not a French ship in origin. The *Hatul Bey* should most probably be the *Halil Bey*, which is mentioned on Ahmet Cevdet's list.[460] The valuations of the *Hatul Bey* and the *Salâbetnümâ* by Keith are still confusing if the origins of the ships are taken into consideration. It is also possible that their names were changed after their capture.

There are other ships mentioned, too. It is said that the Ottoman commander Abdulkadir Bey, after capturing Corfu on 2 May 1799, took the French frigate the *Brune* of 28 guns as part of the spoils. In 1801, 28 Ottoman ships were placed under the command of Russian Vice-Admiral F. F. Uschakov. They are said to have included four ships of the line, six frigates (the *Huseyin*, the *Abbas*,[461] the *Zeynel*, the *Süleyman*, the *Herim* (most probably *Kerim*) and the *Ahmed*), four corvettes, and the *Mustafa*, the *Hüseyin*, the *Ali-Bey*, the *Mehmed* and 14 other gunboats.[462]

# 5

# CONCLUSION

Ottoman history, by its very nature, offers a wide range of materials to the scholarly understanding and assessment of historians who are willing to discover the intrigues of the state of science and technology in the Ottoman Empire. The state of naval technology in the Ottoman Empire in the late eighteenth and early nineteenth centuries constituted the general trajectory of this book. The reason behind the preference of this period, apart from irresistible charm of working on something 'undiscovered', 'alien' and 'unpreferred', was the temptation of the tension and fluctuations between old and new, which the late eighteenth century harbours abundantly.

The discussion on the background to the eighteenth century showed that following a protracted and hesitant process that was occasionally accelerated and slowed down by various factors, a systematic use of sailing ships was adopted by the Ottomans from 1682 onwards. The defeat in Çeşme (1770) came both as a shock and a motivating force behind reform movements that would continue until the rise of Selim III. The systematic construction of new types of sailing warships took place in this period. Various imperial edicts were issued by the Sultan Selim in this regard. Two- and three-decked galleons, frigates, corvettes, sloops, gunboats, fire ships and other small crafts began to dominate the Ottoman fleets, rendering the galley-type oared ships obsolete as warships. These new warships were mounted with modern cannons, which rendered the Ottoman navy a deterrent force in the Mediterranean.

In addition to the ships constructed in the Ottoman shipyards, there were other sources from which the Ottomans obtained ships. Purchasing new ships from foreign countries and private traders was a common way to which the Porte had frequently recourse to strengthen its naval power. Ships sent by Muslim countries, as in the case of the Sultan of Morocco, to the Ottoman Sultan as presents to celebrate his ascendance to the Ottoman throne constituted another source. Moreover, prize ships captured as spoils during naval campaigns contributed to the development of the Ottoman navy, since it facilitated comparisons, examination and imitation of the foreign naval technologies.

There is no doubt that the systematic introduction of these new ships, along with the regulations in the naval administration, changed the structure of the Ottoman navy to a great extent. Ottoman naval power not only appeared as a strong entity per *se*, but also came to be a driving force behind the development of Ottoman land forces with its contributions in security, finance, discipline and supplying provision. New ships gave a fresh impetus to the Ottoman fleets so that they waged successful wars in the Mediterranean and Black Seas. The regenerated Ottoman navy managed to challenge and thwart the Russian navy between 1787 and 1791. Ottoman fleets composed of new sailing warships cooperated with Russian and English naval forces against French forces, and played an active role in the transportation and landing of Ottoman troops in Egypt during 1798–1801. They were also active, though partially worn out and far from their previous efficiency, against the British fleet in 1806.

In the late eighteenth century, shipbuilding began to undergo a shift from being a craft to a semi-scientific pursuit. It is termed 'semi-scientific' because it does not mark a watershed in terms of a full adoption of modern naval technology. However, it was a milestone in the sense that it paved the way for the beginning of a resolute transformation in the Ottoman mentality of naval technology. Real change only occurred in the second half of the nineteenth century.

Regarding the raw materials required for shipbuilding and naval works, Ottoman sources do not record a shortage in many of them. On the contrary, in some raw materials such as timber, copper, rope, iron and lead, Ottoman sources seem to have been ample and adequate to meet the needs, and even allowed for some export. However, there appeared to be some problems and delays in the procurement of, for instance, timber, when the Porte ordered the construction of several ships at the same time. On balance, the thesis suggesting that the Ottomans failed to or lagged behind in adopting the modern naval technology due to the difficulties in finding and the constraints of raw materials falls short in describing the late eighteenth century.

One of the striking breakthroughs of the period was the adoption of the systematic sheathing of the hulls and bottoms of ships with copper from 1792–93 onwards. The first noteworthy trials of this technology had taken place in Europe about 30 years earlier. It provided protection from wood-eating worms and an increase in sailing speed that not only reduced voyage times, but also made navigation easier, it held caulking materials in position and it reduced maintenance costs between voyages.

The development of naval cannons was another important subject taken into consideration, since the outcome of any naval battle was closely connected with the gun capacity of ships on both sides. These guns were generally provided by the *Tersâne-i Âmire/Mamûre Kârhânesi* and the *Tophâne-i Amire*. Projectiles made of various materials were used in the cannons on Ottoman galleons and they were mostly manufactured in the shell and shot works at the arsenal and the *Galata Tophanesi*. Marble, granite, heavy stones and metal shells, chain shots/shots joined together by an iron chain and bar shot/iron bars, cartridge bag/grape shot or canister, shells with five holes/carcass (*beş delikli paçavra*) and scissors of metal shells were used as projectiles in the cannons of Ottoman ships. Marble shells were generally provided from the Marmara islands, while iron for shells was supplied from the Samakov (in Bulgaria) and Pravişte mines (Salonika). As a consequence of the interaction with foreign countries (mainly France and England), the Ottomans managed to follow and adopt new naval guns and complementary equipment.

An interesting theme, which seems to be part of a work of literature rather than technology, is the naming of ships. As far as the Ottoman ship names are concerned, the Ottoman sultan was the final authority. As a tradition, the sultan either chose a name from a list that had been prepared and presented to him by the grand admiral, or he commissioned the grand admiral or another high-ranking official to name a ship during its launch. Various factors such as the source of the money provided for the construction of a ship (as in the case of the *Uzunçarşılı*), prominent physical features (colour, stern, bow or hull shapes of the ships), as well as the function and duty of the ship were taken into consideration. Heroic or epic names, the names of wild animals, religious names suggestive of asking heavenly aid and holy war against infidels, the names of naval guns encouraging the Muslims and scaring the enemy, were popular. In some cases, some aesthetic and mythic names were also involved. The names of construction sites and places as well as the names of sunken and scrapped ships were occasionally given to new ships as well. It is interesting that in the time of sailing ships none of the naval ships were named after sultans, Kaptan Pashas, other commanders or the places/wars where glorious victories had been won, until the time of Selim III, when a triple-decked ship called the *Selimiye* was built.

Another important development was the construction of the first dry dock in the Golden Horn. This modern structure, designed by Swedish engineers led by Rhode, was the construction site for many Ottoman warships and is still in use today. In connection with its creation, the Ottoman government entered into negotiations at the very beginning of the nineteenth century to purchase a steam engine from England to be used at the Imperial Naval Arsenal in emptying the large basins in which ships of war were careened and repaired. Although the result of the negotiations is unknown, it indicates that the Porte was aware of the technology in question and willing to adopt it.

The introduction of a new galleon-launching method was another novelty. Introduced by Le Brun and first applied to a 59-*zira* galleon (the *Arslan-ı Bahrî*) on 9 Şa`bân 1209/1794–95, this method enabled the launching of the galleons after the completion of their hulls on stocks up to their gunports and finishing the rest of the construction in the sea itself. This technique supplanted the traditional method, which had required the launching of completed ships into the sea and putting the ships needing repair on stocks. In addition to requiring hard work and a great number of workers, the old method had many disadvantages among which was the collapse of the timbers during launch. The new method not only reduced the pressure on the bottom timbers of the ships during launch, but also brought economic advantages in that it reduced the number of workers. This new system was used for the next 40 years.

Alongside these important developments, were others that contributed to the overall improvement of the Ottoman navy. Among them were the construction of an anchor house (*lengerhâne*) for the production of anchors, the building of a measuring house (*endâzehâne*) for the modelling and drawing of the plans of ships, the adoption of new mast machines for fitting the masts into their places, the adoption of pumps and fire conduits for emptying bilge and rain water from ships and putting out fires aboard, and the introduction of a new kitchen and provisioning system, which brought order to the feeding habits of the crew and provided extra space on ships enabling them to mount more guns.

In navigation, the tradition of keeping logbooks (*seyir defteri* or *seyir jurnali*) was introduced in this period as well. Logbooks covering naval and navigational regulations (*kavâid-i bahriye*) were given to the ships. All the captains carried Pirî Reis' *Kitâb-ı Bahriye* as a guide, and they were charged with annotating and adding new information to this precious book according to their own observations. Among the navigational equipment used on the ships were sounding lead (*iskandil*) for measuring the depth of the sea, hourglasses (*saat-i rîk/kum saati*), newly drawn maps, hand glass/sandglass (*fula*), quadrants (*rub' tahtası*), ship compass (*gemi pusulası*), set square with wood (*gönye maa tahta*), square compass (*çâr kûşe pusula*), a pair of compasses (*pergâr-ı tâm*), illustrated celestial globe of a large size (*musavver kebîr kürre-i semâ*), elevation wood with hand and needle (*akrebli ve ibreli basîte-i âfâkî*), a moving compass of the Austrian type (*müteharrik nemçekârî pusula*) and many other tools, along with maps delineating fortified and strategic sites, and books relating to navigation, shipbuilding and maritime commerce.

Foreign missions played an important part in the modernisation of Ottoman naval technology with the services they rendered specifically from the late eighteenth century onwards in shipbuilding and launching methods, the construction of dry docks and the use of new raw materials, tools and equipment in naval construction. They also contributed much to Ottoman warfare and navigation through their knowledge of naval tactics, manoeuvres and the use of navigational instruments. These technical contributions enabled the Ottomans to wage naval campaigns with a modern fleet, for instance against the French forces invading Egypt.

This discussion of technological developments in the late eighteenth century would be insufficient without the mention of Selim III's international policy. As a result of his diplomatic and political manoeuvres, the reports and activities that he received from the permanent ambassadors in the leading capitals of European countries, Istanbul became a centre of attraction for foreign officers, engineers and technicians. Selim's policy proved so successful that beside the missions sent through foreign official channels, individual men, groups or families, skilled or unskilled, applied to the Porte for technical jobs independent of their countries. This enabled the Porte to choose from a wide spectrum of foreign missions. It is important to note that high wages drew foreigners to Istanbul. Ottoman and foreign documents show that despite some instances where foreigners complained about unpaid, low or irregular salaries, foreign officers and engineers were paid much more than Ottoman subjects or than they would have received for the same work in their own countries.

Cases of conversion to Islam under the pretext of making money in Ottoman lands were not uncommon. For instance, when asked the reasons for his conversion to Islam and if he did not wish to remain a Christian, a physician admitted that 'he hoped to make money among the Ottomans and thought that he could do no less than compliment with his religion'. However, it is unfair to consider all the conversion cases within this framework. It seems that meritocracy stood out as the determining factor for foreigners' employment in the naval shipbuilding sector. The Ottoman authorities dismissed workers hired for jobs requiring skill and technical know-how who failed to carry out their jobs as required, irrespective of their religion.

Selim III's reforms in naval technology brought about two long-term consequences of a controversial nature. First of all, they initiated a pattern of technological dependence on Europe, considering the employment of an increasing number of foreign technicians in all sectors of naval and military technology. Although negative results were not immediately apparent, the period under discussion served as an incubation period, leaving the door ajar to uncontrollable foreign influence.

On the other hand, from a different perspective, the period in question might be considered to have been positive. The increasing employment of foreign technicians and the adoption of new naval technologies paved the way for the development of a fertile platform for the training and rise of prospective native shipwrights, architects and arsenal workers as a consequence of their interaction with foreign engineers and technologies. These foreigners taught Ottoman students in theoretical and practical courses organised within the body of the naval and land engineering schools. Additionally, some Ottoman artisans were given the opportunity to learn the intricacies of their art in master–apprentice relationships during construction projects that were carried out under the supervision of individuals who had already worked on projects under foreigners. For example, it was Abdülhalim Efendi, the chief engineer and a teacher at the *Mühendishâne*, who completed the construction of the second dry dock together with an Ottoman subject, Manol Kalfa, between 1821 and 1825. Also, Vasil Kalfa, an Ottoman subject, constructed a dry dock during 1857–1870 and enlarged the first one in 1874–1876.

In addition to men trained in dock engineering were native shipbuilders who combined their previous experiences with what they learned from the foreigners. İsmail Kalfa/Halîfe (the chief architect at the Imperial Naval Arsenal), Hammâmîzâde Ahmed, Gülşen Bey, İnegöllü Numan Bey, Ahmed Hâce, Seyyid Mustafa Hoca and Konyalı Ebubekir are just a few names to mention. In the following years, native shipbuilders achieved greater works. In 1830 the engineer Mehmet Efendi and the architect Mehmet Usta built the well-known galleon *Mahmûdiye* of 64.48 m, with 128 guns and a crew of 1280, which was considered the greatest ship of the time and became a legend during the bombardment of Sevastopol and honoured with the title '*gâzî*' (war veteran). That year, the same

Mehmet Efendi and the architect Hasan Kalfa completed the frigate *Şerefresân* of 64 guns.

The means and methods by which the Ottomans attempted to keep abreast of European naval technology and know-how seem to have been, more or less, in parallel with those of all the naval powers of the world at the time in question. The principal channels of information were diplomatic and consular representatives and paid agents controlled by them. In addition, there were foreign officers and engineers, who were sent by their own countries or applied for service independently, to work for rival countries. Other important sources were captured ships, gifts and wreckages, since they enabled the state to examine the enemy's technology closely. Sending a ship to look into enemy harbours to count the ships at dock and observe the state of their rigging, construction and repair facilities was an important part of espionage and information gathering methods as well. The accounts and observations of travellers and merchant officers were also taken into consideration, though no reliance could be placed on their accuracy without taking into strict account the education, biases and prejudices of the authors. It seems that these channels served foreign countries much more than they did the Ottomans, who had occasional difficulties in obtaining the required know-how to operate these channels properly.

All in all, these developments show the Porte's willingness to keep pace with the developments in naval technology in Europe. The Ottomans achieved this goal to some extent by the end of the eighteenth century, under Selim III. However, in the final years of his reign, some internal turmoil characterised by a series of rebellions (the Serbs in the Balkans, the Wahhabis in Arabia and those led by provincial administrators and notables such as Pasvandoğlu, Tepedelenli, Tayyar Pasha and Cezzar Ahmed Pasha, who refused to pay taxes), as well as the Kabakçı Revolt on 29 May 1807 are claimed to have had a negative impact on the modernisation movements of Selim III, in combination with the unwillingness of bureaucracy. These factors have not been studied or interconnected yet in terms of the history of naval technology to constitute a satisfactory evidence for the present book.

# NOTES

## Chapter One

1. Brummet, Palmira, 'The Ottomans as a world power: what we don't know about Ottoman-sea-power', in Kate Fleet (ed.), *The Ottomans and the Sea* (Cambridge, 2001), pp. 1–21.

2. İmber, C. H., 'The navy of Süleyman the Magnificent', *Archivum Ottomanicum* 6 (Belgium, 1980), pp. 212–14.

3. Prins, A. H. J., 'Mediterranean ships and shipping, 1650–1850', in Robert Gardiner (ed.), *The Heyday of Sail: The Merchant Sailing Ship 1650–1850* (London, 1995), p. 78.

4. Bostan, İdris, *Osmanlı Bahriye Teşkilatı: VII. Yüzyılda Tersâne-i Âmire* (Ankara, 1992), p. 94.

5. Katip Çelebi's account depicts well the Ottomans' quest for a navy to measure up with enemy fleets composed of galleons. In a meeting chaired by the Grand Vizier Koca Mehmet Pasha in 1644, naval matters were taken up. Some present mentioned the difficulty of withstanding the enemy galleons aided by wind and said that the Ottomans had to adopt galleons as well. Then Katip Çelebi was invited to the meeting to share his advice. He drew attention to the glorious naval battles that the Ottomans had won with galleys against galleons in the past and suggested that if some people still insisted on the use of galleons as a necessity, then there should be no problem to build them, complete the artillery and provisions as well as recruit expert soldiers and gunners. Kâtip Çelebi, *Tuhfetu'l Kibâr fî Esfâri'l Bihâr* (edited by Orhan Şaik Gökyay) (Istanbul, 1973), pp. 124–25.

6. Uzunçarşılı, İsmail Hakkı, *Osmanlı Devletinin Merkez ve Bahriye Teşkilatı* (Ankara, 1988), p. 470.

7. Panzac, 'The manning of the Ottoman navy in the heyday of sail (1600–1850)', in Eric J. Zürcher (ed.), *Arming the State Military Conscription in the Middle East and Central Asia 1775–1925* (London and New York, 1999), pp. 41–57.

8. Bostan: *Osmanlı Bahriye Teşkilatı*, p. 103.

9. Murphey, Rhoads, 'Osmanlıların Batı Teknolojisini Benimsemedeki Tutumları: Efrenci Teknisyenlerin Sivil ve Askeri Uygulamalardaki Rolü', in Ekmeleddin İhsanoğlu (ed.), *Osmanlılar ve Batı Teknolojisi* (İstanbul, 1992), pp. 7–20.

10. Bamford, Paul Walden, *Fighting Ships and Prisons: The Mediterranean Galleys of France in the Age of Louis XIV* (Minneapolis, 1973), p. 14.

11. Grant, Jonathan, 'Rethinking the Ottoman decline: military technology diffusion in the Ottoman Empire, fifteenth to eighteenth centuries', *Journal of World History* 10 (1999), p. 187.

12. Özbaran, Salih, 'Galata Tersanesinde Gemi Yapımcıları 1529–1530', *Güney-Doğu Avrupa Araştırmaları Dergisi* 8–9 (İstanbul, 1980), p. 97.

13. Grant: 'Rethinking the Ottoman decline', p. 187.

14. Çizakça, Murat, 'The Ottoman Empire: recent research on shipping and shipbuilding in the sixteenth to nineteenth Centuries', *Research in Maritime History*, no. 9 (December 1995), p. 213.

15. İmber: 'The navy of Süleyman', p. 215.

16. Pryor, John H., *Geography, Technology and War: Studies in the Maritime History of the Mediterranean 649–1571* (Cambridge and New York: 1992), p. 177. William Thompson and George Modelski suggest that in the period they call 'the pre-ship of the line warship era', 1494–1654, corresponding to a period characterized by the decline of the galleys as the mainstay of some navies and the emergence of sailed warships specifically in the Atlantic, the Ottomans declined in terms of naval power because of their refusal to give up their galleys and because of the geographical location. See W. Thompson and G. Modelski, *Seapower and Global Politics, 1494–1993* (London, 1988), p. 50.

17. Guilmartin, John F., *Gunpowder and Galleys: Changing Technology and Mediterranean Warfare at Sea in the 16th Century* (London, 1980), p. 39. For more information on galleys, see Robert Gardiner (ed.), *The Age of Galley: Mediterranean Oared Vessels since Pre-classical Times* (London, 1995), especially J. E. Doston, 'The economics and logistics of galley warfare', in Robert Gardiner (ed.), pp. 213–23.

18. Guilmartin, John F., 'The early provision of artillery armament on Mediterranean war galleys', *The Mariner's Mirror*, 59 (London, 1973), pp. 257–80.

19. *Ibid.*

20. Alpagut, Ali Haydar and Fevzi Kurtoğlu, *Türkler'in Deniz Harp Sanatına Hizmetleri* (İstanbul, 1936), p. 9.

21. İmber: 'The navy of Süleyman', p. 216.

22. For more on the Algerian navy, see Moulay Belhamissi, *Histoire de la marine algérienne (1516–1830)*, 3 vols (Algiers: E.N.A.L., 1983).

23. Andrew C. Hess suggests that Muslim corsairs on the frontier in North Africa learned this technology from English and Dutch privateers. See 'The evolution of the Ottoman sea-borne empire in the age of the oceanic discoveries, 1453–1525', *American Historical Review* 75/7 (December 1970), p. 1918, and 'Firearms and the decline of Ibn Khaldun's military elite', *Archivum Ottomanicum* 4 (1971), pp. 173–201.

24. Alpagut and Kurtoğlu: *Türkler'in Deniz*, pp. 8–14.

25. Panzac: 'The manning of the Ottoman navy', p. 44. For more information on the ships of the North African corsairs, see also Daniel Panzac, *Barbary Corsairs: The End of the Legend 1800–1820* (Brill-Leiden-Boston, 2005).

26. Soucek, Svat, 'Ottoman naval policy in the Indian Ocean', *X. Türk Tarih Kongresi, 22–26 Eylül 1986, Kongreye Sunulan Bildiriler* (Ankara, 1993), pp. 1444–45; Özbaran, Salih, 'Osmanlı Imparatorluğu ve Hindistan Yolu', *İstanbul Üniversitesi Türkiyat Dergisi*, no. 31 (Mart 1977), p. 96.

27. Cipolla, Carlo, *Guns, Sails and Empires. Technological Innovation and the Early Phases of European Expansion 1400–1700* (New York, 1965), p. 81.

28. Çizakça: 'The Ottoman Empire', p. 221.

29. Panzac: 'The manning of the Ottoman navy', p. 46.

30. Karal, Enver Ziya, 'Selim III Devrinde Osmanlı Bahriyesi Hakkında Vesikalar', *Tarih Vesikaları* 1/3 (1941), pp. 203–11.

31. Panzac: 'The manning of the Ottoman navy', p. 46.

32. Marx, Robert F., *The Battle of Lepanto 1571* (Ohio, 1996), p. 32.

33. Uzunçarşılı: *Merkez ve Bahriye*, pp. 498–501.

34. Aktepe, M. Münir, 'Çeşme Vakası', *TDV Islam Ansiklopedisi*, vol. 8 (İstanbul: Türkiye Diyanet Vakfı, 1991), p. 289. For a detailed account of the war, see R. C. Anderson, *Naval Wars in the Levant (1559–1853)* (Liverpool, 1952), pp. 277–307.

35. Kaçar, Mustafa, 'Osmanlı İmparatorluğu'nda Askeri Teknik Eğitimde Modernleşme Çalışmaları ve Mühendishanelerin Kuruluşu (1808'e Kadar)', *Osmanlı Bilimi Araştırmaları II* (İstanbul, 1998), pp. 82–93.

36. Schmitd, Jan, *Per koets naar Constantinopel: De Gezatschapsreis van Baron van Dedem van de Gelder naar Istanbul in 1785* (Zutphen, 1998) (English summary).

37. Karal, Enver Ziya, 'Osmanlı Tarihine Dair Vesikalar', *Belleten* 4/14–15 (1940), p. 181.

38. PRO (Public Records Office). FO (Foreign Office) 95/8/14 (25 April 1787), pp. 862–63.

39. Gülen, Nejat, *Şanlı Bahriye (Türk Bahriyesinin İkiyüz Yıllık Tarihçesi 1777–1973)* (İstanbul, 2001), p. 35.

40. Safvet, '1205'de Donanmamız', *Tarih-i Osmanî Encümeni Mecmuası* Year 4, vol. 3 (İstanbul, 1331), pp. 1300-77.

### Chapter Two

1. When Sidney Smith arrived in Istanbul in 1799, he presented Selim III with gifts from King George III. Among these gifts were a model of a ship of the line — the *Royal George* — 12 portable brass 3-pounder cannons for carrying on camel back and paintings of naval battles. See Tom Pocock, *A Thirst for Glory: The Life of Admiral Sir Sidney Smith* (London, 1998), p. 81.

2. Daumas, Maurice and Paul Gille, 'Ships and navigation', *A History of Technology and Invention* (London, 1979), pp. 322–24.

3. Bamford, Paul Walden, *Forests and French Sea Power 1660–1789* (Toronto, 1956), p. 204.

4. A letter from the Earl of Elgin to the Secretary of State says: 'I also received instruction in England, to solicit from the Porte, an exclusive right to cut timber in Albania. A Right might be obtained, and with a promise that it should be exclusive. But I find it were absurd, to expect that this would be against a French intrigue. I wish therefore to know whether I am to make the demand under this circumstance.' See PRO. FO 78/32 (30 May 1801).

5. Albion, Robert Greenhalgh, *Forests and Sea Power: The Timber Problem of the Royal Navy 1652–1862* (Connecticut, 1965), p. 332–33; Crimmin, Patricia K., 'A great object with us to procure this timber...: the Royal Navy's search for ship timber in the Eastern Mediterranean and Southern Russia, 1803–1815', *International Journal of Maritime History* 4/2 (December 1992), pp. 83–115.

6. PRO. FO 78/43 (1 August 1804).

7. BOA. Kamil Kepeci (KK), no. 5734.

8. BOA. Cevdet Bahriye (CB), no. 9360 (8 July 1792).

9. BOA. CB, no. 1310 (28 March 1797). For felling the trees in question properly and in accordance with the given measures and diameters, two superintendents and two *dağ mimars* (architects in charge of felling trees) were commissioned at 250 *kuruş akçes* each, amounting to 1,000 *kuruş* in total.

10. There were ample sources for *pırnar* trees in the mountains of Biga province in 1211/1796-97. See BOA. CB, no. 1796 (18 January 1797).

11. BOA. CB, no. 8705.

12. For the launching requirement of a frigate of 53 *arşun* (a unit of length equal to 1 *zira*, 1 French *pic*) under construction at the *Tersâne-i Âmire*, ten timbers for slipways (*kızaklık*) and 100 for cross pieces of timber were laid down as part of the ways for a ship (*felenks*). See BOA. CB, no. 10895 (26 September 1796).

13. BOA. CB, no. 1905, 1169, 9501.

14. BOA. Hatt-ı Hümâyûn (HH), no. 9706/A-B (1206/1791–92); PRO. FO 78/12A (24 December 1791), p. 211.

15. Two hundred and ninety-seven large-sized pieces of *kemerelik* pine timber, 17, 18, 19 and 20 *ziras*, were provided from the mountains of Domaniç for the deck beams of a three-decked galleon under construction at the *Tersâne-i Âmire* at the end of Rebî'ul'evvel 1210/14 October 1795. A total of 3,175 *kuruş* (600 *para* each) was paid for the expenses of felling and the transportation of the mentioned timbers. See BOA. CB, no. 10694.

16. BOA. HH, no. 12356.

17. One hundred big pieces of timber for *lata* and 400 pieces of pine timber for *koğuş* were urgently demanded in the year 1801–02 from the administrators of these places for the construction of galleons at the *Tersâne-i Âmire* and dry dock. See BOA. CB, no. 2413.

18. BOA. HH, no. 8775 (14 December 1791).

19. PRO. FO 78/39 (12 March 1803), p. 85.

20. According to the measures required, masts of 40 *zira* in length had to be ten to 11 *karış* at the bottom and six to seven *karış* on the top; the ones of 34 *zira* in length had to be eight to nine *karış* at the bottom and five to six *karış* on top; the ones of 32 *zira* in length had to be seven to eight *karış* at the bottom and five to six *karış* on top. See BOA. CB, no. 6188.

21. Timber in planks was also used in covering or cladding certain parts of the ships. To give an example, for a three-decker being constructed at the Imperial Naval Arsenal, 2,500 pieces of oak timber were demanded from Ahyolu and its surrounding area in 1212/1797–98. BOA. CB, no. 4512.

22. BOA. CB, no. 7720 (18 August 1802).

23. BOA. CB, no. 9981.

24. BOA. CB, no. 6336.

25. The timbers were seven *zira* in length, 22 *kanâ* in width and 21 *parmak* in thickness. BOA. CB, no. 2407.

26. *Lata* (lath) is a long, narrow, thinnish board made of pine timber. See Henry Kahane and Andreas Tietze, *The Lingua Franca in the Levant: Turkish Nautical Terms of Italian Origin* (İstanbul, 1988), pp. 272-73. *Lata* was also used in the construction of the big dry dock at the Imperial Naval Arsenal. 12,601 *kuruş* were paid for the felling and transfer of 55 pieces of lath timber supplied from Iznikmid through Nuh Bey in 1211/1796-97. See BOA. CB, no. 1585.

27. BOA. D. BŞM. TRE, no. 15412.

28. *Koğuş* was generally made of pine tree and used for covering the distance between ports in 1800-01. BOA. CB, no. 4511.

29. Güler, İbrahim, 'XVIII. Yüzyılda Sinop'ta Gemi İnşa Teknolojisinin Altyapı, İstihkâm, İstihdâm, Üretim ve Pazarlama Sorunu', in Emre Dölen and Mustafa Kaçar (eds), *1. Türk Bilim ve Teknoloji Tarihi Kongresi Bildirileri (15–17 Kasım 2001)* (İstanbul, 2003), p. 33.

30. These types were taken from a register covering the required timbers and their number for a *kapak kaldırı* (a second-rate, two-decked man-of-war with 80 to 110 guns and with two gun decks below the spar deck) galleon of 63 *zira* and with 80 guns as well as a corvette of 36.5 *zira*, with 26 guns, both under construction at the *Tersâne-i Âmire*. The required timber was provided from Iznikmid. See BOA. CB, no. 10896.

31. BOA. CB, no. 10252.

32. Güler: 'XVIII', p. 43.

33. Feza Günergun argues that the earliest comparisons of measures of length between French and Ottoman were most probably realised at the end of the eighteenth century and adds that one Ottoman *arşın* equalled 1.176 French *kadem*. See 'Osmanlı Ölçü ve Tartılarının Eski Fransız ve Metre Sistemlerindeki Eşdeğerleri: İlk Karşılaştırmalar ve Çevirme Cetvelleri', in Feza Günergun (ed.), *Osmanlı Bilimi Araştırmaları II (Studies in Ottoman Science II)* (İstanbul, 1998), p. 25.

34. Bostan: *Osmanlı Bahriye Teşkilatı*, p. 121.

35. Katip Çelebi: *Tuhfetu'l Kibâr fî Esfâri'l Bihâr*, p. 308.

36. BOA. HH, no. 12356. Samakoçak/Samakovcuk (a village administratively attached to Midye district in 1675 and responsible for providing raw iron until the end of the seventeenth century when this amount was reduced to 200 *kantar*) should not be confused with Samakov (a district of Bulgaria).

37. BOA. CB, no. 2223. In 1808 1,000 *kantars* of raw iron were purchased from Samakovcuk and Ine/Ayna Adası. Each *kantar* cost 11 *kuruş*, and half of the total cost (5,500 *kuruş*) was paid from the Treasury of the *Tersâne-i Âmire*. See BOA. CB, no. 9297 (29 June 1808).

38. BOA. CB, no. 3365 (1803-04).

39. It was also called 'kedge anchor'. It was a kind of anchor thrown from the stern to sea, attached to a wire in order to keep the ship in a certain direction. See Mustafa Zaloğlu, *Gemici Dili* (İstanbul, 1988), p. 373, and Kahane and Tietze: *Lingua Franca*, p. 584.

40. Fid, or *kaşkaval*, is a square bar to support the weight of the topmast. See Kahane and Tietze: *Lingua Franca*, p. 130.

41. They mostly consisted of double blocks with three sheaves and were used to lift very heavy objects. See Zaloğlu: *Gemici Dili*, p. 139.

42. BOA. D. BŞM. TRE, no. 15211 (15 January 1791); HH, no. 10011 (1790–91); KK, nos. 5724 (1790–91) and 5726 (1790–91); CB, nos. 9418 (1797–98), 2223 (1800–01), 2379 (1799–1800) and 2186 (1807).

43. 2,150 *kantars* of raw iron was spent for a 51-*zira* galleon built in Bodrum, 1,200 *kantars* for two galleons of 53 and 51 *ziras* respectively in Sinop, 350 *kantars* for a 55-*zira* galleon in Gemlik and finally 770 *kantars* for a 45-*zira* frigate constructed in Karabiga in 1791–92. See BOA. CB, no. 2194. On the other hand, 57 *lodra* of raw iron were provided by the *mahzen-i sürb* on 18 June 1804 for this purpose. See BOA. CB, no. 7769.

44. Shaw, Stanford J., *Between Old and New: The Ottoman Empire under Selim III (1789–1807)* (Cambridge, Massachusetts, 1971), p. 56.

45. BOA. CB, no. 11461 (13 October 1792). Five hundred *kantars* of iron were needed for the construction of a 54-*zira* galleon in Rhodes. See Şemim Emsen, 'Selim III devrinde Osmanlı donanması' (undergraduate thesis in History, İstanbul Üniversitesi Kütüphanesi, no. 1118), p. 11.

46. BOA. HH, no. 9646 (1792-93).

47. BOA. CB, no. 4437; BOA. CB, no. 11461.

48. BOA. CB, no. 11461.

49. BOA. CB, no. 1796.

50. For the construction of a frigate of 51 *zira* in Gemlik, 30 ironsmiths came from Bursa in 1791–92. See BOA. CB, no. 4397. Sometimes Jewish ironsmiths were employed in the cutting of nails. In order to complete a galleon under construction in Bodrum quickly, two Jewish ironsmiths were demanded on 4 August 1791 from the Kadi of Gelibolu and Ayan of Gelibolu Seyyid Mustafa, to replace the ones who had fallen ill. See BOA. CB, no. 8070.

51. The copper nails produced in 1796-97 according to the methods of Le Brune were different from the previous ones. Since they were smaller, needed filing after casting and therefore required more workmanship. BOA. CB, no. 4436.

52. BOA. CB, no. 5747.

53. BOA. CB, no. 12603.

54. BOA. CB, no. 7013.

55. BOA. CB, no. 1261.

56. BOA. CB, no. 7021.

57. BOA. CB, no. 4436.

58. Bostan: *Osmanlı Bahriye Teşkilatı*, p. 125.

59. For the equipment of naval ships, 113 *vukıyyes* (a unit of weight equal to 1.283 kg) of raw copper were provided from the *mahzen-i sürb* on 18 June 1804. BOA. CB, no. 7769.

60. 750 *kantars* of raw copper were bought from Russian traders on 6 September 1796. See BOA. CB, no. 9258.

61. BOA. KK, no. 5724 (1790–91).

62. Bostan: *Osmanlı Bahriye Teşkilatı*, p. 126.

63. BOA. HH, no. 11386.

64. Bostan: *Osmanlı Bahriye Teşkilatı*, pp. 126-27.

65. BOA. CB, no. 9360.

66. BOA. CB, no. 7356.

67. BOA. CB, no. 1418.

68. BOA. CB, no. 1591. It is understood that 50,000 *kıyyes* of lead were ready on the Alaiye wharf and 150,000 *kıyyes* on the way to the wharf, to arrive in 20-30 days in 1797.

69. BOA. CB, no. 5136.

70. BOA. CB, no. 2181.

71. BOA. CB, no. 2325.

72. BOA. CB, no. 5791.

73. BOA. CB, no. 7274.

74. BOA. CB, no. 1295.

75. Bostan: *Osmanlı Bahriye Teşkilatı*, p. 154. Also see Mehmet Genç, *Osmanlı İmparatorluğunda Devlet ve Ekonomi* (İstanbul, 2000), p. 248.

76. Genç: *Osmanlı*, p. 251.

77. Çizakça: 'The Ottoman Empire', pp. 220–21.

78. BOA. CB, no. 2289.

79. BOA. CB, no. 2360. The document states that 500 *kantars* of hemp (*kendir*) at 20,000 *kuruş* from Tire and 6,350 rolls of sailcloth at a cost of 13,450 *kuruş* were to be purchased.

80. *Mahmud Râif Efendi ve Nızâm-ı Cedîd'e Dâir Eseri*, Kemal Beydilli and İlhan Şahin (eds and translators) (Ankara, 2001), p. 56.

81. BOA. KK, no. 5724.

82. BOA. KK, no. 5726.

83. BOA. CB, no. 5747. Forty to fifty *kantars* of pitch and 15 *kantars* of tar were urgently needed for a certain galleon under construction in the Midilli region in 1793–94.

84. BOA. HH, no. 57599.

85. A pin or thole inserted vertically into the sides of a boat to allow the oar to be fastened. See Kahane and Tietze: *Lingua Franca*, pp. 572–73.

86. Güler says that pitch and tar were mainly provided by the people of Kazık and Akçekenise, attached to the district of Saray in Sinop. See Güler: 'XVIII', p. 35.

87. BOA. CB, no. 1297.

88. BOA. CB, no. 2360.

89. BOA. CB, no. 1549.

90. Bostan: *Osmanlı Bahriye Teşkilatı*, p. 135.

91. BOA. CB, no. 6229.

92. BOA. CB, no. 1297.

93. BOA. CB, no. 5209.

94. Bostan: *Osmanlı Bahriye Teşkilatı*, p. 133.

95. Ware, Chris, *The Bomb Vessel: Shore Bombardment Ships of the Age of Sail* (Annopolis, Maryland, 1994), p. 75.

96. İmber: 'The navy of Süleyman', p. 235.

97. Bostan: *Osmanlı Bahriye Teşkilatı*, p. 133.

98. Rycaut, Paul, *The Present State of the Ottoman Empire* (London, 1668), p. 213.

99. Twenty thousand *kintals* of tallow were provided from Varna and Galatz in March 1803. See PRO. FO 78/39 (12 March 1803), p. 25 onwards.

100. BOA. CB, no. 2643.

101. Bostan: *Osmanlı Bahriye Teşkilatı*, p. 135.

102. Tezel, Hayati, *Anadolu Türkleri'nin Deniz Tarihi*, vol. 1 (İstanbul, 1973), p. 612.

103. BOA. CB, no. 2494.

104. BOA. CB, no. 6056.

105. BOA. CB, no. 4398.

106. Güler: 'XVIII', p. 34.

107. BOA. CB, no. 2360.

108. BOA. CB, no. 4398.

109. BOA. CB, no. 2246.

110. BOA. CB, no. 6056.

111. BOA. CB, no. 1337.

112. BOA. CB, no. 4513.

113. Kahane and Tietze: *Lingua Franca*, pp. 577–78; Bostan: *Osmanlı Bahriye Teşkilatı*, p. 146; Zaloğlu: *Gemici Dili*, p. 385.

114. For the demand of oakum from the *Tersâne-i Âmire* on 8 July 1792, see BOA. CB, no. 9360.

115. '*Üstübi cemi zamanda Mısır Kahire'den olunageldiği beyanıyla*' (see the document dated 13 November 1791, BOA. CB, no. 2229). Another document, dated 1 August 1792, shows that 100 *kantars* of oakum were not enough for the upper deck of a galleon, and so 2,500 *kantars* more were demanded from Egypt and Hire (see BOA. CB, no. 12193).

116. *Mahmud Raif Efendi ve Nızâm-ı Cedîd'e Dâir Eseri*, p. 57.

117. Pakalın, Mehmet Zeki, *Osmanlı Tarih Deyimleri ve Terimleri Sözlüğü*, vol. 3 (Ankara, 1993), p. 90.

118. Du-Plat-Taylor, Francis Maurice, *The Design, Construction and Maintenance of Docks, Wharves and Piers* (Great Britain, 1933), p. 169.

119. Platt, Richard, *Man-of-war* (London, 1993), p. 11.

120. For extreme examples, see Kahane and Tietze: *Lingua Franca*, p. 562.

121. BOA. CB, no. 8008.

122. Kahane and Tietze: *Lingua Franca*, p. 31.

123. A *çekeleve* was a light coastal vessel with spritsail whose prow and poop were alike. See *ibid.*, p. 563.

124. Since the winter season affects the felling of timber and its transportation activities negatively, the galleon *Tevfîk-i Hudâ* was commissioned in November–December 1796 for the transfer of a large amount of timber for a three-decked frigate being constructed at the *Tersâne-i Âmire* before the winter. See BOA. CB, no. 8709.

125. PRO. FO 78/15 (1794).

126. BOA. CB, no. 3032.

127. In an edict addressed to the leading administrators of Cide and Amasra on 2 May 1801, the supply of necessary timber was ordered. See BOA. CB, no. 1292.

128. It is understood that 85,900 *kuruş* was paid for the construction of the galleon and 41,346.5 *kuruş*h for the engineers. See BOA. CB, no. 2684.

129. Nahum, Jean, 'Geleneksel Türk Kayıkçılığı ve Gemiciliği' (Graduation thesis, İstanbul, 1971), p. 3.

130. Tengüz, Hüsnü, *Osmanlı Bahriyesinin Mazisi* (İstanbul, 1995), p. 24.

131. von Pivka, Otto, *Navies of the Napoleonic Era* (Newton Abbot, 1980), pp. 312–13.

132. Shaw: *Between Old and New*, p. 151.

133. Cipolla: *Guns, Sails and Empires*, p. 103.

134. Rees, Gareth, 'Copper sheathing: an example of the technological diffusion in the English merchant fleet', *Journal of Transport History*, New Series 1/2 (September, 1971), p. 93.

135. Alaaddin Bobat refers to the hazardous effects of timber boring and fouling worms. He proves that two types, *lyrodus pedicellatus* and *teredo utriculus*, are more effective in the Mediterranean Sea, while *bankia carinata* is less effective and *teredo navalis* was the only worm discovered in the Black Sea. Referring to other studies, he says that *teredo navalis* was found specifically in the depths of the Marmara Sea, the Eastern Black Sea and almost all over the Turkish seas. In addition, he mentions research indicating that Amasra, Beykoz, Akbaş (Çanakkale), İzmir, and Mersin harbours contain the *nototerado norvegia* type of weeds densely, and the *limnoria tripunctata* and *chelura terabans* types in smaller quantities. See Alaaddin Bobat, 'Emprenyeli Ağaç Malzemenin Kapalı Maden Ocaklarında ve Deniz İçinde Kullanımı ve Dayanma Süresi' (Ph.D. dissertation, Trabzon, 1994), pp. 23-25.

136. BOA. HH, no. 151210.

137. Oared vessels built in narrow and delicate forms, operating not in seas but in relatively bigger rivers such as the Tigris and the Euphrates. They had various functions such as the transportation of guns, soldiers, animals, construction materials and provisions, communication, escorting and guarding, and acting as warships. See Cengiz Orhonlu, 'Gemicilik', *Türkiyat Mecmuası* 15 (İstanbul, 1969), p. 158. For a more recent and illustrated book fully dedicated to the subject, see Rasim Ünlü, *İnce Donanma* (İstanbul, 2005).

138. BOA. HH, no. 15212.

139. Emsen: 'Selim III', p. 17.

140. *Mahmud Raif Efendi ve Nızâm-ı Cedîd'e Dâir Eseri*, p. 57.

141. Naval actions resulting in the establishment of the Republic of Seven Islands in 1800 explains the Ottomans' superiority over the Russian navy in terms of the adoption of copper-sheathing technology, maintenance of the ships, construction and design. 'The Black Sea fleet (Russian) was short of funds for supplies and ships were in a bad state of repair. Most of the ships were veterans of the last Russo–Ottoman War of 1787–91. All of the capital ships under Ushakov's command had serious construction flaws. Only a few of them had copper sheaths that protected the lower portion of the hulls

so as to extend the period of service... During an inspection tour on 12 September, Ushakov realized that the Ottoman ships were superior to Russian ships in terms of design and construction materials although they were undermanned. They were built in the recent French design and equal in number and size to the Russian ships.' See N. E. Saul, *Russia and the Mediterranean 1797–1807* (Chicago and London, 1970), pp. 57–58, 67, 78–79, 88–89. I tender my thanks to my colleague Kahraman Şakul from George Town University for kindly informing me of this passage.

142. Bostan: *Osmanlı Bahriye Teşkilatı*, p. 9.

143. BOA. CB, no. 1588.

144. The *seferiyye akçesi* is a temporary treasury for wartime expenses. BOA. CB, no. 1775.

145. BOA. CB, no. 9362.

146. BOA. CB, no. 4454.

147. Tızlak, Fahrettin: 'Osmanlı Devleti'nde Ham Bakır İşleme Merkezleri Olarak Tokat ve Diyarbakır', Belleten 59/226 (1995), p. 651.

148. BOA. CD (Cevdet-Darphâne), no. 463. For more information about the copper mines, see Tızlak, Fahrettin, *Osmanlı Döneminde Keban-Ergani Yöresinde Madencilik (1775–1850)* (Ankara, 1997).

149. From the mid-eighteenth century, raw copper, after first being processed in the mines in Ergani, was made into pure copper. This raw copper was sent to the *kalhane* (processing house) in Tokat to undergo its last process and to be given its last form. From this time on, Tokat came to be the leading city in the copper metallurgy. See Genç: *Osmanlı*, p. 288.

150. BOA. CD, no. 95. A document dated 16 June 1797 explains this process. Yusuf Ziya Pasha was the *Maadin-i Humayun Emini* (Superintendent of the Imperial Mines), responsible for the supply of copper and administration of copper mines at the time, while Es-Seyyid Hasan was the *nuhas emini* (superintendent of copper supply) in Tokat. The number of carriages required for transporting the copper from Tokat to Samsun wharf was 500–600 *vukıyyes* and this was provided from Canik, Kavak and Ezine Pazari.

151. Tızlak: 'Osmanlı Devleti'nde Ham Bakır İşleme Merkezleri', p. 650.

152. BOA. CD, no. 59. This document shows the total copper requirements for the *Tophâne-i Âmire, Hasköy Furunları* and imperial naval galleons. It is understood that 380,160 *vukıyyes* of copper for the guns to be cast in *Tophâne-i Âmire*, 253,440 *vukıyyes* for the guns to be cast in Hasköy, 30,000 *vukıyyes* for *Cebehane*, 60,000 *vukıyyes* and

26,400 *vukıyyes* for unexpected needs were allotted. The total annual copper needs appear to have been 750,000 *vukıyyes*. Another document dated 23 March 1803 (BOA. Cevdet Askeriye (CA), no. 48831) confirms the same sources and routes for copper supply for the imperial galleons. It mentions 500–600 wagons to be provided from Ezine and Kovan to carry the copper in question, as well as some other wagons and pack animals from Sivas, Tokat and Amasya.

153. For this purpose, an imperial *firman* wrote to the Governor of Erzurum and Meadin Emiri, vizier Yusuf Pasha. See BOA. HH, no. 10721.

154. Güleryüz, Ahmet, *Kadırgadan Kalyona Osmanlıda Yelken, Mikyas-ı Sefain* (İstanbul, 2004), p. 107.

155. The initial wage per *vukıyye* was 50 *akçes*, and five *vukıyyes* of *hark-ı nâr* was added to each 100 *vukıyyes*. After copper merchants complained about the wages, it was increased to 79 *akçes*. See BOA. CB, no. 12216.

156. BOA. CB, no. 1860.

157. Emsen: 'Selim III', p. 10.

158. BOA. CB, no. 8267.

159. A document dated 1 May 1796 indicates the establishment of a new *haddehâne* to process the copper to be fastened onto imperial ships' hulls. It says that the production and preparation of the copper had often been done in the *Humbarahâne* (shell production house) and then transferred to the foundry of the naval arsenal (*Tersâne-i Amire Temurhanesi*) to be processed through the *hadde*. In order to prevent the waste of copper in the *Humbarahâne*, construction of a *Nühashâne* (copper processing house) within the *Temurhâne* was planned as a four-walled room with three furnaces. See BOA. CB, no. 1261.

160. It seems that the Ottomans learned through experience that nails made of copper–zinc alloy were superior to nails made of copper alone in fastening copper plates onto the hulls of galleons. According to French shipbuilder Le Brun's measures and plans, these nails were produced as two types. The cost of the smaller ones was 65 *akçes*, while that of the bigger ones was 60 *akçes* per *vukıyye*. Note that the smaller ones needed more workmanship. See BOA. CB, no. 4437 (1796).

161. *Great Britain Parliamentary Papers 1799-1800*, II (London, 1800), pp. 205-07.

162. Bostan, İdris, 'Osmanlı Bahriyesinde Modernleşme Hareketleri I:

Tersanede Büyük Havuz İnşası (1794-1800)', *150. Yılında Tanzimat* (1992) p. 70.

163. The word *kana* refers to draught marks or an instrument of the wharf workers for measuring length. See Kahane and Tietze: *Lingua Franca*, p. 139. Cevdet Pasha says that 1 *zira-i mimari* = 24 *parmak*, and 1 zira (formerly used) = 24 *kana*, and *kana* is a little bigger than *parmak* because 1 *zira-i mimârî* consisted of 24 *parmak* = 75,8 cm = 37 French *pus*. And 1 *zira* (formerly used) consisted of 24 *kana* = 30 French *pus*. Therefore 1 *zira* (formerly used) is 3 *parmak* longer than the 1 *zira-i mimari* meaning 27 *parmak*. See Ahmed Cevdet, *Târih-i Cevdet*, vol. 6 (İstanbul, 1309), p. 144.

164. The first launching took place on 30 Saturday 1794. Although it was the beginning of the month of Ramadan, Selim III participated in the launching ceremony, took his place in a stand prepared on a galleon and watched the launching. See Emsen: 'Selim III', p. 15.

165. Later on, this method was replaced by another when it was understood that the real problem was caused by the fact that the bow of a galleon carried much more timber in comparison with the stern. Indeed, when the bow first launched into the sea, it raised up straight away and accelerated the immediate lowering of the stern into the sea, causing tension and imbalance of weight. The new method dictated that ships be launched into the sea backwards, while some cables and cords were used to keep them in balance. Following these developments, ships were constructed and completed fully on land and then launched into sea. See Cevdet: *Tarih-i Cevdet*, vol. 4, pp. 143–44, and Uzunçarşılı: *Merkez ve Bahriye*, pp. 502–03.

166. *Mahmud Raif Efendi ve Nızâm-ı Cedîd'e Dâir Eseri*, p. 57.

167. Alpagut and Kurtoğlu: *Türkler'in Deniz*, p. 48; Işın, İ. Bülent, *Osmanlı Bahriyesi Kronolojisi 1299–1920* (Ankara, 2004), p. 152.

168. Zaloğlu: *Gemici Dili*, p. 347.

169. BOA. KK, no. 5726 (6 July 1791).

170. *Fuğla* means lookout post on the foremast (see Kahane and Tietze: *Lingua Franca*, p. 489). However, when it is spelled *fula*, it means 'hand glass' (a kind of sandglass). See Zaloğlu: *Gemici Dili*, p. 141.

171. BOA. CB, no. 10123. Newly invented compasses and oil lamp with rotating glass of English production (*İngilizkârî devir ayna camlı fânus*) all together cost 2223 *kuruş* and 30 *para*. See BOA. CB, no. 11181 (12 April 1798).

172. For a full account of the lists, see Kemal Beydilli, *Türk Bilim ve Matbaacılık Tarihinde Mühendishane, Mühendishane Matbaası ve Kütüphanesi 1776-1826* (İstanbul, 1995), pp. 374-77.

173. Shaw, Stanford J., 'Selim III and the Ottoman navy', *Turcica: Revue d'études turques* 1 (1969) p. 220.

174. Alpagut and Kurtoğlu: *Türkler'in Deniz*, p. 48; Tezel: *Anadolu Türkleri'nin Deniz Tarihi*, p. 622.

175. Gencer, Ali Ihsan, *Bahriye'de Yapılan Islahat Hareketleri ve Bahriye Nezareti'nin Kuruluşu (1789-1867)* (İstanbul, 2001), p. 44. With regard to *Tableau des nouveaux règlements de l'Empire ottoman*, Beydilli claims that Mahmud Raif Efendi did not write the French version of the book, based on the fact that the words '*maltız ocakları*' in the Turkish text (which he wrote himself), meaning the kind of stove that was used for cooking, were wrongly translated as '*les esclaves maltais*' (the Maltese prisoners) in the French version. Therefore, someone else must have translated the Turkish text into French, since it is impossible for Mahmud Raif Efendi to have written two unrelated words as synonyms in the Turkish and French texts. This mistake continues in the Turkish and German translations made from the French version. For a detailed discussion of the issue, see Beydilli: *Türk Bilim*, pp. 155–59.

176. FO 78/15, no. 31 (25 December 1794). See also *Mahmud Raif Efendi ve Nızâm-ı Cedîd'e Dâir Eseri*, p. 57.

177. Shaw: *Between Old and New*, p. 56.

178. FO 78/15, no. 31 (25 December 1794).

179. Shaw: 'Selim III and the Ottoman navy', p. 224.

180. Mahmud Raif Efendi, *Osmanlı İmparatorluğu'nda Yeni Nizamların Cedveli* (translated and edited by Arslan Terzioğlu and Hüsrev Hatemi) (İstanbul, 1789), p. 29.

181. BOA. CB, no. 3883.

182. Hovannesyan, Serkis Sarraf, *Payitaht İstanbul'un Tarihçesi* (İstanbul, 1997).

183. Kaçar, Mustafa, 'Osmanlı Devleti'nde Bilim ve Eğitim Anlayışındaki Değişmeler ve Mühendishânelerin Kuruluşu' (Ph.D. dissertation, İstanbul, 1996), p. 87.

184. When they got old, wooden ships tended to strain and leak. Rain water also penetrated the decks. Therefore, chain pumps were fitted to larger ships. Beside them, common hand pumps were mounted on the ships to supplement the chain pumps. Naish, George P. B., 'Ships and shipbuilding' in Charles Singer, E. J. Holmyard, A. R. Hall and Trevor I. Williams (eds), *A History of Technology*, vol. 3 (Oxford, 1957), p. 484.

185. Winfield, Rif, *The 50-gun Ship* (Great Britain, 1997), p. 101.

186. This bowl was called *yangın tası*, meaning 'fire bowl', and was used as a helmet for protection from fire. The *Tulumbacıbaşı*'s bowl was made of silver, while the personnel's were of copper. See İsmail Hakkı Uzunçarşılı, *Kapıkulu Ocakları I* (Ankara, 1943), p. 83.

187. A fire pump was called *sandık* among people who used the pumps. See Pakalın: *Osmanlı Tarih Deyimleri*, vol. 3, p. 532.

188. BOA. CB, no. 1913.

189. BOA. CB, no. 2421.

190. BOA. CB, no. 4010.

191. Swann, D., 'The engineers of English port improvements 1660-1830: Part I', *Transport History* 1/2 (July 1968), pp. 153–68; 'The engineers of English port improvements 1660–1830: Part II', *Transport History* 1/3 (November 1968), pp. 261–76.

192. Coad, Jonathan G., 'Historic architecture of the Royal Navy, 1650–1850', in Martine Acerra, José Merino and Jean Meyer (eds), *Les Marines de guerre européennes XVIIème–XVIIIème siècles* (Paris, 1985), p. 17.

193. PRO. FO 78/46, pp. 242–44.

194. *Ibid.*

195. BOA. CB, no. 4010.

196. PRO. FO 78/46, pp. 242–44.

197. Tann, Jennifer and M. J. Breckin, 'The international diffusion of the Watt engine, 1775-1825', *Economic History Review* 31/4, 2nd Series, 1978, p. 560.

198. Aksoy, İsmail Hakkı, 'Osmanlı Döneminde Kullanılan Eski Su Boşaltma ve İnşaat Araçları', *Proceedings of the First International Congress on the History of Turkish Islamic Science and Technology*, vol. 3 of 5 vols (Istanbul, Technical University), p. 49; Aksoy, İsmail Hakkı, 'İstanbul'da Tarihi Yapılarda Uygulanan Temel Sistemleri' (Ph.D dissertation, İstanbul, 1982), p. 19.

199. He was an official charged with the administration of the institution concerning the palace animals, their harnesses, feeding, raising and training. He was also charged with the personnel, which consisted of the servants of imperial stables, *sarrac*s (men who produce harnesses), *yedekçi*s, *sarban*s dealing with Sultan's camels, mule raisers called *harbende*, as well as with groves and stud farms. See Pakalın: *Osmanlı Tarih Deyimleri*, vol. 3, p. 542.

200. BOA. CB, no. 4077.

201. Müller-Wiener, Wolfgang, '15-19. Yüzyılları Arasında İstanbul'da İmalathane ve Fabrikalar', in Ekmeleddin İhsanoğlu (ed.), *Osmanlılar ve Batı Teknolojisi* (İstanbul, 1992), p. 77.

202. Bronze sheaves required for the galleons were sometimes cast in the *Humbarahâne*. See BOA. CB, no. 6792. (27 September 1800).

203. BOA. CB, no. 1354.

204. BOA. CB, no. 11292 (6 December 1797).

205. BOA. CB, no. 6872.

206. BOA. CB, no. 3365.

207. BOA. HH, no. 9646.

208. It is known that there was a new crane of 120 *ayak* (c. 40 meters) in height with a single crank in 1770. See Müller-Wiener: '15-19', p. 80.

209. Ragıp Efendi was in charge of constructing carriages at the *hâcegân-ı divan-ı Hümâyûn humbaracılar kışlası demirhanesi* (iron foundry at the barracks of the bombardiers of the Imperial Council) in 1213/1798-99. The total cost (raw iron, timber, blocks with bronze sheaves and others) for the construction of two cranes (*macuna/macula*) amounted to 986 *kuruş*. With regard to the types of timber in the construction of the two cranes, bent brace made of oak (*eğri meşe kemer*) and box for gunstocks (*kundaklık dolap*) were used. See BOA. CB, no. 2172.

210. *Mahmud Raif Efendi ve Nızâm-ı Cedîd'e Dâir Eseri*, p. 57.

211. Kahane and Tietze: *Lingua Franca*, p. 283.

212. Alpagut, Ali Haydar, *Marmarada Türkler* (İstanbul, 1941), pp. 137-41.

213. Tezel: *Anadolu Türkleri'nin Deniz Tarihi*, p. 619. In architectural terminology, Darağacı refers to the elevated scaffolding on which a pulley/block stays in order to raise the drop-hammer used for hitting the piles. See Pakalın: *Osmanlı Tarih Deyimleri*, vol I, p. 393

214. *Mahmud Raif Efendi ve Nizâm-ı Cedîd'de Dair Eseri*, p. 57; Emsen: 'Selim III', p. 15.

215. Işın: *Osmanlı Bahriyesi Kronolojisi*, p. 151.

216. Müller-Wiener: '15-19', pp. 83-84.

217. Tezel: *Anadolu Türkleri'nin Deniz Tarihi*, p. 655.

218. Tutel, Eser, *Gemiler...Süvariler...İskeleler...* (İstanbul, 1998), p. 152.

219. BOA. CB, no. 7720.

220. Naish: 'Ships and shipbuilding', p. 581.

221. Ismail Ferruh Efendi said that sheaves for pulleys (*makara dilleri*) in England were made from a tree called 'Limbo Santo', which was provided from America only. He further says that the 'Limbo Santo' was useful in manufacturing pulley equipment (*makara takımı*). See BOA. HH, no. 6085 (1799-1800).

222. Güleryüz: *Kadırgadan Kalyona Osmanlıda Yelken*, p. 108.

223. BOA. CB, no. 2287.

224. PRO. FO 78/14 (22 February 1793), p. 78.

225. "*...Makara dili yaptıkları Limbo Santo nâm ağaç Amerika'dan gelmekle gayrı mahalde bulunmayup fil vâki makara takımı imâlinde dahî bunların mahâreti müsellem görünür, her ne ise memuriyyet-i bendegânem üzre cümlesi bir an akdem tedârik ve irsâl olunmasına ...ol tarafa gidecek beylik sefineleri zuhur edüb ona vaz ettirlir ise yahut tüccar sefinesi isticâr ve ona tahmil iderler ise ...ve alel hesab bir miktar meblağ taleb ederler mi mühimmât-ı mezkûreyi sigorta etmek iktizâ eder mi ne vechile olacağı henüz mechûl-i bendegânem olmaktan nâşi...*" Ismail Ferruh Efendi's use of the words '*sigorta etmek*' (to insure) is interesting for the time. See BOA. HH, nos. 6085 and 6086 (1799–1800).

226. Gilbert, K. R., 'Machine tools', in Charles Singer, E. J. Holmyard, A. R. Hall and Trevor I. Williams (eds), *A History of Technology*, vol. 4 (Oxford, 1958), pp. 426–27.

227. PRO. FO 78/2 (14 April 1781), p. 111.

228. Aksoy: 'İstanbul'da', p. 12.

229. Daumas and Gille: 'Ships and navigation', p. 408.

230. Doorman, G., 'Dredging', in Charles Singer, E. J. Holmyard, A. R. Hall and Trevor I. Williams (eds), *A History of Technology*, vol. 4 (Oxford, 1958), pp. 629-43.

231. Müller-Wiener: '15–19', p. 84.

232. See note 159 above.

233. BOA. CB, no. 1261.

234. *Hadde* is the name of the machine used to produce thin plates and wire out of raw copper and iron. The first *hadde* was ordered from abroad under the reign of Mahmud II. See Pakalın: *Osmanlı Tarih Deyimleri*, vol. 1, pp. 698–99. A *haddehane* operating by steam power was established in 1834 in order to produce copper sheet mills. See Müller-Wiener: '15–19', p. 85.

235. Çetin, Birol, *Osmanlı İmparatorluğu'nda Barut Sanayi 1700–1900* (Ankara, 2001), p. 27.

236. BOA. CB, no. 1888.

237. It is in fact unknown what types of ships were repaired in the late eighteenth century and how often or to what extent. However, we learn from a document (in 1214/1799–1800) that there were seven boats (*çifte piyade kayığı*) with the Kapudan Pasha on board that needed a wide range of repairs and furnishings, because of overuse and wear. When the superintendent of the Imperial Naval Arsenal expressed this need, he was told that there would be no repairs before a four-year period had passed. See BOA. CB, no. 6506.

238. Shaw: 'Selim III and the Ottoman navy', p. 224.

239. Genç: *Osmanlı*, p. 249.

240. Işın: *Osmanlı Bahriyesi Kronolojisi*, p. 153.

241. *Endâze çıkarmak* meant to take a mould of a ship according to drawings by means of thin pieces of pine. The expression *Endazeden çıkmış* was used for the ships put on stocks after their sternposts and broadsides had been raised, levelled, braced and formed. Ships whose construction came to this stage were called *kafes halinde* (in the form of a cage). Finally, the term *Endâze Güvertesi* was used for the wide and flat floors on which the pictures of the ships to be constructed were drawn and their moulds taken according to these drawings. See Pakalın: *Osmanlı Tarih Deyimleri*, vol. 1, p. 533.

242. BOA. CB, no. 5850.

243. *Mahmud Raif Efendi ve Nızâm-ı Cedîd'e Dâir Eseri*, p. 57.

244. Currier, Betty Nelson, *Anchors* (London, 1999), pp. 62–63.

245. BOA. CB, no. 7212.

246. Kahane and Tietze: *Lingua Franca*, pp. 251–53.

247. BOA. CB, no. 7825.

248. BOA. CB, no. 5891

249. Ship anchors, especially ones for galleys, came from Samakov in Bulgaria. Five anchors were needed for a galley. Anchors were made of 7–16 *kantars* of iron. See Uzunçarşılı: *Merkez ve Bahriye*, p. 453.

250. BOA. CB, no. 3359.

251. BOA. CB, no. 2379.

252. BOA. CB, no. 2223.

253. BOA. HH, no. 14076.

254. BOA. CB, no. 2186.

255. Winklareth, Robert J., *Naval Shipbuilders of the World: From the Age of Sail to the Present Day* (London, 2000), p. 362.

256. Merino, José P., 'Graving docks in France and Spain before 1800', *The Mariner's Mirror* 71 (London, 1985), p. 49.

257. PRO. FO 261/1, no. 22 (9 October 1784).

258. Bostan: 'Osmanlı Bahriyesinde Modernleşme Hareketleri I', p. 71.

259. *Ibid.*, pp. 69–90.

260. Toğrol, Ergün and İ. H. Aksoy, 'Drydocks of Istanbul Golden Horn shipyard', *Proceedings of I. International Congress on the History of Turkish-Islamic Science and Technology, İTÜ, 14–18 September 1981* (İstanbul, 1981), pp. 58–59.

261. Bostan: 'Osmanlı Bahriyesinde Modernleşme Hareketleri I', pp. 74–75. An Ottoman document dated 13 October 1796 mentions the

names of two specific regions providing *boçlana* for the big dry dock: Covitya and Kanam. The spelling of the names should be regarded with some reserve. See BOA. CB, no. 2320.

262. For the construction of the dry dock (1211/1796–97), the necessary oak from Ayna island wharf was transferred to the Imperial Naval Arsenal by a certain Yorgaki's *çekeleve* (a light transport vessel with two short masts) and quality timber from Kidros by ships of such *zimmis* as Kosta and Napalon, as well as *hornbeam lata* from Iznikmid by Yani and Yorgi Reis' *Çenber Sefines* (a kind of transport vessel). The total expense for the transportation and storage (*icâre-i hammâliye*) appears as 3,185 *kuruş*. Two thousand pieces of *kanatlık tahta* (timber for the wings) out of the 3,000 stored for the construction of the big dry dock were bought from Bartin ships, with a cost of 20 *akce* per timber, amounting to 3,665 *kuruş* in 1211/1796–97. The ones bought were stored in the *Kirpashâne* (sailcloth house) in the old naval arsenal. See BOA. CB, nos. 1169 and 9501.

263. For the extraction of *tomruk taşları* (rough-hewn stone blocks), mining (*lağım*) with gunpowder was necessary. The required gunpowder was provided from the *Cebehâne-i Âmire* in 1796. See BOA. CB, no. 1683.

264. Bostan: 'Osmanlı Bahriyesinde Modernleşme Hareketleri I', pp. 76–78.

265. BOA. CB, no. 10103.

266. Puzzolana is composed of active silica and a certain amount of active alumina, and when it is used together with lime it becomes binding. For more information, see M. Süheyl Akman, *Deniz Yapılarında Beton Teknolojisi* (Istanbul, 1992), p. 41.

267. Aksoy: 'İstanbul'da', p. 73.

268. Merino: 'Graving docks', p. 47.

269. Aksoy: 'İstanbul'da', p. 72.

270. Bostan: 'Osmanlı Bahriyesinde Modernleşme Hareketleri I', pp. 78–79.

271. BOA. CB, no. 5315.

272. Aksoy: 'İstanbul'da', p. 15. The original statement in the document referred to by Aksoy is '*deniz dürbinlerinin zîrine vaz' olulan iskele ve ücret-i kadem: bahâ-i tel, ücret-i kadem and baha-i câm 1100 para*'. The document also mentions *mismâr, ağaç, kırmız, şem-i sorh, şem-i ruğan, sancaklık, ıhlamur yeke, tunç boru* etc. among the tools and equipment purchased for the construction of a model dry dock and underwater glass and gives the total cost as 3,220 *paras* ('*Havuz*

*resmi ve deniz dürbinleri inşası lazıması içün mübayaa olunan eşya bahası*'). Additionally, the cost for the *kürek-i âhen* (iron shovel) and *örs-i âhen* (iron anvil) to be used in *Demürcü Ocağı*, reconstructed in Âlât Meydanı, was 2,600 and 3,010 *paras* respectively. For the travel allowance of Said Çavuş commissioned to bring *boçlana* soil from Değirmenlik and Santron Adaları, 6,000 *paras* were paid. The *Demürciyân-ı Tersâne* and *Demürciyan-ı Françelû*, who worked in the production of iron tools and equipment for the dry dock, received 12,780 *paras*. Materials such as *seng, çelik, seng-i bileği* and *eğe-i kol* were used by the *demürciyân* for the production of iron tools, and 400, 5192, 400 and 232 *paras* were spent, respectively. The *lağımcıyân, ser-lağımcıyân, çavuş, mutemed, rençberân, hammâlân-ı kereste, neccâr Manol* and his assistant were employed in the construction of the gates of the dry dock on 30 August 1795 and they received 32,635 *paras* in total. Beside these workers, there were a *Tavşan* and a *Nakkâşân* working in the manufacture of the modal dry dock and underwater glass, who received 22,640 *kuruş* and 80 *paras*, respectively. In a nutshell, it seems that the total cost for all kinds of expenditures amounted to 2,255 *kuruş* and 9 *paras* on 30 August 1795. See BOA. CB, no. 10103.

273. Aksoy: 'Osmanlı Döneminde', p. 49, and also Aksoy: 'İstanbul'da', p. 19.
274. PRO. FO 78/46, pp. 242–44.
275. Toğrol and Aksoy: 'Drydocks of Istanbul', pp. 58–59.
276. Tutel, Eser, 'Tersâne-i Amire', *Dünden Bugüne İstanbul Ansiklopedisi*, vol. 7 (İstanbul, 1994), p. 255.
277. BOA. CB, no. 5791.
278. Timber would be used for the revolving parts of the gates (*kapının devri içün*), the spindles of the gate (*kapının milleri içün*) and the spine of the feet of the gate (*kapının ayakları içün omurga*). See BOA. CB, no. 2155.
279. Aksoy: 'İstanbul'da', p. 73.
280. The settlement from Azapkapı towards Kasımpaşa is essential for present-day enumeration of the dry docks. See Tutel: 'Tersâne-i Amire', p. 137.
281. Aksoy: 'İstanbul'da', pp. 71–82.
282. Erendil refers to Muneccimbashi Ahmed Dede for this information. See Erendil, Muzaffer, *Topçuluk Tarihi* (Ankara, 1988), p. 83.
283. Guilmartin: 'The early provision of artillery armament', p. 261.
284. Erendil: *Topçuluk Tarihi*, p. 87.

285. For a detailed account of the activities of the *Tophâne* from the fourteenth to the sixteenth centuries, see Salim Aydüz, 'Osmanlı Devleti'nde Tophâne-i Âmire'nin Faaliyetleri ve Top Döküm Teknolojisi, XIV–XVI. Y*üzy*ıllar' (İstanbul: Ph.D. dissertation, İstanbul University, 1998).

286. *Ibid.*, p. 412.

287. Alpagut and Kurtoğlu: *Türkler'in Deniz*, p. 40.

288. Bostan: *Osmanlı Bahriye Teşkilatı*, p. 175.

289. Panzac, Daniel, 'Armed peace in the Mediterranean 1736–1739: a comparative survey of the navies', *The Mariner's Mirror* 84/1 (London, 1997), pp. 44–45.

290. Panzac: 'Armed peace in the Mediterranean', p. 55.

291. Panzac, referring to Çelebizade, argues that the first three-deckers of the Ottoman fleet were built in 1725 during the reign of Ahmed III. See Panzac: 'Armed peace in the Mediterranean', pp. 42–43.

292. BOA. HH, nos. 8168 and 14076 (1802–03).

293. We know that such a process was carried out for two galleons, one built at the *Tersâne-i Âmire* and the other in Sinop, as well as new sloops in 1789–90. See BOA. CB, no. 5832. Twenty newly cast cannons were loaded onto the ships in the same year (see BOA. HH, no. 56099) and two new cannons were planned to be tested and installed on ships in 1790–91. See BOA. HH, no. 57562-krt. 329.

294. Beydilli: *Türk Bilim*, p. 181.

295. Alpagut and Kurtoğlu: *Türkler'in Deniz*, p. 45.

296. BOA. HH, no. 9792.

297. BOA. HH, no. 11753.

298. BOA. D. BŞM. TRE, no. 15328.

299. Bostan: *Osmanlı Bahriye Teşkilatı*, p. 177. See also Aydüz: 'Osmanlı Devleti'nde Tophâne-i Âmire'nin Faaliyetleri', p. 416.

300. Aydüz: 'Osmanlı Devleti'nde Tophâne-i Âmire'nin Faaliyetleri', p. 415.

301. İnalcık, Halil, 'The socio-political effects of the diffusion of firearms in the Middle East', in V. J. Parry and M. E. Yapp (eds), *War, Technology and Society in the Middle East* (London, 1975), p. 203.

302. Erendil: *Topçuluk Tarihi*, p. 70; see also Bostan: *Osmanlı Bahriye Teşkilatı*, pp. 84, 85, 96 and 174.

303. Tekindağ, Şahabeddin, 'Haliç Tersanesi'nde Yapılan İlk Osmanlı Donanması ve Cafer Kapudan'ın Arizası', *Belgelerele Türk Tarihi Dergisi* 48 (İstanbul, 2001), p. 28.

304. Kahane and Tietze: *Lingua Franca*, pp. 99–100.

305. Agoston, Gabor, 'Ottoman artillery and European military technology

in the 15th to 17th centuries', *Acta Orientalia Academiae Scientiarum Hungaricae*, vol. 47 (1994), pp. 39–40.

306. Aydüz: 'Osmanlı Devleti'nde Tophâne-i Âmire'nin Faaliyetleri', p. 417. Also see Erendil: *Topçuluk Tarihi*, pp. 70–71.

307. Erendil: *Topçuluk Tarihi*, pp. 70–71.

308. Kahane and Tietze: *Lingua Franca*, p. 110.

309. As understood from the regulations for *Humbaraci* class in 1792–93, newly invented *obus* guns were to be used to fire projectiles during military campaigns when there was no proper location to manufacture *humbaras* (mortars). See Tahsin Esencan, *Türk Topçuluğu ve Kaynakları* (Ankara, 1946), p. 62. It is understood from an edict dated 23 March 1791 that the casting of 50 *obüs* and *sürat* guns in the *Tophâne-i Âmire* was demanded for a *trabago* and some other ships constructed at the *Tersâne-i Âmire*, and that for casting these guns, 72 *kantars* of *kali-yi İngilizî* (British tin) were required. See BOA. CB, no. 1454.

310. The *balyemez* was a long-range battering gun. Three hundred *kantars* of copper were needed to make this cannon in 1782. This cannon was also made from bronze and could fire balls of 24 *okkas* each in 1694. See Kahane and Tietze: *Lingua Franca*, pp. 99–100.

311. BOA. CB, no. 1474.

312. BOA. CB, no. 12282.

313. BOA. HH, no. 55529.

314. Tezel: *Anadolu Türkleri'nin Deniz Tarihi*, pp. 618–19.

315. Emsen: 'Selim III', p. 47.

316. In 1790–91 stonemasons in the Marmara region were ordered to cut, prepare and send 610 large marble cannonballs for naval guns. Five hundred and fifty *kuruş* were paid just for workers cutting marbles. See BOA. CB, no. 6143. Marble shells with diameters of 65, 44, and 22 were also demanded from the Marmara islands in 1792–93 for the new galleons, whose construction nearly came to be completed at the *Tersâne-i Amire*. Two hundred marble shells from each of the above-mentioned diameters were needed. See BOA. CB, no. 5848.

317. During the British expedition under the command of Duckwoth to pass through the Dardanelles in 1807, the Ottomans used mortars that could throw huge cannonballs made of marble and granite. These cannonballs were made from the columns of Greek and Roman temples. One of the cannonballs was brought back to Portsmouth as a trophy because of its epic quality. A stone ball of 800 pounds cut through the mainmast of the *Windsor Castle* and another, two feet

and six inches in diameter, caused a fire and explosion in the *Standard*, killing eight and wounding 47. See Pocock: *A Thirst for Glory*, pp. 203–04.

318. The Ottomans, for instance, used them during Napoleon's siege of the town of Acre on 9 May 1799. See Nicholas Tracy (ed.), *The Naval Chronicle: The Contemporary Record of the Royal Navy at War*, vol. 2 (1799–1804) (London, 1998), p. 24.

319. In addition to the marble shells of different diameters, metal shells with diameters of 18, 9 and 5 were also used in naval cannons. The document dated 4 January 1793 shows that the manufacture and cast of 200 metal shells of 18, 400 of 9 and 400 of 5, which amounts to 1,000 metal shells in total, were demanded from the *Humbarahâne* and the *Tersâne-i Atik* for a galleon almost completed. See BOA. CB, no. 6381.

320. BOA. HH, no. 11753.

321. In a document dated 11 September 1800, the manufacture of shells with five holes, common shells and grape shot was ordered by an imperial edict. See BOA. CB, no. 7163.

322. As revealed by a document of 1801–02, scissors of metal shells (*maden toplu mikrazlar*) made of mortar metal were also used in the cannons of Ottoman ships. It seems that stocks of mortar metal ran out in the *Humbarahâne* of the *Tersâne-i Amire*. Because of the urgent need, 300 *kantars* were provided from the *Humbarahâne* of Haskoy. See BOA. CB, no. 3609.

323. BOA. KK, no. 5724.

324. BOA. KK, no. 5726.

325. BOA. D. BŞM. TRE, no. 15211.

326. PRO. FO 78/14 (22 February 1793), p. 78.

327. *Ibid.*, p. 79.

328. *Ibid.*, p. 38 (10 January 1793 to 31 December 1793).

329. *Ibid.*, p. 78.

330. PRO. FO 78/28 (16 February 1800), p. 111.

331. Ademoğlu, Ebru, 'Yahya Naci Efendi ve Fırlatılan Cisimlerin Hareketleriyle İlgili Eseri: Risale-i Hikmet-i Tabiiyye (1809)', in Feza Günergun (ed.), *Osmanlı Bilimi Araştırmaları*, vol. 4, no. 1 (İstanbul, 2002), pp. 25–56.

332. For more detail, see Ekmeleddin İhsanoğlu, *Başhoca İshak Efendi, Türkiye'de Modern Bilimin Öncüsü* (Ankara, 1989).

333. Kaçar, Mustafa, 'Osmanlılarda Deniz Torpidoları Hakkında İlk Tercüme Eser: E'r-Risaletü'l Berkiye fî Alâti'r- Ra`diye', in Emre Dölen

and Mustafa Kaçar (eds), *1. Türk Bilim ve Teknoloji Tarihi Kongresi Bildirileri (15–17 Kasım 2001)* (İstanbul, 2003), pp. 155–63.

334. BOA. HH, no. 8024.

335. BOA. CB, no. 2357.

336. BOA. CD, no. 2921 and CA, no. 48831.

337. BOA. HH, nos. 1592 (1799–1800) and 6644 (3 July 1799).

338. Wick was provided from Egypt (Mısır), therefore it was called *fitil-i mısrî* (Egyptian wick). See Alpagut and Kurtoğlu: *Türkler'in Deniz*, p. 33.

339. See the tables in BOA. KK, nos. 5724 and 5726, and in D. BŞM. TRE, no. 15211.

340. BOA. CB, no. 1354.

341. BOA. CB, no. 11292 (24 October 1801).

342. The term *sudagabu* was an expression used in the second half of the eighteenth century. There is no evidence of earlier use. See Uzunçarşılı: *Merkez ve Bahriye*, p. 489.

343. BOA. HH, no. 10560.

344. Altıer, Selim Sırrı, *Osmanlı Bahriyesinin Yelken Devri ve Türk Korsanları* (İstanbul, no date), p. 28.

345. BOA. HH, nos. 10093, 10253, 10259, 10270 and 10401.

346. BOA. CB, no. 9418.

347. BOA. HH, no. 8168.

348. '*Bizim donanmada top talimi idecek adam yoktur, bilenlerin kimi donanmada kimi Vidindedir, talim hususu bir rezalet olmasun. Yalnız gemileri gezdiği kifayet eder, her ne yapılacak ise yapılub Çarşanba günü kalksunlar, bin altun azdır, iki bin verilsün.*' See BOA. HH, no. 14638.

349. PRO. FO 78/15 (25 December 1794).

350. Uzunçarşılı, İsmail Hakkı, 'Ondokuzuncu asır başlarına kadar Türk-İngiliz münasebatına dair vesikalar', *Belleten* 13 (1949), pp. 583–84.

351. Danışman, Günhan, 'Anadolu Enerji Teknolojileri Tarihçesi ve 18. Yüzyıl Sonunda Osmanlı Yönetiminin Sanayileşmede Kaçırdığı Fırsatın Yeniden Değerlendirilmesi', in Emre Dölen and Mustafa Kaçar (eds), *1. Türk Bilim ve Teknoloji Tarihi Kongresi Bildirileri (15–17 Kasım 2001)* (İstanbul, 2003), pp. 95–113.


**Chapter Three**


1. *Tâife-i Efrenciyân* was a group of non-Muslim technicians employed temporarily for a certain task or project in the Sultan's palace. See Rhoads Murphey: 'Osmanlıların Batı Teknolojisini Benimsemedeki Tutumları', pp. 7–20.

2. For some non-Muslim consultant physicians and scholars of other branches serving in the Ottoman palace, see Ekmeleddin İhsanoğlu, *Büyük Cihad'dan Frenk Fodulluğluna* (İstanbul, 1996), pp. 85–138 and 213–16.

3. İhsanoğlu, Ekmeleddin, 'Ottoman science in the classical period and early contacts with European science and technology', in Ekmeleddin İhsanoğlu (ed.), *Transfer of Modern Science and Technology to the Muslim World* (İstanbul, 1992), pp. 1–49.

4. Shaw: *Between Old and New*, p. 141.

5. Beydilli: *Türk Bilim*, p. 85.

6. PRO. FO 261/1, no. 22. (9 October 1784).

7. PRO. FO 78/8, pp. 30-31 (23 February 1787).

8. PRO. FO 78/7 (24 July 1786).

9. A French officer and astronomer serving the French embassy who taught astronomy, geometry, cartography, the use of sea watches and graphometers as well as map drawing with compasses at the *Mühendishâne*. His book, entitled *Traité du pilotage et de la manúuvre* (*Treatise on Pilotage and Manoeuvres*), was translated by Kapudane Hasan Efendi, but was not published. See Kazım Çeçen, 'Mühendishâne-i Bahrî-i Hümâyûn', *Dünden Bugüne İstanbul Ansiklopedisi*, vol. 6 (İstanbul, 1994), p. 14, and Kaçar: 'Osmanlı ımparatorluğu'nda Askeri Teknik', p. 94.

10. Uzunçarşılı: *Merkez ve Bahriye*, p. 508.

11. For more information about him, see Virginia H. Aksan, 'Choiseul-Gouffier at the Sublime Porte 1784–1792', in *Studies on Ottoman Diplomatic History* (Istanbul, 1992).

12. 'The administration of various maneuvers and tactics of the naval ships is a science which explains the ways and methods with which warships are put in order during campaigns. Furthermore, it includes the administration of sails, anchors, cannons, and all war equipment. The 96-page narrative part is supported by thirteen plates at the end of the book featuring drawings of ships in various maneuvers.' See the copy (no. ŞK. 1666) in the Istanbul Archeological Museums Library.

13. Kaçar: 'Osmanlı Devleti'nde Bilim', p. 87.

14. Roche, Max, *…ducation, assistance et culture françaises dans l'Empire ottoman* (Istanbul, 1989), p. 17; Duparc, Pierre, *Recueil des instructions* (Paris, 1969), pp. 477–94.

15. Kaçar: 'Osmanlı Devleti'nde Bilim', p. 88.

16. *Ibid.*

17. Le Roy is reported to have said in despair that every piece of wood and each pound of nails was an object of negotiations during his assignment at the Imperial Naval Arsenal. See Avigdor Levy, 'Military reform and the problem of centralization in the Ottoman Empire in the eighteeth century', *Middle Eastern Studies* 18 (1982), p. 236.

18. Kaçar: 'Osmanlı Devleti'nde Bilim', p. 90.

19. Günergun, Feza, 'Osmanlı Ölçü ve Tartılarının Eski Fransız ve Metre Sistemlerindeki Eşdeğerleri: ılk Karşılaştırmalar ve Çevirme Cetvelleri', in Feza Günergun (ed.), *Osmanlı Bilimi Araştırmaları II (Studies in Ottoman Science II)* (İstanbul, 1998), p. 24.

20. Kaçar argues that Le Roy stayed in Istanbul for six years. In the year 1792, he worked as an assistant in naval constructions in France. He was arrested during the French Revolution and later on commissioned to naval constructions in Toulon. He changed his name and adopted the name of 'Abouzir'. In 1795 he became Chief Naval Commissioner in Le Havre and participated in Napoleon's campaign in Egypt in 1798. He was appointed as consul to Hamburg. In 1811 he went to Copenhagen to deal in the shipbuiding and timber trade. Following his retirement, he passed away on 17 February 1825 in Paris. See Kaçar: 'Osmanlı Devleti'nde Bilim', p. 87.

21. Bamford: *Forests and French Sea Power*, p. 204.

22. Tracy: *The Naval Chronicle*, p. 306..

23. Kaçar: 'Osmanlı Devleti'nde Bilim', pp. 87–88.

24. Shaw, Stanford J., 'The established Ottoman army corps under Selim III (1789-1807)', *Der Islam* 40 (1965) p. 171.

25. Shaw: 'Selim III and the Ottoman Navy,' p. 222.

26. *Ibid.* See also Roche: *...ducation, assistance et culture françaises*, p. 19, and Müller-Wiener, *Bizans'tan Osmanlı'ya İstanbul Limanı* (İstanbul, 1998), p. 82.

27. FO 78/15 (1794).

28. BOA. HH, no. 14666 (1205/1790-91).

29. BOA. HH, no. 10588 (1790-91).

30. Roche: *...ducation, assistance et culture françaises*, p. 19. See also Shaw: 'Selim III and the Ottoman navy', p. 222.

31. BOA. HH, no. 14666 (1205/1790-91).

32. Bostan, İdris, 'Osmanlı Bahriyesi'nin Modernleşmesinde Yabancı Uzmanların Rolü', *İstanbul Üniversitesi Edebiyat Fakültesi Tarih Dergisi-Prof. Dr. Hakkı Dursun Yıldız Hatıra Sayısı* (İstanbul, 1994), pp. 179–182. Kemal Beydilli referring to a document from Maliyeden Müdevver Defteri, no. 10426, p. 110, mentions a man named Monier and

suggests that he was Le Brun's brother. He further argues that Le Brun and Monier started work in the capacity of shipbuilding engineers at salaries of 500 *kuruş*. See Beydilli: *Türk Bilim*, pp. 8–9.

33. These cranes are reported to have been built in the old fashion way with big pulleys. See Müller-Wiener: *Bizans'tan Osmanlı'ya İstanbul Limanı*, pp. 83–84.

34. Karal: 'Selim III Devrinde Osmanlı Bahriyesi', pp. 206–209.

35. Karal: 'Selim III Devrinde Osmanlı Bahriyesi', p. 208.

36. The *Şucâ-ı bahrî* was among the naval ships at the *Tersâne-i Âmire* in 1810. It appears among the list of the auxiliary fleet of the navy at the *Tersâne-i Âmire* in 1810. See Bahri S. Noyan, 'Eski Gemilerimizin İsimleri', *Hayat Tarih Mecmuası* 1/1, Year 14 (İstanbul, 1978), p. 93.

37. The date 22 December 1798 is given for the launching of the *Sâika-i bâd* and the *Âteşfeşân*. See Işın: *Osmanlı Bahriyesi Kronolojisi*, p. 154.

38. FO 78/15, no. 31, pp. 338-346 (25 December 1794).

39. FO 78/15, no. 4, p. 29 (25 February 1794).

40. Bostan: 'Osmanlı Bahriyesi'nin Modernleşmesinde Yabancı Uzmanların Rolü', p. 180.

41. BOA. CB, no. 4436.

42. BOA. CB, no. 4437.

43. BOA. CB, no. 5849.

44. For the details of Le Brun's proposals, see Kaçar: 'Osmanlı Devleti'nde Bilim', pp. 118–120.

45. Shaw: 'Selim III and the Ottoman Navy,' pp. 222-223.

46. Kaçar: 'Osmanlı Devleti'nde Bilim', p. 122.

47. BOA. HH, no. 4503 (1799–1800). Regarding Le Brun's escape, Abdülkadir Paşa Layihası says that he escaped to his country, without mentioning Russia, during the military campaign following the Porte's declaration of war against France in the face of Napoleon's attack on Egypt, and that Benoit replaced him. See Uzunçarşılı: *Merkez ve Bahriye*, pp. 537–39.

48. BOA. HH, no. 2495.

49. FO 78/28 (17 February 1800), pp. 151-152.

50. BOA. CB, no. 2260.

51. BOA. CB, no. 1214.

52. BOA. CB, no. 12281.

53. Bostan: 'Osmanlı Bahriyesi'nin Modernleşmesinde Yabancı Uzmanların Rolü,' p. 182.

54. BOA. HH, no. 2495.

55. BOA. CB, no. 9418 (28 July 1797).

56. BOA. CB, nos. 2808 and 8714. See also Bostan: 'Osmanlı Bahriyesi'nin Modernleşmesinde Yabancı Uzmanların Rolü', p. 182.

57. Daumas and Gille: 'Ships and navigation', pp. 281–82.

58. Müller-Wiener: *Bizans'tan Osmanlı'ya İstanbul Limanı*, p. 82.

59. FO 78/18, no. 14, pp. 153–54 (15 June 1797). See also Roche: ...*ducation, assistance et culture françaises*, p. 17.

60. FO 78/ 18, no. 14, p. 155 (15 June 1797).

61. No original French version of his name is available. Our best given is Toissaint Dument.

62. BOA. Cevdet-Hariciye (CH), no. 4411.

63. Bostan: 'Osmanlı Bahriyesi'nin Modernleşmesinde Yabancı Uzmanların Rolü', p. 185.

64. Müller-Wiener: *Bizans'tan Osmanlı'ya İstanbul Limanı*, p. 82.

65. *Ibid.*

66. BOA. CB, no. 1033.

67. BOA. CB, no. 1033. These names are read differently by Beydilli, using Maliyeden Müdevver Defteri, no. 10421 (11 February 1797). *Sharlo* appears as *Salolu*; *Antuvan* as *Anton*; *Petro* as *Peter*. See Beydilli: *Türk Bilim*, p. 90.

68. This is the Ottoman spelling of the name in the document.

69. BOA. Cevdet-Sıhhiye (CS), no. 1355.

70. BOA. CB, no. 1129.

71. Shaw: 'Selim III and the Ottoman Navy,' pp. 228-29.

72. Beydilli, Kemal, 'ılk Mühendislerimizden Seyyid Mustafa ve Nizâm-ı Cedîd'e Dair Risalesi', *Tarih Enstitüsü Dergisi* 13 (İstanbul, 1987), p. 402.

73. See Küçük Hüseyin Paşa Layihası (3 February 1797) in Kaçar: 'Osmanlı İmparatorluğu'nda Askeri Teknik', p. 131.

74. Uzunçarşılı: *Merkez ve Bahriye Teşkilatı*, p. 508.

75. *Ibid.*, p. 538.

76. BOA. CB, no. 7472.

77. BOA. CB, no. 5264.

78. BOA. CB, no. 7753.

79. BOA. CB, no. 8389.

80. BOA. CB, no. 9269.

81. BOA. CB, no. 1250.

82. BOA. CB, no. 12232.

83. BOA. CB, no. 12383.

84. PRO, FO 78/15, p. 341.

85. Beydilli: *Türk Bilim*, p. 88.

86. Kaçar: 'Osmanlı İmparatorluğu'nda Askeri Teknik', p. 107.

87. Kuban, Doğan, 'Kauffer François', *Dünden Bugüne İstanbul Ansiklopedisi*, vol. 4 (İstanbul, 1994), pp. 492–93. For more information about his life and work in Istanbul during the time of Selim III, see Frédéric Hitzèl, 'François Kauffer (1751–1801): ingénieur-cartogaphe français au service de Selim III', in Ekmeleddin İhsanoğlu (ed.), *Science in Islamic Civilisation* (İstanbul, 2000), pp. 233–41.

88. Kuban: 'Kauffer François,' pp. 492-93.

89. Karal, Enver Ziya, *Selim III'ün Hatt-ı Hümayunları* (Ankara, 1999), p. 98.

90. Beydilli, Kemal, 'Ignatius Mouradgea D'Ohsson (Muradcan Tosunyan)', *İstanbul Üniversitesi Edebiyat Fakültesi Tarih Dergisi* 34 (İstanbul, 1983–84) pp. 263–65. For a different assessment of D'Ohsson, see also Carter V. Findley, 'Mouradgea D'Ohsson (1740–1807): liminality and cosmopolitanism in the author of the Tableau général de l'Empire ottoman', *The Turkish Studies Association Bulletin* 22/1 (Spring 1998), pp. 21–35.

91. PRO. FO 78/11, (31 October 1790), p. 281.

92. PRO. FO 78/11, (20 November 1790), p. 299.

93. PRO. FO 78/11, (10 November 1791), p. 177.

94. PRO. FO 78/12A, (21 December 1791), p. 203.

95. On 10 July 1795, they began to be paid a regular salary. See BOA. CB, no. 1209.

96. Bostan: 'Osmanlı Bahriyesi'nin Modernleşmesinde Yabancı Uzmanların Rolü,' p. 183.

97. Müller-Wiener: *Bizans'tan Osmanlı'ya İstanbul Limanı*, p. 82.

98. Aksoy: 'İstanbul'da', p. 72.

99. FO 78/18, no.14, (15 June 1797), p. 155.

100. Bostan: 'Osmanlı Bahriyesi'nin Modernleşmesinde Yabancı Uzmanların Rolü', p. 183. But Müller-Wiener gives the date 1793 for the arrival of Rhodé to Turkey. See Müller-Wiener: *Bizans'tan Osmanlı'ya İstanbul Limanı*, p. 82.

101. Beydilli: *Türk Bilim*, p. 91.

102. Bostan: 'Osmanlı Bahriyesi'nin Modernleşmesinde Yabancı Uzmanların Rolü', p. 183.

103. Gencer: *Bahriye'de Yapılan Islahat Hareketleri*, p. 49.

104. BOA. CB, no. 9981.

105. BOA. CB, no. 10103.

106. Aksoy: *İstanbul'da*, p. 15. See also Chapter 2 in the present book.

107. BOA. CB, no. 12603.

108. For his work and 150 *kuruş* salary between the years 1796–97 and

1803–04, see BOA. CB, nos. 906, 2190, 4451, 1520, 5264, 5801 and 10824.

109. BOA. CB, no. 5264.

110. Bostan: 'Osmanlı Bahriyesinde Modernleşme Hareketleri I', p. 76.

111. He is mentioned as *gemi inşa ettirici mimâr-ı sânî* in an Ottoman document. See BOA. CB, no. 1204.

112. Bostan: 'Osmanlı Bahriyesi'nin Modernleşmesinde Yabancı Uzmanların Rolü,' p. 183.

113. It cost 23,308 *kuruş* in total. See BOA. CB, no. 2144 (26 July 1797).

114. Karal: 'Selim III Devrinde Osmanlı Bahriyesi', p. 209.

115. BOA. CB, no. 1408 (21 July 1800).

116. BOA. CB, no. 1638.

117. Bostan: 'Osmanlı Bahriyesi'nin Modernleşmesinde Yabancı Uzmanların Rolü,' p. 183.

118. Tezel, *Anadolu Türkleri'nin Deniz Tarihi*, p. 656.

119. BOA. CB, no. 1204.

120. BOA. CB, no. 2463.

121. BOA. CB, no. 1204. (December-January 1794-95).

122. BOA. HH, no. 9080 (1203).

123. PRO. FO 78/14, p. 24 (22 February 1793).

124. BOA. HH, no. 15370 (1794-95)

125. Beydilli: *Türk Bilim*, p. 89.

126. PRO. FO 78/16 (25 June 1795), p. 168.

127. PRO. FO 78/17 (10 July 1796), p. 102.

128. Beydilli: *Türk Bilim*, p. 89.

129. Shaw: 'Selim III and the Ottoman Navy', p. 223.

130. He refers to the anonynous French 'Essai sur la puissance navale des Turcs' (A E Mémoires et Documents, Turquie, no. 30, fol. 355). See Shaw: 'Selim III and the Ottoman navy', p. 225.

131. Karal: 'Selim III Devrinde Osmanlı Bahriyesi', p. 206.

132. Tom Pocock writes that the vessel *Tigre*, a former French prize taken by Lord Bridport in 1796, had brought out a team of English shipwrights in October 1799, who were instructing the Ottomans in the building of not only gunboats, but also ships of the line. See Pocock: *A Thirst for Glory*, p. 84.

133. For the letter from the Earl of Elgin at Constantinople to Secretary of State Lord Grenwille, see PRO. FO 78/28, no. 33 (18 March 1800), pp. 313–16.

134. FO 78/28 (17 March 1800), p. 317

135. FO 78/28 (17 March 1800), pp. 317-318

136. PRO. FO 78/28, no. 36 (26 March 1800), p. 338. This diplomatic correspondence can also be followed in a French document dated 18 March 1800, written to Alexander de Sutzo, *Interprète de la Sublime Porte ottomane*, by B. Pisani. See PRO, FO 78/28 (18 March 1800), p. 319.

137. PRO. FO 78/15, p. 338.

138. Shaw gives his name as 'Volla'. See Shaw: *Between Old and New*, p. 140.

139. Beydilli: *Türk Bilim*, p. 89.

140. BOA. HH, no. 9792.

141. BOA. CB, no. 1638.

142. BOA. CB, no.12738.

143. *Tavşan*, meaning 'rabbit' in modern Turkish, in seamanship means a carpenter dealing with delicate pieces of workmanship. See Uzunçarşılı: *Merkez ve Bahriye*, p. 474.

144. Tezel: *Anadolu Türkleri'nin Deniz Tarihi*, p. 656.

145. BOA. CB, nos. 1124, 1534, 1638, 2478 and 8098.

146. Karal: 'Selim III Devrinde Osmanlı Bahriyesi', p. 209.

147. BOA. CB, no. 8389.

148. BOA. CB, no. 9269.

149. BOA. CB, no. 1250.

150. BOA. CB, no. 1611.

151. Tezel: pp. 666-667.

152. Aksoy: *İstanbul'da*, pp. 71-82.

153. BOA. CB, nos. 330 and 642.

154. BOA. CB, no. 330.

155. BOA. CB, no. 1611; Aksoy: *İstanbul'da*, pp. 71-82.

156. BOA. CB, no. 330.

157. BOA. CB, no. 6300.

158. BOA. CB, no. 1611 (28 July 1800).

159. Tezel: *Anadolu Türkleri'nin Deniz Tarihi*, pp. 666-67.

160. Karal: 'Selim III Devrinde Osmanlı Bahriyesi', p. 207.

161. *Ibid.*, p. 206.

162. *Ibid.*

163. BOA. HH, no. 56625 (1791-92).

164. Karal: 'Selim III Devrinde Osmanlı Bahriyesi', p. 208.

165. BOA. CB, no. 12232 (2 September 1797). Tezel mentions a certain Komyanus working in the construction of the dry dock in the arsenal. See Tezel: *Anadolu Türkleri'nin Deniz Tarihi*, p. 656.

166. Gencer, Ali İhsan, 'İstanbul Tersânesinde Açılan İlk Tıb Mektebi,' *Türk Denizcilik Tarihi Araştırmaları* 41, (İstanbul, 1978), p.54.

167. BOA. CB, no. 1575.

168. BOA. HH, no.14666 (1790–91). The document compares İsmail Halîfe and Le Brun with respect to their competence in building a 57.5 *zira* galleon at the Imperial Naval Arsenal. It seems that although İsmail Efendi's high capacity, experience and success in shipbuilding was recognised by the authorities, Le Brun was preferred to him.

169. Karal: 'Selim III Devrinde Osmanlı Bahriyesi', p. 207.

170. BOA. CB, no. 330.

171. BOA. CB, no. 642.

172. For some of his duties, see BOA. HH, no. 9707/A-B. (1790-91).

173. Karal: 'Selim III Devrinde Osmanlı Bahriyesi', p. 209.

174. Emsen: 'Selim III', p. 22.

175. Karal: 'Selim III Devrinde Osmanlı Bahriyesi', p. 209.

176. Emsen: 'Selim III', p. 16.

177. Tezel: *Anadolu Türkleri'nin Deniz Tarihi*, pp. 666–67. See also Emsen: 'Selim III', p. 25.

178. Alpagut and Kurtoğlu: *Türkler'in Deniz*, p. 31; Emsen: 'Selim III', p. 11.

179. BOA. CB, no. 5849; see also BOA. HH, no. 10405.

180. Karal: 'Selim III Devrinde Osmanlı Bahriyesi', p. 206.

181. Uzunçarşılı: *Merkez ve Bahriye*, p. 534.

182. Mahmud Raif Efendi: *Osmanlı İmparatorluğu'nda Yeni Nizamların Cedveli* (see the appendix).

183. Uzunçarşılı: *Merkez ve Bahriye*, p. 535.

184. BOA. HH, no. 2529-a (1803-04).

185. Beydilli: 'ılk Mühendislerimizden Seyyid Mustafa ve Nizâm-ı Cedîd'e Dair Risalesi,' pp. 422-423.

186. The adjective '*büyük*' is added by Beydilli to separate him from Seyyid Mustafa, the writer of a monologue on *Nizâm-ı Cedîd*. For the discussion of the misunderstanding, see *Ibid.*, pp. 387–479.

187. *Ibid.*, p. 400.

188. Karal: 'Selim III Devrinde Osmanlı Bahriyesi', p. 206.

189. Uzunçarşılı: *Merkez ve Bahriye*, pp. 534–35.

190. BOA. CB, no. 3032.

191. BOA. HH, no. 2529-a (1803-04).

192. Beydilli: 'İlk Mühendislerimizden Seyyid Mustafa ve Nizâm-ı Cedîd'e Dair Risalesi', pp. 406–07.

193. *Ibid.*, pp. 408–09.

194. Ergin, Osman Nuri, *Türkiye Maarif Tarihi*, vols 1–2 (İstanbul, 1977), p. 322. See also PRO. FO 78/15 (1794), p. 342.

195. Beydilli: *Türk Bilim*, p. 53.
196. PRO. FO 78/15 (1994), p. 342. Beydilli says that Selim Efendi was commissioned to repair the fort of İsmail on 3 Şa`bân 1208/6 March 1794. Also he was employed in the repairs of the forts Yergˆğü and Niş as well as some other fortified places. He applied geometrical methods to these places. See Beydilli: *Türk Bilim*, p. 53.
197. Beydilli: *Türk Bilim*, pp. 53 and 254.
198. Çeçen: 'Mühendishâne-i Bahrî-i Hümâyûn', p. 14.
199. Beydilli: *Türk Bilim*, p. 53.
200. *Ibid.*
201. İhsanoğlu, Ekmeleddin, 'Osmanlı Havacılığına Genel Bir Bakış', in Ekmeleddin İhsanoğlu and Mustafa Kaçar (eds), *Çağını Yakalayan Osmanlı-Osmanlı Devleti'nde Modern Haberleşme ve Ulaşım Teknikleri* (İstanbul, 1995), pp. 502–04.
202. BOA. CB, no. 4010.
203. PRO. FO 78/46 (2 December 1805) and (11 December 1805).
204. Beydilli: *Türk Bilim*, p. 53.
205. Mustafa Kaçar, referring to *Menâkıb-ı Kethüdâzâde Mehmed Ârif Efendi*, writes that Selim Efendi came to Istanbul during the reign of Selim III. He was capable of melting iron through works and making some iron tools such as chains used on ships. He embraced Islam, since he loved Muslim clothes and customs (*âdet*). Following his conversion, some leading figures with whom he met and spoke without any difficulty earlier on, began to insult him later because of his wearing Muslim clothes. Therefore, he left the country, saying, 'Now I find out that knowledge is in my hat, not in my head.' Kaçar goes on, quoting from Arif Efendi, who said, 'If we did not fail to show respect to him and employ him, we would have perfect iron works, but unfortunatelly we lost him.' See Kaçar: 'Osmanlı ımparatorluğu'nda Askeri Teknik', p. 108.
206. Çeçen: 'Mühendishâne-i Bahrî-i Hümâyûn', p. 14.
207. BOA. HH, no. 9792.
208. Gencer: *Bahriye'de Yapılan Islahat Hareketleri*, p. 53.
209. BOA. CB, no. 330.
210. He built, together with Mühendis Ali Efendi, the *Hıfzürrahman* of 64 guns in 1825. See Tezel: *Anadolu Türkleri'nin Deniz Tarihi*, p. 666.
211. BOA. HH, no. 2529-a (1803-04).
212. Tezel: *Anadolu Türkleri'nin Deniz Tarihi*, p. 656.
213. Gencer: *Bahriye'de Yapılan Islahat Hareketleri*, pp. 65–89.
214. Cezar, Yavuz, 'Osmanlı Devleti'nin Mali Kurumlarından Tersâne-i Amire Hazinesi ve Defterdarlığı'nın 1805 Tarihli Kuruluş Yasası ve Eki', *Istanbul Universitesi ıktisat Fakültesi Mecmuası* 41/1–4 (İstanbul, 1985), pp. 361–88.

**Chapter Four**

1. For the evaluation of the Ottoman historiography of the sea from a literary point of view, see Caludia Römer, 'The sea in comparisons and metaphors in Ottoman historiography in the sixteenth century', in Kate Fleet (ed.), *The Ottomans and the Sea* (Cambridge, 2001), pp. 233–44, and Victoria Holbrook, 'Oceanic feeling, narcissism and the post classical image', in Kate Fleet (ed.), *The Ottomans and the Sea*, pp. 245–54.
2. Noyan: 'Eski Gemilerimizin İsimleri', pp. 91-94.
3. Tutel: *Gemiler...*, p. 140.
4. Tezel: *Anadolu Türkleri'nin Deniz Tarihi*, p. 617.
5. Panzac: 'Armed peace in the Mediterranean', pp. 44-45.
6. Panzac: 'Armed peace in the Mediterranean', p. 55.
7. BOA. HH, no. 9658.
8. Manning, Thomas Davys and Charles Fredric Walker, *British Warship Names* (London, 1959), p. 28.
9. Woodman, Richard, *The Story of Sail* (London, 1999), p. 103.
10. Manning and Walker: *British Warship Names*, p. 28.
11. Woodman: *The Story of Sail*, pp. 102–09.
12. *Ibid.*, p. 115.
13. Manning and Walker: *British Warship Names*, pp. 32–33.
14. Tezel: *Anadolu Türklerinin Deniz Tarihi*, p. 617.
15. Winfield: *The 50-gun Ship*, p. 67.
16. Tezel: *Anadolu Türklerinin Deniz Tarihi*, pp. 617–18.
17. Manning and Walker: *British Warship Names*, p. 27.
18. Noyan: 'Eski Gemilerimizin İsimleri', p. 92.
19. Tezel: *Anadolu Türklerinin Deniz Tarihi*, pp. 617–18.
20. For more details, see Ware: *The Bomb Vessel*.
21. Tezel: *Anadolu Türklerinin Deniz Tarihi*, pp. 617–18.
22. von Pivka: *Navies of the Napoleonic Era*, p. 214.
23. Tezel: *Anadolu Türklerinin Deniz Tarihi*, pp. 617–18.
24. BOA. HH, no. 9658 (1791-92).
25. Manning and Walker: *British Warship Names*, p. 32.
26. Grenville, Henry, *Observations sur l'état actuel de l'Empire ottoman* (edited by Andrew S. Ehrenkreutz and Ann Arbor) (Michigan, 1965), p. 3.
27. Ahmet Vasıf Efendi, *Mehâsinu'l-Âsâr ve Hakâiku'l Ahbâr* (Ankara, 1994), p. 393.
28. Among these names were new ones as well as the ones of ships formerly scrapped. See Noyan: 'Eski Gemilerimizin İsimleri', p. 93.
29. BOA. HH, no. 14141.

30. BOA. HH, nos. 10679 (1790–91), 11264 (March–April 1793–94), 14486 (July–August 1794) and 14523 (1805), and BOA. CB, no. 7210. For the launching ceremonies in Britain, see Margaretta Lincoln, 'Naval ship launches as public spectacle 1773-1854', *The Mariner's Mirror* 83/4 (London, 1997), pp. 466-72.

31. This practice appears among the traditional duties of the chief astronomers. See Salim Aydüz, 'Osmanlı Devleti'nde Müneccimbaşılık', *Osmanlı Bilimi Araştırmaları* (İstanbul, 1995), pp. 159–207.

32. Uzunçarşılı: *Merkez ve Bahriye*, p. 490.

33. Before the launching ceremony of a three-decked galleon, red broad-cloth (*al çuka*), cotton for cushions (*minderlik kutn*) and pink fabric (*pembe*) for furnishing the throne of the Sultan were planned for purchase. The total cost for all these preparations amounted to 380.5 *kuruş* in 1802-03. See BOA. CB, no. 1281.

34. It is known that during a ceremony attended by Abdulhamid I, the Grand Vizier, the Sheikhulislam and the Kapudan Pasha (Gazi Hasan Pasha), on the occasion of the launching of the galleon *Bed'-i Nusret* on Thursday, 24 *Receb* 1199, the Qur'anic verse *bismillahi mecrâhâ ve mursâhâ*, referring to the Prophet Noah and meaning '...embark therein; in the name of Allah will be its (moving) course and its (resting) anchorage', was recited. See Ahmet Vasıf Efendi: *Mehâsinu'l Asâr*, p. 260.

35. For more information on Divanhâne, see Rasim Ünlü, *Bahriye'nin Haliç Serüveni: İstanbul'un Fethinden Son Divanhaneye* (İstanbul: Deniz Basımevi, 2006).

36. Tezel: *Anadolu Türklerinin Deniz Tarihi*, p. 619.

37. *Mahmud Raif Efendi ve Nızâm-ı Cedîd'e Dâir Eseri*, p. 55.

38. Karal: 'Selim III Devrinde Osmanlı Bahriyesi', pp. 210–11.

39. von Pivka: *Navies of the Napoleonic Era*, p. 212.

40. Morriss, Roger (ed.), *The Channel Fleet and the Blockade of Brest, 1793–1801* (Aldershot, 2001), p. 541.

41. PRO. FO 78/55, no. 10 (27 January 1807), p. 122.

42. Panzac, referring to Çelebizade, says that the first three-deckers of the Ottoman fleet were built in 1725 during the reign of Ahmed III. See Panzac: 'Armed peace in the Mediterranean', pp. 42-43.

43. Uzunçarşılı: *Merkez ve Bahriye*, pp. 473-74.

44. Karal: 'Osmanlı Tarihine Dair Vesikalar', p. 181.

45. PRO. FO 95/8/14, pp. 862-63.

46. von Pivka: *Navies of the Napoleonic Era*, p. 212.

47. Gencer: *Bahriye'de Yapılan Islahat Hareketleri*, p. 81.

48. PRO. FO 78/55, no. 10 (27 January 1807), p. 122.

49. Uzunçarşılı: *Merkez ve Bahriye*, p. 472.

50. BOA. CB, no. 10896.

51. Gencer: *Bahriye'de Yapılan Islahat Hareketleri*, p. 82.

52. PRO. FO 78/55, no. 10 (27 January 1807), p. 122.

53. Kahane and Tietze: *Lingua Franca*, p. 238.

54. Henderson, James, *The Frigates* (London, 1998), pp. 16–17.

55. Henderson: *The Frigates*, p. 19.

56. PRO. FO 78/4, pp. 48–49.

57. Karal: 'Osmanlı Tarihine Dair Vesikalar', p. 181.

58. PRO. FO 95/8/14, pp. 862–63.

59. PRO. FO 78/10.

60. For the seven frigates constructed in Ereğli between 1799 and 1806, see Sinan Yakay, *Kdz. Ereğli'de Tersâneciliğin Tarihi ve Tersâneci Ağalar* (İzmit, 2004), pp. 31–34.

61. Karal: 'Selim III Devrinde Osmanlı Bahriyesi', pp. 210–211. Yakay says that seven frigates were constructed in Ereğli between 1799 and 1806, and he gives the names of the constructors as Hacı Mehmet Emin Ağa, Midilli Nazırı Hacı İsmail Ağa, Orta Bostancıbaşısı Mehmet Emin Ağa, Hacı İsmail Ağa, Viranşehir Voyvodası Çalıkzade Hüseyin Ağa and Kassabbaşısı Osman Aağa. See Yakay: *Kdz. Ereğli'de*, pp. 31–32.

62. Cevdet: *Târih-i Cevdet*, vols 7–8, pp. 349–51.

63. von Pivka: *Navies of the Napoleonic Era*, p. 212.

64. General Sebastiani's report to Napoleon states that the Ottoman navy consisted of 27 big warships and 20 frigates, and that this naval force was the best among European powers because they had been built by French engineers. See Karal: 'Selim III Devrinde Osmanlı Bahriyesi', pp. 206–09.

65. Gencer: *Bahriye'de Yapılan Islahat Hareketleri*, p. 83.

66. PRO. FO 78/55, no. 10 (27 January 1807), p. 122.

67. Uzunçarşılı: *Merkez ve Bahriye*, p. 468.

68. Karal: 'Selim III Devrinde Osmanlı Bahriyesi', pp. 210–11.

69. Gencer: *Bahriye'de Yapılan Islahat Hareketleri*, p. 83.

70. PRO. FO 78/55, no. 10 (27 January 1807), p. 122.

71. Uzunçarşılı: *Merkez ve Bahriye*, pp. 467–68.

72. BOA. CB, no. 2779.

73. Uzunçarşılı: *Merkez ve Bahriye*, p. 466.

74. A Greek master builder at the Imperial Naval Arsenal built two new sloops of 22 guns. PRO. FO 78/8 (23 February 1787), p. 38.

75. Two sloops constructed in Biga Gümrüğü in 1206/1791–92. BOA. CB,

no. 1206 (1791–92).

76. PRO. FO 78/7 (26 June 1786), p. 193.

77. Five sloops were completed in Sinop in 1789–90. To rig and equip them, some materials were demanded. See BOA. CB, no. 1751 (29 March 1790).

78. For 12 sloops of war with 14–16 guns built at Idra, see PRO. FO 78/9 (1 May 1788), p. 118.

79. An American-built sloop was sold by British merchants to the Ottomans, see PRO. FO 78/10 (15 March 1789), p. 71.

80. A Camilla sloop reformed from the British navy and purchased from British merchants. PRO. FO 78/10 (1 March 1789), p. 58.

81. BOA. CB, no. 5832 (1204/1789–90).

82. PRO. FO 95/8/14, pp. 862–63.

83. *Mahmud Raif Efendi ve Nızâm-ı Cedîd'e Dâir Eseri*: p. 57.

84. PRO. FO 78/8 (25 May 1787), p. 84.

85. PRO. FO 78/7 (25 October 1786), p. 293.

86. PRO. FO 78/11 (8 April 1790), p. 63.

87. PRO. FO 78/9 (1 May 1788), p. 118.

88. PRO. FO 78/9 (15 December 1789), p. 356.

89. PRO. FO 78/10.

90. BOA. HH, no. 9792 (17 October 1790).

91. PRO. FO 261/7 (22 May 1791), p. 23.

92. PRO. FO 78/9 (15 December 1788).

93. BOA. HH, no. 12418 (1205/1790–91).

94. BOA. HH, no. 9658 (1206/1791–92).

95. PRO. FO 78/8 (10 November 1787), pp. 238–42.

96. BOA. HH, no. 3446-e (13 April 1801).

97. Lyon, David J., 'British warships: types and building policy', in Martine Acerra, José Merino and Jean Meyer (eds), *Les Marines de guerre européennes XVIIème-XVIIIème siècles* (Paris: Presses de l'Université de Paris-Sorbonne, 1985), p. 152.

98. See Uzunçarşılı: *Merkez ve Bahriye*, p. 466; Bostan: *Osmanlı Bahriye Teşkilatı*, pp. 96–97.

99. For more information about fireships, see William C. Chapman, 'Prelude to Chesme', *The Mariner's Mirror* 52 (London, 1966), pp. 61–77, and Pakalın: *Osmanlı Tarih Deyimleri*, vol. 1, p. 164.

100. PRO. FO 78/9 (22 February 1788), p. 45.

101. BOA. HH, no. 14011 (1793–94).

102. It is reported that a vessel of the late Mavroyeni's was thought to be quite adequate for conversion into a fire ship and so was prepared for that purpose. Five fireships were to be prepared at Vidin, eight at

Nicopoli, ten at Rushtchuk and ten at Silistria, all carrying four 32-pounders: 30–40 gunboats of the remains of the previous year. PRO. FO 78/12-A, p. 46.

103. Uzunçarşılı: *Merkez ve Bahriye*, p. 467; Zaloğlu: *Gemici Dili*, p. 383.

104. BOA. CB, no. 1751 (29 March 1790).

105. Uzunçarşılı: *Merkez ve Bahriye*, p. 459.

106. Kahane and Tietze: *Lingua Franca*, p. 440.

107. BOA. HH, no. 11282.

108. BOA. CB, no. 1454.

109. Woodman: *The Story of Sail*, p. 89.

110. PRO. FO 95/8/14 (25 April 1787), pp. 862–63.

111. PRO. FO 78/8 (23 February 1787), pp. 30–31, (10 March 1787), p. 47.

112. PRO. FO 78/8 (10 May 1787), p. 79.

113. PRO. FO 78/8 (25 May 1787), p. 84.

114. PRO. FO 78/8 (10 November 1787), pp. 238–42; FO 261/6 (25 March 1788), p. 65.

115. PRO. FO 78/8 (25 April 1787), p. 70; FO 261/6 (11 February 1788), p. 10; FO 78/9 (1 April 1788), p. 45.

116. PRO. FO 78/7 (10 May 1786), p. 124, and (10 April 1786), p. 98.

117. PRO. FO 78/8 (9 August 1787), p. 147; FO 78/9 (22 February 1788), p. 81; FO 261/1, no. 22 (9 October 1784); FO 78/5 (25 November 1784), pp. 217–18; FO 78/10 (22 March 1789), p. 78; FO 78/9 (May 1789), p. 136.

118. PRO. FO 78/8 (9 June 1787), p. 95.

119. PRO. FO 261/7 (22 May 1791), p. 23.

120. PRO. FO 78/7 (23 December 1786), p. 367.

121. Kahane and Tietze: *Lingua Franca*, p. 111.

122. The *Tılsım-ı bahri* of 30 *zira* and the *Şihâb-ı sâkıb* of 30 *zira* are both described as *firkateyn-i bomba* (bomb frigates). See BOA. HH, no. 9658 (1791–92).

123. Two gunboats upon a new construction, each carrying a small mortar, were among the ships in the fleet under the Captan Pasha proceeding for the Dardanelles. See PRO. FO 78/7 (10 May 1786), p. 124.

124. PRO. FO 78/8 (9 June 1787), p. 95.

125. PRO. FO 78/9 (15 March 1788), pp. 66–67; FO 261/6 (25 March 1788), p. 65.

126. PRO. FO 78/9 (22 February 1788), p. 45.

127. PRO. FO 78/8 (9 August 1787), p. 147; FO 261/6 (11 February 1788), p. 10.

128. PRO. FO 78/10 (22 March 1789), p. 78.

129. PRO. FO 78/8 (10 November 1787), pp. 238–42.

130. PRO. FO 261/1, no. 16 (23 July 1784).

131. PRO. FO 78/6 (10 October 1785), p. 207; FO 261/2, no. 21 (10 October 1785).

132. PRO. FO 78/28 (18 March 1800), p. 316.

133. PRO. FO 95/8/14 (25 April 1787), pp. 862–63; FO 78/8 (23 February 1787), pp. 30–31, and (10 March 1787), p. 47.

134. PRO. FO 78/8 (10 May 1787), p. 87, and (9 August 1787), p. 147; FO 78/9 (25 March 1788), p. 75.

135. PRO. FO 78/9 (1 May 1788), p. 118.

136. PRO. FO 78/10 (1789), p. 136.

137. PRO. FO 78/12A (24 March 1791), p. 46.

138. PRO. FO 78/16 (25 June 1795), p. 168.

139. Woodman: *The Story of Sail*, p. 244.

140. Sami, Şemseddin, *Kâmus-ı Türkî* (Istanbul: Bedir Yay, n.d.), p. 769.

141. PRO. FO 261/4 (25 Nov. 1782), pp. 412–13.

142. 'They are sharp built and swift, but so light as not to stand the broadside of a good frigate. Their guns are of different calibers, unskillfully pointed and worked. The vessels illy maneuvered, but crowded with men, one third Turks, the rest Moors, of determined bravery, and resting their sole hopes on boarding. But two of these vessels belong to the government, the rest being private property. If they come out of harbour together, they separate immediately in quest of prey; and it is said that, they were never known to act together in any instance. Nor do they come out at all, when they know there are vessels cruising for them. They perform three cruises a year, between the middle of April and November, when they unrig and lay up for the winter. When not confined within the straits, they rove northwardly to the channel, and westwardly to the westward islands. They are at peace at present with France, Spain, England, Venice, the United Netherlands, Sweden, and Denmark; and at war with Russia, Austria, Portugal, Naples, Sardinia, Genoa and Malta...' See 'Report of the Secretary of State relative to the Mediterranean trade' (December 28, 1790) in *State Papers and Publick Documents of the United States from the Accession of George Washington to the Presidency, Exhibiting a Complete View of Our Foreign Relations Since That Time*, vol. 10 (Boston, 1819), pp. 41–47.

143. PRO. FO 78/4, p. 112.

144. PRO. FO 78/10, p. 136.

145. PRO. FO 78/10, pp. 271–72.

146. PRO. FO 78/11, p. 63.

147. *Kile* was a unit of measurement used for grains in the Ottoman Empire. There were various types of *kile*, such as *İstanbul kilesi*, approximately 25 kilos, and *İbrail kilesi*, around 100 kilos. In the period of sailing ships, *kile* assumed a new meaning and was used in the same way that we use ship 'tonnage' today. Thirty-six *kiles* was equal to one tonnage (*tonilato*). See Pakalın: *Osmanlı Tarih Deyimleri*, vol. 1, p. 281.

148. BOA. CB, nos. 2779 and 2216.

149. For the etymological analysis and comparisons of the various derivatives of the name, see Kahane and Tietze: *Lingua Franca*, pp. 149–51.

150. De Souza, Philip, *Seafaring and Civilization: Maritime Perspectives on the World History* (London, 2001), p. 17.

151. Gardiner, Robert and Richard Ugner (eds), *Cogs, Caravels and Galleons: The Sailing Ship 1000–1650* (London, 1994), pp. 91–98.

152. Cipolla: *Guns, Sails and Empires*, p. 81.

153. Uzunçarşılı: *Merkez ve Bahriye*, p. 469.

154. Prins, A. H. J., 'Mediterranean ships and shipping, 1650–1850', in Robert Gardiner (ed.), *The Heyday of Sail: The Merchant Sailing Ship 1650–1850* (London, 1995), p. 78.

155. Uzunçarşılı: *Merkez ve Bahriye*, p. 469.

156. Tezel: *Anadolu Türklerinin Deniz Tarihi*, p. 727.

157. PRO. FO 78/6 (10 June 1785), pp. 118–19.

158. PRO. FO 78/7 (25 January 1786), p. 19.

159. PRO. FO 261/7 (22 May 1791), p. 23.

160. Karal: 'Selim III Devrinde Osmanlı Bahriyesi', p. 207. Noyan gives 1793 for its construction date. See Noyan: 'Eski Gemilerimizin İsimleri', p. 92.

161. BOA. HH, no. 55529.

162. In the second half of the eighteenth century, they were paid 46 *kuruş*. Uzunçarşılı: *Merkez ve Bahriye*, p. 484.

163. BOA. CB, no. 1913.

164. Shaw refers to FO 78/15, no. 31 (25 December 1794). See Shaw: 'Selim III and the Ottoman navy', p. 220.

165. Tezel: *Anadolu Türklerinin Deniz Tarihi*, p. 622.

166. Gencer: *Bahriye'de Yapılan Islahat Hareketleri*, p. 44.

167. BOA. CB, no. 12602.

168. Cevdet: *Târih-i Cevdet*, vols 7–8, pp. 349–51.

169. A galleon of 51 *zira* was completed in Sinop and sent to Istanbul. In addition, another galleon of 47.5 zira was under construction on 13

*Rebî`u'l-âhir* 1204/29 March 1790 in Sinop. For the requirement of the galleon, sliding ways (*kızak*), cross pieces of timber (*felenk*), raw iron, tallow, wire and anchor were demanded. See BOA. CB, no. 1751.

170. Karal: 'Selim III Devrinde Osmanlı Bahriyesi', p. 207.

171. PRO. FO 78/10, pp. 294–95.

172. BOA. HH, no. 9644-A.

173. BOA. CB, no. 1913.

174. BOA. CB, no. 1479.

175. Cevdet: *Târih-i Cevdet*, vols 7–8, pp. 349–51.

176. Emsen: 'Selim III', p. 41.

177. Noyan: 'Eski Gemilerimizin İsimleri', p. 93.

178. Karal: 'Selim III Devrinde Osmanlı Bahriyesi', p. 207.

179. BOA. HH, no. 9658.

180. BOA. HH. no. 8845.

181. BOA. CB, no. 2194.

182. BOA. CB, no. 8705.

183. Noyan gives 1746 for the construction date. See Noyan: 'Eski Gemilerimizin İsimleri', p. 92.

184. Karal: 'Selim III Devrinde Osmanlı Bahriyesi', p. 207.

185. BOA. HH, no. 9644-A.

186. BOA. CB, no. 1913.

187. Karal: 'Selim III Devrinde Osmanlı Bahriyesi', p. 207.

188. BOA. CB, no. 1913.

189. Karal: 'Selim III Devrinde Osmanlı Bahriyesi', p. 209.

190. Noyan: 'Eski Gemilerimizin İsimleri', p. 93.

191. Noyan gives 1792 for its construction date. See Noyan: 'Eski Gemilerimizin İsimleri', p. 92.

192. BOA. HH, no. 14666.

193. Karal: 'Selim III Devrinde Osmanlı Bahriyesi', p. 207. See also BOA. HH, no.14666.

194. Emsen: 'Selim III', p. 12.

195. Emsen: 'Selim III', p. 8.

196. BOA. CB, no. 1913.

197. Cevdet: *Târih-i Cevdet*, vols 7–8, pp. 349–51.

198. Emsen: 'Selim III', pp. 41–44.

199. Noyan: 'Eski Gemilerimizin İsimleri', p. 93.

200. BOA. HH, no.14666.

201. Karal: 'Selim III Devrinde Osmanlı Bahriyesi', p. 206. See also BOA. HH, no.14666.

202. Emsen: 'Selim III', p. 17.

203. BOA. CB, no. 2194.

204. BOA. CB, no. 10514.

205. BOA. CB, no. 9360.

206. Cevdet: *Târih-i Cevdet*, vols 7–8, pp. 349–51.

207. Noyan: 'Eski Gemilerimizin İsimleri', p. 93.

208. Noyan gives 1776 for its construction date. See Noyan: 'Eski Gemilerimizin İsimleri', p. 92.

209. Karal: 'Selim III Devrinde Osmanlı Bahriyesi', p. 206.

210. BOA. CB, no. 5136.

211. Cevdet: *Târih-i Cevdet*, vols 7–8, pp. 349–51.

212. Emsen: 'Selim III', p. 41.

213. Noyan: 'Eski Gemilerimizin İsimleri', p. 93.

214. Karal: 'Selim III Devrinde Osmanlı Bahriyesi', p. 206.

215. Emsen: 'Selim III', p. 8.

216. Tezel: *Anadolu Türklerinin Deniz Tarihi*, p. 651.

217. BOA. HH. no. 9658.

218. Cevdet: *Târih-i Cevdet*, vols 7–8, pp. 349–51.

219. Emsen: 'Selim III', p. 41.

220. Noyan: 'Eski Gemilerimizin İsimleri', p. 93.

221. Karal: 'Selim III Devrinde Osmanlı Bahriyesi', p. 208.

222. Emsen: 'Selim III', p. 8.

223. Tezel: *Anadolu Türklerinin Deniz Tarihi*, p. 622. Shaw also draws attention to the application of this new system to the *Bahr-i Zafer*, without mentioning the *Hümây-ı Zafer*. See Shaw: 'Selim III and the Ottoman navy', p. 220.

224. BOA. CB, no. 1913.

225. Cevdet: *Târih-i Cevdet*, vols 7–8, pp. 349–51.

226. Noyan: 'Eski Gemilerimizin İsimleri', p. 93.

227. Karal: 'Selim III Devrinde Osmanlı Bahriyesi', p. 208.

228. Cevdet: *Târih-i Cevdet*, vols 7–8, pp. 349–51.

229. Noyan: 'Eski Gemilerimizin İsimleri', p. 93.

230. BOA. CB, no. 1913.

231. Karal: 'Selim III Devrinde Osmanlı Bahriyesi', p. 208.

232. Cevdet: *Târih-i Cevdet*, vols 7–8, pp. 349–51.

233. Emsen: 'Selim III', p. 13.

234. Karal: 'Selim III Devrinde Osmanlı Bahriyesi', p. 206.

235. Emsen: 'Selim III', pp. 8 and 11.

236. BOA. CB, no. 6229.

237. BOA. CB, no. 8085 (18 July 1797).

238. Cevdet: *Târih-i Cevdet*, vols 7–8, pp. 349–51.

239. Emsen: 'Selim III', p. 41.

240. Noyan: 'Eski Gemilerimizin İsimleri', p. 93.

241. Karal: 'Selim III Devrinde Osmanlı Bahriyesi', p. 209.

242. Cevdet: *Târih-i Cevdet*, vols 7–8, pp. 349–51.

243. Karal: 'Selim III Devrinde Osmanlı Bahriyesi', p. 209.

244. Çeçen: 'Mühendishâne-i Bahrî-i Hümâyûn', p. 14.

245. Karal: 'Selim III Devrinde Osmanlı Bahriyesi', p. 206.

246. Noyan gives 1752 for its construction date. See Noyan: 'Eski Gemilerimizin İsimleri', p. 92.

247. Cevdet: *Târih-i Cevdet*, vols 7–8, pp. 349–51.

248. Emsen: 'Selim III', p. 41.

249. Noyan: 'Eski Gemilerimizin İsimleri', p. 93.

250. Mahmud Raif Efendi: *Osmanlı İmparatorluğu'nda Yeni Nizamların Cedveli* (see the appendix).

251. Shaw: 'Selim III and the Ottoman Navy,' p. 225. The number of guns is mentioned both as 62 (probably by mistake) and 122 in Karal: 'Selim III Devrinde Osmanlı Bahriyesi', p. 206.

252. Emsen: 'Selim III', p. 15.

253. The French *Royal Louis*, with 100 guns, was built in 1759. It was one of three-deckers constructed for the French navy and was very similar to the British first rates. It also shows the important changes that had occurred in replacing the aging ships of Louis XIV's fleet. The hull sheer is much flatter, and less emphasis placed upon decoration. The quarterdeck is extended, while increased draught and beam have made a more stable gun-platform and a more weather-resistant hull with higher freeboard. There seems to have been significant alteration in basic ship rig, too. The spirit-topsail has gone; doubling it with a jib boom extends the bowsprit. It retains its square sails, often useful for pulling a demasted battleship out of the line, but now supports a series of jibs that are complemented by staysails set between the masts. Above the deep-gored topsails with three rows of reefing points, are set topgallants and royals. Most interesting is the spanker with its vertical leech, which, although it retains its long, vestigial lateen yard (carried as a spare lower yard), it has shed the area of sail forward of the mast. See Woodman: *The Story of Sail*, p. 99. Unlike the information given above, James Pritchard refers to the *Royal Louis* as having 116 guns on board and states that by the spring of 1758 its keel and stem- and sternposts had been laid down at Brest and frames were being mounted, but the ship was only completed late in

1761. See James Pritchard, *Louis XV's Navy 1748–1762: A Study of Organization and Administration* (Kingston and Montreal, 1987). For a general account of the French navy, see Ernest H. Jenkis, *A History of the French Navy, from Its Beginnings to the Present Day* (London, 1973).

254. FO 78/15, p. 346.

255. BOA. CB, no. 6188.

256. He refers to the anonymous French 'Essai sur la puissance navale des Turcs' (A E Mémoires et Documents, Turquie, no. 30, fol. 355). See Shaw: 'Selim III and the Ottoman navy', p. 225.

257. Karal: 'Selim III Devrinde Osmanlı Bahriyesi', p. 206.

258. Goodwin, Godfrey, *The Janissaries* (London, 1997), p. 107.

259. The document states that the *Selimiye* had all the improvements, thanks to the Captain Pasha's extreme attention to naval matters and his ability. See FO 78/34 (6 November 1799), p. 22

260. In another letter from the Earl of Elgin at Constantinople to the secretary of state on 21 April 1800, the Captain Pasha is said to have sailed from Constantinople on Saturday 26th on his own ship (the *Selimiye*) of 132 guns, together with six other ships of the line and four 50's, as well as six smaller ships of war. See FO 78/29 (21 April 1800), pp. 78–79.

261. James, William, *The Naval History of Great Britain*, vol. 3 (London, 1886), p. 87.

262. Emsen: 'Selim III', p. 41.

263. BOA. HH, no. 3446-e (13 April 1801)

264. Cevdet: *Târih-i Cevdet*, vols 7–8, pp. 349–51.

265. Emsen: 'Selim III', p. 41.

266. Noyan: 'Eski Gemilerimizin İsimleri', p. 93.

267. Tezel: *Anadolu Türklerinin Deniz Tarihi*, p. 655.

268. Karal: 'Selim III Devrinde Osmanlı Bahriyesi', p. 206.

269. Cevdet: *Târih-i Cevdet*, vols 7–8, pp. 349–51.

270. Emsen: 'Selim III', p. 41.

271. Noyan: 'Eski Gemilerimizin İsimleri', p. 93.

272. Çeşmî-zâde Mustafa Reşîd, *Çeşmî-zâde Tarihi* (İstanbul, 1993), p. 23.

273. Karal: 'Selim III Devrinde Osmanlı Bahriyesi', p. 207.

274. Cevdet: *Târih-i Cevdet*, vols 7–8, pp. 349–51.

275. BOA. CB, no. 9274.

276. Emsen: 'Selim III', p. 41.

277. Noyan: 'Eski Gemilerimizin İsimleri', p. 93.

278. Noyan gives 1779 for its construction date. See Noyan: 'Eski

Gemilerimizin İsimleri', p. 92.

279. Karal: 'Selim III Devrinde Osmanlı Bahriyesi', p. 208.

280. Cevdet: *Târih-i Cevdet*, vols 7–8, pp. 349–51.

281. Karal: 'Selim III Devrinde Osmanlı Bahriyesi', p. 208.

282. Emsen: 'Selim III', p. 9.

283. Cevdet: *Târih-i Cevdet*, vols 7–8, pp. 349–51.

284. Karal: 'Selim III Devrinde Osmanlı Bahriyesi', p. 208.

285. Cevdet: *Târih-i Cevdet*, vols 7–8, pp. 349–51.

286. Noyan: 'Eski Gemilerimizin İsimleri', p. 93.

287. Mahmud Raif Efendi: *Osmanlı İmparatorluğu'nda Yeni Nizamların Cedveli* (see the appendix).

288. Karal: 'Selim III Devrinde Osmanlı Bahriyesi', p. 208.

289. Cevdet: *Târih-i Cevdet*, vols 7–8, pp. 349–51.

290. Emsen: 'Selim III', p. 41.

291. Noyan: 'Eski Gemilerimizin İsimleri', p. 93.

292. Karal: 'Selim III Devrinde Osmanlı Bahriyesi', p. 209.

293. BOA. CB, no. 2144 (26 July 1797).

294. BOA. CB, no. 8085.

295. Cevdet: *Târih-i Cevdet*, vols 7–8, pp. 349–51.

296. BOA. CB, no. 8085.

297. Karal: 'Selim III Devrinde Osmanlı Bahriyesi', p. 209.

298. Cevdet: *Târih-i Cevdet*, vols 7–8, pp. 349–51.

299. BOA. HH, no. 9658.

300. Uzunçarşılı: *Merkez ve Bahriye*, pp. 467–68.

301. A sailing craft used in the Levant, with two short masts that lean forward. See Kahane and Tietze: *Lingua Franca*, p. 563.

302. BOA. CB, no. 8709.

303. Tezel: *Anadolu Türklerinin Deniz Tarihi*, pp. 392–93.

304. Güleryüz: *Kadırgadan Kalyona Osmanlıda Yelken*, p. 98.

305. Karal: 'Selim III Devrinde Osmanlı Bahriyesi', p. 208.

306. Cevdet: *Târih-i Cevdet*, vols 7–8, pp. 349–51.

307. Karal: 'Selim III Devrinde Osmanlı Bahriyesi', p. 208.

308. Cevdet: *Târih-i Cevdet*, vols 7–8, pp. 349–51.

309. Karal: 'Selim III Devrinde Osmanlı Bahriyesi', p. 208.

310. Cevdet: *Târih-i Cevdet*, vols 7–8, pp. 349–51.

311. Emsen: 'Selim III', p. 41.

312. Noyan: 'Eski Gemilerimizin İsimleri', p. 93.

313. Karal: 'Selim III Devrinde Osmanlı Bahriyesi', p. 208.

314. Cevdet: *Târih-i Cevdet*, vols 7–8, pp. 349–51.

315. Noyan: 'Eski Gemilerimizin İsimleri', p. 93.

316. Karal: 'Selim III Devrinde Osmanlı Bahriyesi', p. 206.

317. Cevdet: *Târih-i Cevdet*, vols 7–8, pp. 349–51.

318. Karal: 'Selim III Devrinde Osmanlı Bahriyesi', p. 206.

319. BOA. CB, no. 2287.

320. Cevdet: *Târih-i Cevdet*, vols 7–8, pp. 349–51.

321. Karal: 'Selim III Devrinde Osmanlı Bahriyesi', p. 206. See also Alpagut and Kurtoğlu: *Türkler'in Deniz,,* p. 30.

322. Emsen: 'Selim III', p. 41.

323. Noyan: 'Eski Gemilerimizin İsimleri', p. 93.

324. Karal: 'Selim III Devrinde Osmanlı Bahriyesi', p. 207.

325. Alpagut and Kurtoğlu: *Türkler'in Deniz*, p. 31.

326. Cevdet: *Târih-i Cevdet*, vols 7–8, pp. 349–51.

327. Karal: 'Selim III Devrinde Osmanlı Bahriyesi', p. 208.

328. See the pictures at the end of *Mahmud Raif Efendi ve Nızâm-ı Cedîd'e Dâir Eseri*.

329. Karal: 'Selim III Devrinde Osmanlı Bahriyesi', p. 208.

330. BOA. CB, no. 1897.

331. Noyan: 'Eski Gemilerimizin İsimleri', p. 93.

332. Karal: 'Selim III Devrinde Osmanlı Bahriyesi', p. 206.

333. Işın: *Osmanlı Bahriyesi Kronolojisi*, p. 154.

334. BOA. HH, no. 3446-e (13 April 1801).

335. Cevdet: *Târih-i Cevdet*, vols 7–8, pp. 349–51.

336. Emsen: 'Selim III', p. 41.

337. Noyan: 'Eski Gemilerimizin İsimleri', p. 93.

338. Karal: 'Selim III Devrinde Osmanlı Bahriyesi', p. 207.

339. BOA. CB, nos. 1860 and 2359.

340. Cevdet: *Târih-i Cevdet*, vols 7–8, pp. 349–51.

341. Işın: *Osmanlı Bahriyesi Kronolojisi*, p. 155.

342. Karal: 'Selim III Devrinde Osmanlı Bahriyesi', p. 207.

343. BOA. CB, nos. 1860 and 2359.

344. Emsen: 'Selim III', p. 36.

345. Cevdet: *Târih-i Cevdet*, vols 7–8, pp. 349–51.

346. Emsen: 'Selim III', p. 41.

347. Tezel suggests that this was a galleon of 53.5 *zira* rather than a frigate of 53 *zira* and that its hull cost 48,529 *kuruş*. See Tezel: *Anadolu Türklerinin Deniz Tarihi*, p. 611.

348. Karal: 'Selim III Devrinde Osmanlı Bahriyesi', p. 207.

349. Cevdet: *Târih-i Cevdet*, vols 7–8, pp. 349–51.

350. Karal: 'Selim III Devrinde Osmanlı Bahriyesi', p. 207.

351. *Ibid.*, p. 209.

352. *Ibid.*

353. Cevdet: *Târih-i Cevdet*, vols 7–8, pp. 349–51.

354. Emsen: 'Selim III', p. 41.

355. Noyan: 'Eski Gemilerimizin İsimleri', p. 93.

356. BOA. HH, no. 3446-e (13 April 1801)

357. Cevdet: *Târih-i Cevdet*, vols 7–8, pp. 349–51.

358. This phrase is a part of a verse referring to the prophet Noah, meaning 'And he [Noah] said: Embark therein: in the name of Allah will be its (moving) course and its (resting) anchorage. Surely, my Lord is Oft-Forgiving, Most Merciful.' See *The Noble Qur'an*, 11/41.

359. Ahmet Vasıf Efendi: *Mehâsinu'l-Âsâr*, p. 260.

360. BOA. HH, no. 10011.

361. BOA. CB, no. 1913.

362. Cevdet: *Târih-i Cevdet*, vols 7–8, pp. 349–51.

363. BOA. HH, no. 10631.

364. BOA. HH, no. 1205.

365. BOA. HH, no. 10011.

366. BOA. HH, no. 9644-A.

367. Tezel: *Anadolu Türklerinin Deniz Tarihi*, p. 651.

368. BOA. HH, no. 10011.

369. BOA. HH. No. 9658.

370. Noyan gives 1780 for its construction date. See Noyan: 'Eski Gemilerimizin İsimleri', p. 92.

371. Tezel: *Anadolu Türklerinin Deniz Tarihi*, p. 651.

372. Cevdet: *Târih-i Cevdet*, vols 7–8, pp. 349–51.

373. BOA. HH, no. 10011.

374. BOA. CB, no. 1913.

375. BOA. HH, no. 10011.

376. BOA. HH. no. 9658.

377. Cevdet: *Târih-i Cevdet*, vols 7–8, pp. 349–51.

378. Emsen: 'Selim III', p. 41.

379. Noyan: 'Eski Gemilerimizin İsimleri', p. 93.

380. BOA. HH. no. 9658.

381. BOA. CB, no. 1164.

382. BOA. HH. no. 9658.

383. Noyan: 'Eski Gemilerimizin İsimleri', p. 92.

384. BOA. CB, no. 3040 (17 June 1801).

385. BOA. CB, no. 1897.

386. Cevdet: *Târih-i Cevdet*, vols 7–8, pp. 349–51.

387. Noyan: 'Eski Gemilerimizin İsimleri', p. 93.

388. Cevdet: *Târih-i Cevdet*, vols 7–8, pp. 349–51.

389. Emsen: 'Selim III', p. 23.

390. *Ibid.*, p. 41.

391. Noyan: 'Eski Gemilerimizin İsimleri', p. 93.

392. BOA. HH, no. 3446-e (13 April 1801).

393. BOA. Kamil Kepeci (KK), no. 5726.

394. BOA. HH, no. 10011.

395. BOA. CB, no. 2335.

396. BOA. CB, no. 1913.

397. Noyan gives 1785 for its construction date. See Noyan: 'Eski Gemilerimizin İsimleri', p. 92.

398. (Altınay), Ahmet Refik, 'Onsekizinci Asırda Fransa ve Türk Askerliği', *Türk Tarih Encümeni Mecmuası*, yeni seri 1/4 (İstanbul, 1930), p. 32. See also Çeçen: 'Mühendishâne-i Bahrî-i Hümâyûn', p. 14. Vasif Efendi confirms that a French architect built it in two to three years. He says that it was launched into the sea as a 59-*zira* galleon on Wednesday (31 May 1787). Some statesmen attended the launching ceremony and its architect was given a sable fur because he was a foreigner. Then the vessel was named the *Mukaddeme-i Zafer* as it was a tradition to give a name for newly constructed ships. Ahmet Vasıf Efendi: *Mehâsinu'l-Âsâr*, p. 393.

399. BOA. CB, no. 2373.

400. BOA. HH, no. 9644-A.

401. Uzunçarşılı: *Merkez ve Bahriye*, p. 484.

402. BOA. CB, no. 5849; HH, no. 10405.

403. BOA. CB, no. 2373.

404. Gencer: *Bahriye'de Yapılan Islahat Hareketleri*, p. 27.

405. BOA. HH, no. 9644-A.

406. Gülen suggests that it was built in 1798 and launched into the sea. See Gülen: *Şanlı Bahriye*, p. 63.

407. Tezel: *Anadolu Türklerinin Deniz Tarihi*, p. 665.

408. Cevdet: *Târih-i Cevdet*, vols 7–8, pp. 349–51.

409. BOA. CB, no. 1295.

410. Emsen: 'Selim III', p. 41.

411. Noyan: 'Eski Gemilerimizin İsimleri', p. 93.

412. Cevdet: *Târih-i Cevdet*, vols 7–8, pp. 349–51.

413. Emsen: 'Selim III', p. 24.

414. Emsen: 'Selim III', p. 41.

415. Emsen: 'Selim III', pp. 41-45.

416. Noyan: 'Eski Gemilerimizin İsimleri', p. 93.

417. BOA. HH, no. 9658.

418. Emsen: 'Selim III', p. 13.

419. BOA. HH, no. 9658.

420. *Aktarma* had two meanings: a river ship (mostly the ones on the Danube) escorting a fleet, and a captured and towed enemy ship. See Çelebi: *Tuhfetü'l kibâr fî esfâri'l bihâr*, p. 295. Also see Bostan: *Osmanlı Bahriye Teşkilatı*, p. 90.

421. Alpagut and Kurtoğlu: *Türkler'in Deniz*, p. 31, and Emsen: 'Selim III', p. 11.

422. Emsen: 'Selim III', pp. 11–15.

423. The *duba* was a vessel used to transport goods and in the construction of the feet of bridges. See Zaloğlu: *Gemici Dili*, p. 110.

424. Alpagut and Kurtoğlu: *Türkler'in Deniz*, p. 31.

425. Karal: 'Selim III Devrinde Osmanlı Bahriyesi', p. 209.

426. Some ship constructors were awarded *kapucubaşı*, *mirimiran*, *paşa* etc. See Yakay: *Kdz. Ereğli'de*, p. 82.

427. BOA. KK, no. 5734.

428. PRO. FO 261/1, no. 3w.

429. PRO. FO 78/5, pp. 18-19 (10 February 1784).

430. PRO. FO 261/1, no. 22.

431. PRO. FO 261/1, no. 22, p. 209.

432. Tezel: *Anadolu Türklerinin Deniz Tarihi*, p. 649.

433. BOA. CB, no. 1913.

434. BOA. HH, no. 9658.

435. PRO. FO 78/8 (25 September 1787), p. 197.

436. PRO. FO 78/9, p. 118

437. PRO. FO 78/10, p. 53.

438. PRO. FO 78/10, pp. 71.

439. BOA. HH, no. 8083 (1789–90).

440. Karal: 'Selim III Devrinde Osmanlı Bahriyesi', p. 209.

441. Güleryüz: *Kadırgadan Kalyona Osmanlıda Yelken*, p. 98. The same ship is referred as a galleon. See Cevdet: *Târih-i Cevdet*, vols 7–8, pp. 349-51.

442. BOA. CB, no. 6055. This document mentions that the ships were of 60–70 guns and that five of them never left the harbour as they needed some equipment and tools to sail off. The one with 60 guns sailed off for an expedition around the surrounding areas. It also mentions that these ships could only be purchased after they had arrived in the Ottoman harbours and had been examined carefully there.

443. Gencer: *Bahriyede Yapilan Islahat Hareketleri*, p. 57.

444. BOA. D. BŞM. TRE, no. 15211.

445. BOA. HH, no. 9210.

446. PRO. FO 78/14, p. 223.

447. Uzunçarşılı: 'Ondokuzuncu asır başlarına kadar Türk-İngiliz', pp. 582–83.

448. PRO. FO 78/39, p. 25.

449. *Mahmud Raif Efendi ve Nizâm-ı Cedîd'e Dair Eseri*: p. 58.

450. Karal: 'Selim III Devrinde Osmanlı Bahriyesi', p. 209.

451. BOA. HH, no. 8686.

452. PRO. FO 78/10 (22 September 1789).

453. BOA. CB, no. 5832.

454. PRO. FO 78/50 (26 June 1806).

455. Clowes, William Laird, *The Royal Navy: A History*, vol. 4 (New York, 1996), p. 458.

456. Anderson: *Naval Wars*, pp. 391–92.

457. James: *The Naval History of Great Britain*, vol. 3, p. 93.

458. Lloyd: *The Keith Papers*, vol. 2, pp. 358–59.

459. Karal: 'Selim III Devrinde Osmanlı Bahriyesi', p. 209.

460. Cevdet: *Târih-i Cevdet*, vols 7–8, pp. 349–51.

461. This might be the *Abbas Kaptan Gemisi*, on which Mehmed, a galleon sailor, was injured in one of his eyes while trying to disjoint a cannon and was granted 10–25 *akçe* in 1792–93. See BOA. HH, no. 8905.

462. von Pivka: *Navies of the Napoleonic Era*, p. 214.

# BIBLIOGRAPHY

## Archival sources

### *Başbakanlık Osmanlı Arşivi/Prime Ministerial Archives (BOA)*
Bâb-ı Defterî-Baş Muhasebe Kalemi, Tersâne-i Âmire (D. BŞM. TRE), no.
15211, 15328, 15412

### *BOA. Cevdet Askeriye (CA), no. 48831*
BOA. Cevdet Bahriye (CB), no. 186, 330, 642, 906, 1033, 1124, 1129, 1164,
1169, 1204, 1206, 1209, 1214, 1250, 1261, 1281, 1292, 1295, 1297, 1310,
1337, 1354, 1408, 1418, 1454, 1474, 1479, 1520, 1534, 1549, 1575, 1585,
1588, 1591, 1611, 1638, 1683, 1751, 1775, 1796, 1860, 1888, 1897, 1905,
1913, 2144, 2155, 2172, 2181, 2186, 2190, 2194, 2216, 2223, 2229, 2246,
2260, 2287, 2289, 2320, 2325, 2335, 2357, 2359, 2360, 2373, 2379, 2407,
2413, 2421, 2463, 2478, 2494, 2684, 2779, 2808, 3032, 3359, 3365, 3609,
3883, 4010, 4077, 4397, 4398, 4411, 4436, 4437, 4451, 4454, 4511, 4512,
4513, 4918, 5136, 5209, 5264, 5315, 5747, 5791, 5801, 5832, 5848, 5849,
5850, 5891, 6055, 6056, 6143, 6188, 6229, 6300, 6336, 6381, 6505, 6506,
6792, 6872, 7013, 7163, 7210, 7212, 7274, 7356, 7472, 7720, 7753, 7769,
7825, 8008, 8070, 8076, 8085, 8098, 8267, 8389, 8705, 8709, 8714, 9258,
9269, 9274, 9297, 9360, 9362, 9418, 9501, 9646, 9981, 10103, 10123, 10252,
10514, 10824, 10895, 10896, 11181, 11461, 11292, 12193, 12216, 12232,
12281, 12282, 12383, 12602, 12738, 14076.
BOA. Cevdet Darphâne (CD), no. 59, 95, 463, 2921.
BOA. Cevdet Hariciye (CH), no. 4411.
BOA. Cevdet Sıhhiye (CS), no. 1355
BOA, Hatt-ı Hümâyûn (HH), no. 1205, 1592, 2495, 2529-a, 3446-e, 4503,
4563, 4592, 6085, 6086, 6644, 8024, 8083, 8168, 8686, 8775, 8845, 8905,
9080, 9210, 9644-A, 9646, 9658, 9706/A-B, 9792, 10011, 10093, 10253,
10259, 10270, 10401, 10405, 10560, 10588, 10631, 10679, 10689, 10721,

11264, 11282, 11386, 11753, 12356, 12418, 14011, 14076, 14141, 14486, 14523, 14638, 14666, 151210, 15212, 15370, 55150, 55529, 56099, 56625, 57562-krt. 329, 57599.

BOA. Kamil Kepeci (KK), no. 5724, 5726, 5734

### Public Record Office, London
### (FO) Foreign Office Archives

78/2 (14 Apr. 1781), 78/4 (26 March 1783), 78/5 (10 Feb. 1784), 78/7 (24 July 1786), 78/8 (23 February 1787) pp. 30–31, 78/9 (1 May 1788), 78/10 (22 Sep. 1789), 78/10 (15 March 1789), p. 71, FO 78/10 (1 March 1789), p. 58, 78/11 (31 Oct. 1790), 78/11 (20 Nov. 1790), 78/11 (10 Nov. 1791), 78/12A (21 Dec. 1791), 78/12A (24 Dec. 1791), 78/14 (22 Feb. 1793), 78/15 (25 Feb. 1794), 78/15 (25 Dec. 1794), 78/16 (25 June 1795), 78/17 (10 July 1796), 78/18 (15 June 1797), 78/21 (22 March 1799), 78/25 (26 Oct. 1798), 78/25 (27 Oct. 1798), 78/25 (9 Nov. 1798), 78/26 (27 May 1799), 78/27 (9 January 1800 to 30 December 1800), 78/27 (12 April 1800), 78/28 (16 Feb. 1800), 78/28 (17 Feb.1800), 78/28 (17 March 1800), 78/28 (18 March 1800), 78/28 (26 March 1800), 78/29 (21 April 1800), 78/32 (30 May 1801), 78/34 (6 Nov. 1799), 78/39 (25 Feb. 1803), 78/39 (12 March 1803), 78/43 (1 Aug. 1804), 78/46 (2 Dec. 1805), 78/46 (11 Dec. 1805), 78/50 (26 June 1806), 78/55, no. 10 (27 Jan. 1807), 78/57 (22 June 1804), 78/59 (6 April 1807), 95/8/14 (25 April 1787), pp. 862-63, 261/1, no. 20 (10 Sept. 1784), FO 261/1, no. 16 (23 July 1784), 261/1, no. 22 (9 Oct. 1784), 261/4 (25 Nov. 1782), 261/5 (12 Sept. 1784), FO 261/6 (25 March 1788), p. 65, 261/6 (11 February 1788), p. 10, 261/7 (22 May 1791), p. 23.

*Great Britain Parliamentary Papers 1799–1800*, II. London: House of Commons, 1800.

*State Papers and Publick Documents of the United States, from the Accession of George Washington to the Presidency, Exhibiting a Complete View of Our Foreign Relations Since That Time*, vol. 8 (Boston: Thomas B. Wait, 1819), pp. 200–201, 218–219 and 232, and vol. 10 (Boston: Thomas B. Wait, 1819), pp. 41–55 and 464–65.

### Primary sources

Ahmed Cevdet, *Târih-i Cevdet*, vols 5, 6, 7, 8 and 12 (İstanbul: Matbaa-i Osmaniye, 1309).

Ahmet Vasıf Efendi, *Mehâsinu'l-Âsâr ve Hakâiku'l Ahbâr* (Published by Mücteba İlgürel) (Ankara: TTK, 1994).

Çeşmî-zâde Mustafa Reşîd, *Çeşmî-zâde Tarihi* (Published by Bekir

Kütükoğlu) (İstanbul: İstanbul Fetih Cemiyeti, 1993).

De Truguet, *Usûlü'l-ma`arif fî vech-i Tasfif-i Sefâyin-i Donanma ve Fenn-i Tedbîr-i Harekâtuhâ* (the copy in the Archeological Museum in Istanbul, no. ŞK. 1666).

Kâtip Çelebi, *Tuhfetü'l Kibâr fî Esfâri'l Bihâr* (edited by Orhan Şaik Gökyay) (İstanbul: Milli Eğitim Basımevi, 1973).

_____ *History of the Maritime Wars of the Turks* (translated by James Mitchell) (London, 1831).

Şemseddin Sami, *Kâmus-ı Türkî* (İstanbul: Bedir Yay, n.d.).

## Secondary sources

Acerra, Martine, José Merino and Jean Meyer (eds), *Les Marines de guerre européennes XVIIème–XVIIIème siècles* (Paris: Presses de l'Université de Paris-Sorbonne, 1985).

Ademoğlu, Ebru 'Yahya Naci Efendi ve Fırlatılan Cisimlerin Hareketleriyle İlgili Eseri: Risale-i Hikmet-i Tabiiyye (1809)', in Feza Günergun (ed.), *Osmanlı Bilimi Araştırmaları*, vol. 4, no. 1 (İstanbul: İstanbul Üniversitesi Edebiyat Fakültesi Yayını, 2002), pp. 25–56.

Adıvar, A. Adnan, *Osmanlı Türklerinde İlim* (İstanbul: Remzi Kitabevi, 1971).

Agoston, Gabor, 'Ottoman artillery and European military technology in the 15th to 17th centuries', *Acta Orientalia Academiae Scientiarum Hungaricae*, vol. 47 (1994).

_____ 'Gunpowder for the Sultan's Army', *Turcica: Revue d'études turques* 25 (1993).

_____ 'Osmanlı İmparatorluğu'nda Harp Endüstrisi ve Barut Teknolojisi (1450–1700), *Yeni Türkiye*, Year 6, no. 31 (January–February 2000), pp. 630–41.

_____ 'Merces Prohibitae: The Anglo-Ottoman trade in war material and the dependence theory', in Kate Fleet (ed.), *The Ottomans and the Sea* (Cambridge: Skilliter Center for Ottoman Studies & Istituto per l'Oriente C. A. Nallino, 2001), pp. 177–92.

_____ '1453–1826 Avrupa'da Osmanlı Savaşları', in Jeremy Black (ed.), *Top, Tüfek ve Süngü, Yeniçağ Savaş Sanatı 1453–1815* (translated by Yavuz Alogan) (İstanbul: Kitap Yayınevi, 2003), pp. 30–51.

Akıncı, Gündüz, *Türk-Fransız Kültür İlişkileri (1701–1859). Başlangıç Dönemi* (Erzurum: Atatürk Üniversitesi Edebiyat Fakültesi Yayını, 1973).

Akman, M. Süheyl, *Deniz Yapılarında Beton Teknolojisi* (İstanbul: İTÜ Gemi İnşaatı ve Deniz Bilimleri Fakültesi Yay, 1992).

Aksan, Virginia H., 'Ottoman sources of information on Europe in the eighteenth century', *Archivum Ottomanicum* 11, 1986 (1988), pp. 5-16.

____'Choiseul-Gouffier at the Sublime Porte 1784–1792', in Sinan Kuneralp (ed.), *Studies on Ottoman Diplomatic History* (Istanbul: The Isis Press, 1992).

____'Ottoman military recruitment strategies in the late 18th century', in Eric J. Zürcher (ed.), *Arming the State Military Conscription in the Middle East and Central Asia 1775–1925* (London and New York: I. B. Tauris, 1999), pp. 21–39.

____'Breaking the spell of the Baron de Tott: reframing the question of military reform in the Ottoman Empire, 1760–1830', *The International History Review* 24/2 (June 2002), pp. 254–77.

Aksoy, İsmail Hakkı, 'İstanbul'da Tarihi Yapılarda Uygulanan Temel Sistemleri' (İstanbul: Ph.D. dissertation, İTÜ İnşaat Fakültesi Matbaası, 1982).

____'Osmanlı Döneminde Kullanılan Eski Su Boşaltma ve İnşaat Araçları', *Proceedings of the First International Congress on the History of Turkish İslamic Science and Technology*, vol. 3 of 5 vols (Istanbul: Technical University, pp. 47–56).

Aktepe, M. Münir, 'Çeşme Vakası', *TDV Islam Ansiklopedisi*, vol. 8 (İstanbul: Türkiye Diyanet Vakfı, 1991), p. 289.

Albion, Robert Greenhalgh, *Forests and Sea Power: The Timber Problem of the Royal Navy 1652–1862* (Connecticut: Archon Books, 1965).

Alpagut, Ali Haydar, *Marmarada Türkler* (İstanbul: Deniz Matbaası, 1941).

Alpagut, Ali Haydar and Fevzi Kurtoğlu, *Türkler'in Deniz Harp Sanatına Hizmetleri* (İstanbul: Deniz Matbaası, 1936).

(Altınay) Ahmet Refik, 'Onsekizinci Asırda Fransa ve Türk Askerliği', *Türk Tarih Encümeni Mecmuası*, yeni seri 1/4 (İstanbul 1930), pp. 17–33.

____*On ikinci Ası-ı Hicrî'de İstanbul Hayatı (1689–1785)* (İstanbul: Enderun Kitabevi, 1988).

Altıer, Selim Sırrı, *Osmanlı Bahriyesinin Yelken Devri ve Türk Korsanları* (İstanbul: Boğaziçi Yayınları, n.d.).

Anderson, R. C., *Naval Wars in the Levant (1559–1853)* (Liverpool: Liverpool University Press, 1952).

Armytage, W. H. G., *A Social History of Engineering* (London: Faber and Faber, 1976).

Avigdor, Levy, 'Military reform and the problem of centralization in the Ottoman Empire in the 18th century', *Middle Eastern Studies* 18 (1982).

Aydüz, Salim, 'Osmanlı Devleti'nde Müneccimbaşılık', *Osmanlı Bilimi Araştırmaları* (İstanbul: İstanbul Üniversitesi Edebiyat Fakültesi Yayını, 1995), pp. 159–207.

_____ 'Osmanlı Devleti'nde Tophâne-i Âmire'nin Faaliyetleri ve Top Döküm Teknolojisi, XIV–XVI. Yüzyıllar' (İstanbul: Ph.D. dissertation, İstanbul University, 1998).

Bamford, Paul Walden, *Forests and French Sea Power 1660–1789* (Toronto: University of Toronto Press, 1956).

_____ *Fighting Ships and Prisons: The Mediterranean Galleys of France in the Age of Louis XIV* (Minneapolis: The University of Minnesota Press, 1973).

Basch, Lucien, 'A galley in Istanbul: the *Kadirga* ', *The Mariner's Mirror: The Journal of the Society for Nautical Research* 60 (London: Greenwich National Maritime Museum, Society for Nautical Research, 1974), pp. 133–34.

_____ 'The *Kadirga* revisited: a preliminary re-appraisal', *The Mariner's Mirror: The Journal of the Society for Nautical Research* 65 (London: Greenwich National Maritime Museum, Society for Nautical Research, 1979), pp. 39–51.

Belhamissi, Moulay, *Histoire de la marine algérienne (1516–1830)*, 3 vols (Algiers: E.N.A.L., 1983).

Berkes, Niyazi, *The Development of Secularism in Turkey* (Montreal: McGill University Press, 1964).

Beydilli, Kemal, 'Ignatius Mouradgea D'Ohsson (Muradcan Tosunyan)', *İstanbul Üniversitesi Edebiyat Fakültesi Tarih Dergisi* 34 (İstanbul, 1983–84), pp. 247–314.

_____ 'İlk Mühendislerimizden Seyyid Mustafa ve Nizâm-ı Cedîd'e Dair Risalesi', *Tarih Enstitüsü Dergisi* 13 (İstanbul, 1987), pp. 387–479.

_____ *Türk Bilim ve Matbaacılık Tarihinde Mühendishane, Mühendishane Matbaası ve Kütüphanesi 1776–1826* (İstanbul: Eren Yayınları, 1995).

Beydilli, Kemal and İlhan Şahin (eds and translators), *Mahmud Raif Efendi ve Nızâm-ı Cedîd'e Dâir Eseri* (Ankara: TTK, 2001).

Bobat, Alaaddin, 'Emprenyeli Ağaç Malzemenin Kapalı Maden Ocaklarında ve Deniz İçinde Kullanımı ve Dayanma Süresi' (Trabzon: Ph.D. dissertation, Karadeniz Teknik Üniversitesi, Fen Bilimleri Enstitüsü, Orman Endüstri Mühendisliği Anabilim Dalı, 1994).

Bostan, İdris, *Osmanlı Bahriye Teşkilatı: VII. Yüzyılda Tersâne-i Âmire* (Ankara: TTK, 1992).

_____ 'Izn-i Sefine Defterleri ve Karadeniz'de Rusya ile Ticaret Yapan Devlet-i Aliyye Tüccarları', *Marmara Üniversitesi Fen-Edebiyat Fakültesi Türklük Araştırmaları Dergisi* 6 (İstanbul, 1990), pp. 21–44.

_____ 'Osmanlı Bahriyesinde Modernleşme Hareketleri I: Tersanede Büyük Havuz İnşası (1794–1800)', *150. Yılında Tanzimat* (1992), pp. 69–90.

_____ 'Shipyards in the Eastern Mediterranean during the late 18th and early 19th centuries as attested in the Ottoman archival materials', *The Evolution of Wooden Shipbuilding in the Eastern Mediterranean during the 18th and 19th Centuries* (Athens: n. p., 1993).

_____ 'Osmanlı Bahriyesi'nin Modernleşmesinde Yabancı Uzmanların Rolü', *İstanbul Üniversitesi Edebiyat Fakültesi Tarih Dergisi-Prof. Dr. Hakkı Dursun Yıldız Hatıra Sayısı* (İstanbul, 1994), pp. 177–92.

_____ 'XVI–XVII. Yüzyıllarda Osmanlı Tersaneleri ve Gemi İnşa Teknolojisi', *Yeni Türkiye* 6/31 (Ocak-Şubat 2000), pp. 620–29.

_____ *Kürekli ve Yelkenli Osmanlı Gemileri* (İstanbul, 2005).

_____ *Beylikten İmparatorluğa Osmanlı Denizciliği* (İstanbul: Kitap Yayınevi, 2006).

Brummett, Palmira, *Ottoman Seapower and Levantine Diplomacy in the Age of Discovery* (Albany: State University of New York Press, 1994).

_____ 'The Ottomans as a world power: what we don't know about Ottoman-sea-power', in Kate Fleet (ed.), *The Ottomans and the Sea* (Cambridge: Skilliter Centre for Ottoman Studies & Istituto per l'Oriente C. A. Nallino, 2001), pp. 1–21.

Büyüktuğrul, Afif, *Osmanlı Deniz Harp Tarihi ve Cumhuriyet Donanması*, 4 vols (İstanbul: Deniz Basımevi, 1982).

Cezar, Yavuz, 'Osmanlı Devleti'nin Mali Kurumlarından Tersâne-i Amire Hazinesi ve Defterdarlığı'nın 1805 Tarihli Kuruluş Yasası ve Eki', *İstanbul Universitesi İktisat Fakültesi Mecmuası. Ord. Prof. Ömer Lutfu Barkan'a Armağan* 41/1–4 (İstanbul, 1985), pp. 361–88.

Chapman, William C., 'Prelude to Chesme', *The Mariner's Mirror: The Journal of the Society for Nautical Research* 52 (London: Greenwich National Maritime Museum, Society for Nautical Research, 1966), pp. 61–77.

Cipolla, Carlo, *Guns, Sails and Empire. Technological Innovation and the Early Phases of European Expansion 1400–1700* (New York: Minerva Press, 1965).

Clowes, William Laird, *The Royal Navy: A History*, 7 vols (New York: Chatham, 1996).

Coad, Jonathan G., 'Historic architecture of the Royal Navy, 1650–1850', in Martine Acerra, José Merino and Jean Meyer (eds), *Les Marines de guerre européennes XVIIème–XVIIIème siècles* (Paris: Presses de l'Université de Paris-Sorbonne, 1985), pp. 13–19.

Cock, Randolph, 'The finest invention in the world: the Royal Navy's early trials of copper sheathing, 1708–1770', *The Mariner's Mirror: The Journal of the Society for Nautical Research* 87/4 (London: Greenwich National

Maritime Museum, Society for Nautical Research, 2001), pp. 446–59.

Crimmin, Patricia K., 'The royal and the Levant trade, c. 1795–c. 1805,' in Jeremy Black and Philip Woodfine (eds), *The British Navy and the Use of Naval Power in the Eighteenth Century* (UK: Leicester University Press, 1988), pp. 221–36.

_____ 'A great object with us to procure this timber…: the Royal Navy's search for ship timber in the Eastern Mediterranean and Southern Russia, 1803–1815', *International Journal of Maritime History* 4/2 (December 1992), pp. 83–115.

Currier, Betty Nelson, *Anchors* (London: Chatham, 1999).

Çeçen, Kazım, 'Mühendishâne-i Bahrî-i Hümâyûn', *Dünden Bugüne İstanbul Ansiklopedisi*, vol. 6 (İstanbul: Türkiye Ekonomik ve Sosyal Tarih Vakfı, 1994).

Çetin, Birol, *Osmanlı İmparatorluğu'nda Barut Sanayi 1700–1900* (Ankara: Kültür Bakanlığı, 2001).

Çizakça, Murat, 'Ottomans and the Mediterranean: an analysis of the Ottoman shipbuilding industry as reflected by the arsenal registers of Istanbul, 1529–1650', *Le genti del mare Mediterraneo* (n.d.), pp. 773–87.

_____ 'The Ottoman Empire: recent research on shipping and shipbuilding in the sixteenth to nineteenth Centuries', *Research in Maritime History*, no. 9 (December 1995), pp. 213–28.

Çoker, Fahri, 'Osmanlı Bahriyesinde İngiliz Islah Heyetleri', *Bahriyemizin Yakın Tarihinden Kesitler* (Ankara: Deniz Kuvvetleri Komutanlığı Karargah Basımevi, 1994), pp. 166–78.

Danışman, Günhan, 'Anadolu Enerji Teknolojileri Tarihçesi ve 18. Yüzyıl Sonunda Osmanlı Yönetiminin Sanayileşmede Kaçırdığı Fırsatın Yeniden Değerlendirilmesi', in Emre Dölen and Mustafa Kaçar (eds), *1. Türk Bilim ve Teknoloji Tarihi Kongresi Bildirileri (15–17 Kasım 2001)* (İstanbul, 2003), pp. 95–113.

Daumas, Maurice and Paul Gille, 'Ships and navigation', in Maurice Daumas (ed.), *A History of Technology and Invention: Progress through the Ages*, vol. 2 (translated from the French by Eileen B. Hennes) (London: John Murray, 1979), (London, 1979), pp. 322–408.

Davis, Robert Charles, *Shipbuilders of Venetian Arsenal* (Baltimore: John Hopkins University Press, 1991).

Dawson, William, *Naval Guns, and Mounting and Working Heavy Guns at Sea* (London: Mitchell and Co., 1872).

De Souza, Philip, *Seafaring and Civilization: Maritime Perspectives on the World History* (London: Profile Books, 2001).

Demir, Ahmet, *Türkiye'de Gemi Yapım Sanayiinde Kuruluş Yeri* (Ankara:

Ankara Üniversitesi Siyasal Bilgiler Fakültesi Yayınları, 1967).

Doorman, G., 'Dredging', in Charles Singer, E. J. Holmyard, A. R. Hall and Trevor I. Williams (eds), *A History of Technology*, vol. 4 (Oxford: Clarendon Press, 1958), pp. 629–43.

Doston, J. E, 'The economics and logistics of galley warfare', in Robert Gardiner (ed.), *The Age of Galley: Mediterranean Oared Vessels since Pre-classical Times* (London: Conway Maritime, 1995), pp. 217–13.

Du-Plat-Taylor, Francis Maurice, *The Design, Construction and Maintenance of Docks, Wharves and Piers* (Great Britain: Richard Clay & Sons, 1933).

Duffy, Christopher, *The Military Experience in the Age of Reason* (London: Wordsworth, 1998).

Duparc, Pierre, *Recueil des instructions* (Paris: Centre national de la recherche scientifique, 1969).

Emsen, Şemim, 'Selim III devrinde Osmanlı donanması' (undergraduate thesis in History, İstanbul Üniversitesi Kütüphanesi, no. 1118).

Erendil, Muzaffer, *Topçuluk Tarihi* (Ankara: Genelkurmay Basımevi, 1988).

Ergin, Osman Nuri, *Türkiye Maarif Tarihi*, vols 1–2 (İstanbul: Eser Matbaası, 1977).

Ertuğ, Necdet, *Osmanlı Döneminde İstanbul Deniz Ulaşım ve Kayıkçılar* (Ankara: Kültür Bakanlığı Yay., 2001).

Esencan, Tahsin, *Türk Topçuluğu ve Kaynakları* (Ankara: As. Fabrikalar Basımevi, 1946).

Ethem Ziya, *Gemi Topçuluğunun Geçirdiği Safhalar* (İstanbul: Deniz Matbaası, 1934).

Findley, Carter V., 'Mouradgea D'Ohsson (1740–1807): liminality and cosmopolitanism in the author of the Tableau général de l'Empire ottoman', *The Turkish Studies Association Bulletin* 22/1 (Spring 1998), pp. 21–35.

Fleet, Kate (ed.), *The Ottomans and the Sea* (Cambridge: Skilliter Center for Ottoman Studies & Istituto per l'Oriente C. A. Nallino, 2001).

Gardiner, Robert (ed.), *The Age of Galley: Mediterranean Oared Vessels since Pre-classical Times* (London: Conway Maritime, 1995).

Gardiner, Robert and Richard Ugner (eds.), *Cogs, Caravels and Galleons: The Sailing Ship 1000–1650* (London: Conway Maritime Press, 1994).

Gencer, Ali İhsan, 'İstanbul Tersânesinde Açılan İlk Tıb Mektebi', *Tıp Fakültesi Mecmuası* 41 (1978), pp. 732–47.

____ *Bahriye'de Yapılan Islahat Hareketleri ve Bahriye Nezareti'nin Kuruluşu (1789–1867)* (İstanbul: TTK, 2001).

Genç, Mehmet, *Osmanlı İmparatorluğunda Devlet ve Ekonomi* (İstanbul: Ötüken, 2000).

Gibson, Marjorie Hubbel, *H.M.S. Somerset 1746–1778, The Life and Times of an Eighteenth Century British Man-O-War and Her Impact on North Africa* (Cotuit and Mass.: Abbey Gate House, 1992).

Gilbert, K. R., 'Machine tools', in Charles Singer, E. J. Holmyard, A. R. Hall and Trevor I. Williams (eds), *A History of Technology*, vol. 4 (Oxford: Clarendon Press, 1958).

Goodwin, Godfrey, *The Janissaries* (London: Saqi, 1997).

Göçek, Fatma Müge, *East Encounters West: France and the Ottoman Empire in the Eighteenth Century* (New York and Oxford: Oxford University Press, 1987).

Göyünç, Nejad, 'Kapudân-ı Deryâ Küçük Hüseyin Paşa', *İstanbul Üniversitesi Tarih Dergisi* 2/3–4 (İstanbul, 1952), pp. 35–50.

Grant, Jonathan, 'Rethinking the Ottoman decline: military technology diffusion in the Ottoman Empire, fifteenth to eighteenth centuries', *Journal of World History* 10 (1999), pp. 179–201.

Grenville, Henry, *Observations sur l'état actuel de l'Empire ottoman* (edited by Andrew S. Ehrenkreutz and Ann Arbor) (Michigan: The University of Michigan Press, 1965).

Guilmartin, John Francis, 'The early provision of artillery armament on Mediterranean war galleys', *The Mariner's Mirror: The Journal of the Society for Nautical Research* 59 (London: Greenwich National Maritime Museum, Society for Nautical Research, 1973), pp. 257–80.

____*Gunpowder and Galleys: Changing Technology and Mediterranean Warfare at Sea in the 16th Century* (London: Cambridge University Press, 1980).

Gülen, Nejat, *Şanlı Bahriye (Türk Bahriyesinin İkiyüz Yıllık Tarihçesi 1777–1973)* (İstanbul: Kastaş Yayınları, 2001).

Güler, İbrahim, 'XVIII. Yüzyılın İlk Yarısında Askeri Seferlerde Sinop'un Güvenlik ve Asayiş Meselesi', *OMÜ Eğitim Fakültesi Dergisi* 6 (Samsun, 1991), pp. 72–85.

____ 'XVIII. Yüzyılda Sinop'ta Gemi İnşa Teknolojisinin Altyapı, İstihkâm, İstihdâm, Üretim ve Pazarlama Sorunu', in Emre Dölen and Mustafa Kaçar (eds), *1. Türk Bilim ve Teknoloji Tarihi Kongresi Bildirileri (15–17 Kasım 2001)* (Published by Emre Dölen and Mustafa Kaçar) (İstanbul: TBTK and İSKİ, 2003), pp. 29–60.

Güleryüz, Ahmet, *Kadırgadan Kalyona Osmanlıda Yelken, Mikyas-ı Sefain* (İstanbul: Türkiye Sualtı Arkeolojisi Vakfı TINA, Denizler Kitabevi, 2004).

Günergun, Feza, 'Osmanlı Ölçü ve Tartılarının Eski Fransız ve Metre Sistemlerindeki Eşdeğerleri: İlk Karşılaştırmalar ve Çevirme Cetvelleri', in Feza Günergun (ed.), *Osmanlı Bilimi Araştırmaları II (Studies in Ottoman*

*Science II)* (İstanbul, 1998), pp. 23–68.

Hale, William and Ali İhsan Bağış (eds.), *Four Centuries of Turco-British Relations: Studies in Diplomatic, Economic and Cultural Affairs* (London: The Eothen Press 1984).

Henderson, James, *The Frigates* (London: Wordsworth Military Library, 1998).

_____ *Sloops and Brigs: An Account of the Smallest Vessels of the Royal Navy during the Great Wars, 1793 to 1815* (London: Coles, 1972).

Hess, Andrew C., 'The evolution of the Ottoman sea-borne empire in the age of the oceanic discoveries, 1453–1525', *American Historical Review* 75/7 (December 1970), pp. 1892–1919.

_____ 'Firearms and the decline of Ibn Khaldun's military elite', *Archivum Ottomanicum* 4 (1971), pp. 173–201.

Hitzèl, Frédéric, 'Le rôle des militaires français à Constantinople (1784–1798)' (Paris: M.A. dissertation, Université de Paris-Sorbonne (Paris V), 1987).

_____ 'François Kauffer (1751–1801): ingénieur-cartogaphe français au service de Selim III', in Ekmeleddin İhsanoğlu (ed.), *Science in Islamic Civilisation* (İstanbul: IRCICA, 2000), pp. 233–41.

Holbrook, Victoria, 'Oceanic feeling, narcissism and the post classical image', in Kate Fleet (ed.), *The Ottomans and the Sea* (Cambridge: Skilliter Center for Ottoman Studies and Istituto per l'Oriente C. A. Nallino, 2001), pp. 245–54.

Hovannesyan, Serkis Sarraf, *Payitaht İstanbul'un Tarihçesi* (translated by Elmon Hançer) (İstanbul, 1997).

Işın, İ. Bülent, *Osmanlı Bahriyesi Kronolojisi 1299–1920* (Ankara: Dz. K.K. Basımevi, 2004).

İhsanoğlu, Ekmeleddin, *Başhoca İshak Efendi, Türkiye'de Modern Bilimin Öncüsü* (Ankara: Kültür Bakanlığı Yay., 1989).

_____ (ed.), *Transfer of Modern Science and Technology to the Muslim World* (İstanbul: IRCICA, 1992).

_____ 'Osmanlıların Batı'da Gelişen Bazı Teknolojik Yeniliklerden Etkilenmeleri' *Osmanlılar ve Batı Teknolojisi.* (İstanbul: İstanbul Üniversitesi Edebiyat Fakultesi Yay., 1992).

_____ and Mustafa Kaçar (eds), *Çağını Yakalayan Osmanlı-Osmanlı Devleti'nde Modern Haberleşme ve Ulaşım Teknikleri* (İstanbul: IRCICA, 1995).

_____ 'Aviation: the last episode in the Ottoman transfer of Western technology', *Journal of the Japan-Netherlands Institute* 6 (Tokyo, 1996), pp. 189–219.

_____ *Büyük Cihad'dan Frenk Fodulluğuna* (İstanbul: İletişim, 1996)

_____ *Science, Technology and Learning in the Ottoman Empire: Western Influence, Local Institutions and the Transfer of Knowledge* (UK: Ashgate Variorum Collected Studies Series, 2004).

_____ and Ramazan Şeşen, M. Serdar Bekar and Gülcan Gündüz, *Osmanlı Askerlik Tarihi Literatürü*, 2 vols, Ekmeleddin İhsanoğlu (ed.) (İstanbul: IRCICA, 2004).

İlgürel, Mücteba, 'Osmanlı Devleti'nde Ateşli Silahlar', *Yeni Türkiye.* Year 6, no. 31 (January–February 2000), pp. 613–19.

İmber, C. H., 'The navy of Süleyman the Magnificent', *Archivum Ottomanicum* 6 (Belgium, 1980), pp. 211–82.

İnalcık, Halil, 'The socio-political effects of the diffusion of firearms in the Middle East', in V. J. Parry and M. E. Yapp (eds), *War, Technology and Society in the Middle East* (London: Oxford University Press, 1975), pp. 185–217.

James, William, *The Naval History of Great Britain*, vol. 3 (London: R. Bentley and son, 1886).

Jarvis, Rupert C., 'Sources for the history of ships and shipping', *The Journal of Transport History* 3/3 (May 1958), pp. 212–34.

Jenkins, Ernest Harold, *A History of the French Navy, from Its Beginnings to the Present Day* (London: Macdonald and Jane's, 1973).

Kaçar, Mustafa, 'Osmanlı Devleti'nde Bilim ve Eğitim Anlayışındaki Değişmeler ve Mühendishânelerin Kuruluşu', (İstanbul: Ph.D. dissertation, Istanbul University, 1996).

_____ 'Osmanlı İmparatorluğu'nda Askeri Teknik Eğitimde Modernleşme Çalışmaları ve Mühendishanelerin Kuruluşu (1808'e Kadar)', *Osmanlı Bilimi Araştırmaları II* (İstanbul: İstanbul Üniversitesi Edebiyat Fakultesi Yay., 1998), pp. 69–137.

_____ 'The development in the attitude of the Ottoman state towards science and education and the establishment of the engineering schools (Mühendishânes)', *Proceedings of the International Congress of History of Science, Liege, 20–26 July 1997*, vol. 6, in Ekmeleddin İhsanoğlu, Ahmed Djebbar and Feza Günergun (eds), *Science,Technology and Industry in the Ottoman World* (Belgium: Brepols Publisher, 2000), pp. 81–90.

_____ 'Osmanlılarda Deniz Torpidoları Hakkında İlk Tercüme Eser: E'r-Risaletü'l Berkiye fî Alâti'r- Ra`diye', in Emre Dölen and Mustafa Kçar (eds.), *1. Türk Bilim ve Teknoloji Tarihi Kongresi Bildirileri (15-17 Kasım 2001)* (İstanbul, 2003), pp. 155–63.

_____ 'Osmanlı Ordusunda Görevli Fransız Subayı Saint-Rémy'nin İstanbul'-daki Top Döküm Çalışmaları (1785–87)', *Osmanlı Bilimi Araştırmaları*, vol.

5, no. 1 (İstanbul: İstanbul Üniversitesi Edebiyat Fakultesi Yay., 2003), pp. 33–50.

Kahane, Henry and Andreas Tietze, *The Lingua Franca in the Levant: Turkish Nautical Terms of Italian and Greek Origin* (İstanbul: ABC Kitabevi, 1988).

Karal, Enver Ziya, 'Osmanlı Tarihine Dair Vesikalar', *Belleten* 4/14–15 (1940), pp. 175–89.

____ 'İngilterenin Akdeniz Hakimiyeti Hakkında Vesikalar (1798–1805)', *Tarih Vesikaları* 1/2 (1941), pp. 122–34.

____ 'Osmanlı İmparatorluğunda Kaptan Paşalara ve Donanmaya Yapılan Merasim', *Tarih Vesikaları* 1/2 (1941), pp.135–44.

____ 'Selim III Devrinde Osmanlı Bahriyesi Hakkında Vesikalar', *Tarih Vesikaları* 1/3 (1941), pp. 203–11.

____ *Selim III'ün Hatt-ı Hümayunları-Nizam-ı Cedit- 1789–1807* (Ankara: TTK, 1988).

____ *Selim III'ün Hatt-ı Hümayunları* (Ankara: TTK, 1999).

Kazasker Mehmed Hafid Efendi, *Sefînetü'l-Vüzerâ* (published by İsmet Parmaksızoğlu, director of the Ragıp Paşa Library) (İstanbul: Şirket-i Mürettibiye Basımevi, 1952).

Knight, R. J. B., 'The introduction of copper sheathing into the Royal Navy, 1779–1786', *The Mariner's Mirror: The Journal of the Society for Nautical Research* 59 (London: Greenwich National Maritime Museum, Society for Nautical Research, 1973), pp. 299–309.

____ 'The building and maintenance of the British fleet during the Anglo-French Wars: 1688–1815', in Martine Acerra, José Merino and Jean Meyer (eds), *Les Marines de guerre européennes XVIIème–XVIIIème siècles* (Paris: Presses de l'Université de Paris-Sorbonne, 1985), pp. 35–50.

Kuban, Doğan, 'Kauffer François', *Dünden Bugüne İstanbul Ansiklopedisi*, vol. 4 (İstanbul: Türkiye Ekonomik ve Sosyal Tarih Vakfı, 1994), pp. 492–93.

Kurtoğlu, Fevzi, *XVI. Asırda Hind Okyanusunda Türkler ve Portekizler* (İstanbul: Devlet Basımevi, 1937).

____ *Türklerin Deniz Muharebeleri* (İstanbul: Deniz Matbaası, 1932).

____ *Deniz Mektepleri Tarihçesi* (İstanbul: Deniz Matbaası, 1941).

____ *1768–1774 Türk-Rus Harbinde Akdeniz Harekatı ve Cezayirli Gazi Hasan Paşa* (İstanbul: Deniz Matbaası, 1942).

Lethbridge, T. C., 'Shipbuilding', in Charles Singer, E. J. Holmyard, A. R. Hall and Trevor I. Williams (eds), *A History of Technology*, vol. 2 (Oxford: Clarendon Press, 1957), pp. 562-88.

Levy, Avigdor, 'Military reform and the problem of centralization in the

Ottoman Empire in the eighteenth century', *Middle Eastern Studies* 18 (1982), pp. 227–49.

Lincoln, Margaretta, 'Naval ship launches as public spectacle 1773–1854', *The Mariner's Mirror: The Journal of the Society for Nautical Research* 83/4 (London: Greenwich National Maritime Museum, Society for Nautical Research, November 1997), pp. 466–72.

Lloyd, Christopher (ed.), *The Keith Papers*, vol. 2 (London: Navy Records Society, 1950).

Lybyer, A. H., 'The Ottoman Turks and the routes of oriental trade', *The English Historical Review* 30 (1915), pp. 577–88.

Lyon, David J., 'British warships: types and building policy', in Martine Acerra, José Merino and Jean Meyer (eds), *Les Marines de guerre européennes XVIIème–XVIIIème siècles* (Paris: Presses de l'Université de Paris-Sorbonne, 1985), pp. 147–64.

Mahan, Alfred Thayer. *The Influence of Sea Power upon History, 1663–1783* (Boston: Little, Brown and company, 1904).

Mahmud Raif Efendi, *Osmanlı İmparatorluğu'nda Yeni Nizamların Cedveli* (translated and edited by Arslan Terzioğlu and Hüsrev Hatemi) (İstanbul: Türkiye Turing ve Otomobil Kurumu, 1789).

Manning, Thomas Davys and Charles Fredric Walker, *British Warship Names* (London: Putnam, 1959).

Marcus, G. J., *Heart of Oak: Survey of British Sea Power in the Georgian Era* (Oxford: Oxford University Press, 1975).

Marx, Robert F., *The Battle of Lepanto 1571* (Ohio: The World Publishing Company, 1996).

Merino, José P., 'Graving docks in France and Spain before 1800', *The Mariner's Mirror: The Journal of the Society for Nautical Research* 71 (London: Greenwich National Maritime Museum, Society for Nautical Research, 1985), pp. 35–58.

Mitchell, Donald William, *A History of Russian and Soviet Sea Power* (London: Deutsch, 1974).

Morriss, Roger (ed.), *The Channel Fleet and The Blockade of Brest, 1793–1801* (Aldershot: Ashgate for the Navy Records Society, 2001).

Mudie, Rosemary and Colin Rosemary, *The Story of the Sailing Ship* (London and New York: Marchall Cavendish Publications, 1975).

Müller-Wiener, Wolfgang, *Bizans'tan Osmanlı'ya İstanbul Limanı* (İstanbul: Tarih Vakfı Yurt Yayınları, 1998).

_____ '15–19. Yüzyılları Arasında İstanbul'da İmalathane ve Fabrikalar', in E. İhsanoğlu (ed.), *Osmanlılar ve Batı Teknolojisi* (İstanbul: İstanbul Üniversitesi Edebiyat Fakültesi Basımevi, 1992), p. 77.

Murno, David, *Dictionary of the World* (Oxford and New York: Oxford University Press, 1995).

Murphey, Rhoads, 'Tersane-i amire muhasebe icmallerinden seçilmiş Osmanlı gemi inşasına ait belgeler', *Proceedings of the First International Congress on the History of Turkish İslamic Science and Technology*, vol. 3 of 5 vols (İstanbul: Technical University, pp. 179–84).

____ 'Osmanlıların Batı Teknolojisini Benimsemedeki Tutumları: Efrenci Teknisyenlerin Sivil ve Askeri Uygulamalardaki Rolü', in Ekmeleddin İhsanoğlu (ed.), *Osmanlılar ve Batı Teknolojisi* (İstanbul: İstanbul Üniversitesi Edebiyat Fakültesi Yay., 1992), pp. 7–20.

____ *Ottoman Warfare 1500–1700* (London: UCL Press, 1999).

Naish, George P. B, 'Ships and Shipbuilding' in Charles Singer, E. J. Holmyard, A. R. Hall and Trevor I. Williams (eds), *A History of Technology*, vol. 3 (Oxford: Clarendon Press, 1957), pp. 471-500.

____ 'Ship-building' in Charles Singer, E. J. Holmyard, A. R. Hall and Trevor I. Williams (eds), *A History of Technology*, vol. 4 (Oxford: Clarendon Press, 1958), pp. 574-595.

Nahum, Jean, 'Geleneksel Türk Kayıkçılığı ve Gemiciliği' (Robert Kolej Engineering Department thesis, İstanbul, 1971).

Noyan, Bahri S., 'Eski Gemilerimizin İsimleri', *Hayat Tarih Mecmuası* 1/1, Year 14 (İstanbul: Kent Basımevi, 1978), pp. 91–94.

Nutku, Ata, *Ancient Turkish Craft I, Sultan's Galley (Kadırga), İ.T.Ü. Gemi Enstitüsü Bülteni* (İstanbul: İ.T.Ü. Makine Fakültesi Yay., 1957).

Orhonlu, Cengiz, 'Gemicilik', *Türkiyat Mecmuası* 15 (İstanbul: İstanbul Üniversitesi Edebiyat Fakiltesi Yayını, 1969), pp. 157–69.

Orhonlu, Cengiz and Turgut Işıksal, 'Osmanlı Tarihinde Nehir Nakliyatı Hakkında Araştırmalar: Dicle ve Fırat Nehirlerinde Nakliyat', *İstanbul Üniversitesi Edebiyat Fakültesi Tarih Dergisi* 17–18 (İstanbul, 1962–63), pp. 79–102.

____ 'Osmanlı Türkleri Devrinde İstanbul'da Kayıkçılık ve Kayık İşletmeciliği', *İstanbul Üniversitesi Edebiyat Fakultesi Tarih Dergisi* 21 (İstanbul, 1966), pp. 109–34.

Ortzen, Len, *Guns at Sea: The World's Great Naval Battles* (London: Wiedenfeld and Nicolson, 1976).

Ostapchuk, Victor, 'Five documents from the Topkapı Palace archive on the Ottoman defence of the Black Sea against the Cossacks (1639)', *Journal of Turkish Studies* 11 (Halil İnalcık Hatıra Sayısı) (Cambridge Mass., 1987), pp. 49–104.

____ 'The human landscape of the Ottoman Black Sea in the face of the Cossack naval raids', in Kate Fleet (ed.), *The Ottomans and the Sea* (Cambridge: Skilliter Center for Ottoman Studies & Istituto per l'Oriente C.

A. Nallino, 2001), pp. 23–95.

Özbaran, Salih, 'Osmanlı Imparatorluğu ve Hindistan Yolu', *Istanbul Üniversitesi Edebiyat Fakültesi Türkiyat Dergisi*, no. 31 (Mart 1977), p. 96

____ 'Galata Tersanesinde Gemi Yapımcıları 1529–1530', *Güney-Doğu Avrupa Araştırmaları Dergisi* 8–9 (İstanbul: İstanbul Üniversitesi Edebiyat Fakültesi Yayını, 1980), pp. 97–102.

____ '16. Yüzyılda Asya'da ve Afrika'da Ateşli Silahların ve Askeri Teknolojinin Yayılmasında Osmanlıların Rolü' *10. Türk Tarih Kongresi* 4 (1993), pp. 1473–79.

Padfield, Peter, *Guns at Sea: A History of Naval Gunnery* (London: Hugh Evelyn, 1973).

Pakalın, Mehmet Zeki, *Osmanlı Tarih Deyimleri ve Terimleri Sözlüğü*, vols 1–3 (Ankara: MEB, 1993).

Panzac, Daniel, 'XVII. Yüzyılda Osmanlı İmparatorluğu'nda Deniz Ticareti' (translated by Serap Yılmaz), *Tarih İncelemeleri Dergisi* 4 (1989), pp. 179–92.

____ 'Armed peace in the Mediterranean 1736–1739: a comparative survey of the navies', *The Mariner's Mirror: The Journal of the Society for Nautical Research* 84/1 (London: Greenwich National Maritime Museum, Society for Nautical Research, February 1997), pp. 41–55.

____ 'The manning of the Ottoman navy in the heyday of sail (1600–1850)', in Eric J. Zürcher (ed.), *Arming the State Military Conscription in the Middle East and Central Asia 1775–1925* (London and New York: I. B. Tauris, 1999), pp. 41–57.

____ *Barbary Corsairs: The End of the Legend 1800–1820* (Brill-Leiden-Boston, 2005).

Parry, V. J., 'Materials of war in the Ottoman Empire', in M. A. Cook (ed.), *Studies in the Economic History of the Middle East* (London and New York: Oxford University Press, 1970), pp. 219–29.

Petrovi_, Djurdjica, 'Fire-arms in the Balkans on the eve of and after the Ottoman conquests of the fourteenth and fifteenth centuries', in V. J. Parry and M. E. Yapp (eds), *War, Technology and Society in the Middle East* (London: Oxford University Press, 1975), pp. 164–94.

Pinon, Pierre, 'Un épisode de la réception des progrès techniques à Constantinople : l'échec de la mission Ferregeau, ingénieur des Pomts et Chaussées (1796–1799)', *De la révolution française à la Turquie d'Ataturk, Colloque 1989* (Istanbul and Paris: ISIS, 1990), pp. 71–83.

Platt, Richard, *Man-of-war* (London: Conway Maritime, 1993).

Pocock, Tom, *A Thirst for Glory: The Life of Admiral Sir Sidney Smith* (London: Pimlico, 1998).

Polat, Muzaffer, *Kaptan-ı Derya Cezayirli Gazi Hasan Paşa* (İstanbul: Deniz Kuvvetleri Komutanlığı Kuzey Deniz Sahra Komutanlığı, 1989).

____ *Kuzey Deniz Sahra Komutanlığı Karargâh Binası (Bahriye Divanhanesi)* (İstanbul: Deniz Basımevi, 1997), pp. 4–5.

Porter, W., *The History of the Corps of Royal Engineers*, vol. 1 (Great Britain: Chatham, 1977), pp. 228–35.

Prins, A. H. J., 'Two trends of thought in the Turkish maritime culture: the ethical ship and the magical galley', *The Mariner's Mirror: The Journal of the Society for Nautical Research* 70 (London: Greenwich National Maritime Museum, Society for Nautical Research, 1984), pp. 45–58.

____ 'Mediterranean ships and shipping, 1650–1850', in Robert Gardiner (ed.), *The Heyday of Sail: The Merchant Sailing Ship 1650–1850* (London: Conway, 1995).

Pritchard, James, 'The problem of North America in French nautical science during the 17th and 18th centuries', in Martine Acerra, José Merino and Jean Meyer (eds), *Les Marines de guerre européennes XVIIème–XVIIIème siècles* (Paris: Presses de l'Université de Paris-Sorbonne, 1985), pp. 331–44.

____ *Louis XV's Navy 1748–1762: A Study of Organization and Administration* (Kingston and Montreal: McGill-Queen's University Press, 1987).

Pryor, John H., *Commerce, Shipping and Naval Warfare in the Medieval Mediterranean* (London: Variorum Reprints, 1987).

____ *Geography, Technology and War: Studies in the Maritime History of the Mediterranean 649–1571* (Cambridge and New York: Cambridge University Press, 1992).

Ralston, David B., *Importing the European Army: The Introduction of the European Military Techniques and Institutions into the Extra-European World, 1600–1914* (Chicago: University of Chicago Press, 1996).

Rees, Gareth, 'Copper sheathing: an example of the technological diffusion in the English merchant fleet', *The Journal of Transport History* New Series 1/2 (September 1971), pp. 85–93.

Roche, Max, *Éducation, assistance et culture françaises dans l'Empire ottoman* (Istanbul: ISIS, 1989).

Rogers, Hugh Cuthbert Basset, *A History of Artillery* (Secaucus and New Jersey: Citadel, 1975), pp. 59–72.

Römer, Claudia, 'The sea in comparisons and metaphors in Ottoman historiography in the sixteenth century', in Kate Fleet (ed.), *The Ottomans and the Sea* (Cambridge: Skilliter Center for Ottoman Studies & Istituto per l'Oriente C. A. Nallino, 2001), pp. 233–44.

Rycaut, Paul, *The Present State of the Ottoman Empire* (London, 1668).

Safvet, '1205'de Donanmamız', *Tarih-i Osmanî Encümeni Mecmuası* Year 4, vol. 3 (İstanbul, 1331), pp. 1300–77.

Saul, N.E., *Russia and the Mediterranean 1797–1807* (Chicago and London: The University of Chicago Press, 1970).

Say, Yağmur, *Top ve Topçuluğun Tarihsel Gelişimi ve Mühendishâne-i Berrî-i Hümâyûn (1795–1995)* (Ankara: Toçu ve Füze Okulu Matbaası, 1995).

Sayacı, Kenan, *Deniz Harp Okulu Tarihçesi* (Ankara: Deniz Kuvvetleri Komutanlığı, n.d.)

Schmitd, Jan, *Per koets naar Constantinopel: De Gezatschapsreis van Baron van Dedem van de Gelder naar Istanbul in 1785* (Zutphen: Walburg Press, 1998) (English summary).

Seyyid Mustafa, *İstanbul'da Askerlik Sanatı, Yeteneklerin ve Bilimlerin Durumu Üzerine Risale* (translated by Hüsrev Hatemi) (İstanbul: TÜYAP Tüm Fuarcılık Yayını, 1986).

Shaw, Stanford J., 'The established Ottoman army corps under Selim III (1789-1807)', *Der Islam* 40 (1965), 142-184.

_____ 'Selim III and the Ottoman navy', *Turcica: Revue d'études turques* 1 (1969), pp. 212–41.

_____ *Between Old and New: The Ottoman Empire under Selim III (1789–1807)* (Cambridge, Massachusetts: Harvard University Press, 1971).

Soucek, Svat, 'Certain types of ships in the Ottoman-Turkish terminology', *Turcica: Revue d'études turques* 7 (Paris, 1975), pp. 233–49.

_____ 'Ottoman naval policy in the Indian Ocean', *X. Türk Tarih Kongresi, 22–26 Eylül 1986, Kongreye Sunulan Bildiriler* (Ankara: TTK, 1993), pp. 1443–46.

Swann, D., 'The engineers of English port improvements 1660–1830: Part I', *Transport History* 1/2 (July, 1968), pp. 153–68.

_____ 'The engineers of English port improvements 1660–1830: Part II', *Transport History* 1/3 (November 1968), pp. 261–76.

Şakul, Kahraman, 'Ottoman artillery and warfare in the eighteenth century', (İstanbul: M.A. dissertation, Boğaziçi University, 2001).

Şehsuvaroğlu, H., *Deniz Tarihimize Ait Makaleler* (İstanbul: TC Deniz Basımevi, 1965).

Tann, Jennifer and M. J. Breckin, 'The international diffusion of the Watt engine, 1775–1825', *Economic History Review* 31/4, 2nd Series, 1978, pp. 541–64.

Tekindağ, Şahabeddin, 'Haliç Tersanesi'nde Yapılan İlk Osmanlı Donanması ve Cafer Kapudan'ın Arizası', *Belgelerele Türk Tarihi Dergisi* 48 (İstanbul, Ocak 2001), pp. 26–29.

Tengüz, Hüsnü, *Osmanlı Bahriyesinin Mazisi* (İstanbul: Dz.K.K., 1995).

Tezel, Hayati, *Anadolu Türkleri'nin Deniz Tarihi*, vol. 1 (İstanbul: Dz.K.K., 1973).

Tızlak, Fahrettin, 'Osmanlı Devleti'nde Ham Bakır İşleme Merkezleri Olarak Tokat ve Diyarbakır', *Belleten* 59/226 (1995), pp. 641–59.

____ *Osmanlı Döneminde Keban-Ergani Yöresinde Madencilik (1775–1850)* (Ankara: TTK, 1997).

Thompson, William R., 'The military Superiority thesis and the ascendancy of Western Eurasia in the world system', *Journal of World History* 10 (1999), pp. 144–78.

____ and George Modelski, *Seapower and Global Politics, 1494–1993* (London: Macmillan, 1988).

Toğrol, Ergün and İ. H. Aksoy, 'Drydocks of Istanbul Golden Horn shipyard', *Proceedings of I. International Congress on the History of Turkish-Islamic Science and Technology, İTÜ, 14–18 September 1981* (İstanbul, 1981), pp. 57–65.

Tracy, Nicholas (ed.), *The Naval Chronicle: The Contemporary Record of the Royal Navy at War*, vol. 2 (1799–1804) (London: Chatam Publishing, 1998).

Tutel, Eser, 'Tersâne-i Amire', *Dünden Bugüne İstanbul Ansiklopedisi*, vol. 7 (İstanbul: Türkiye Ekonomik ve Sosyal Tarih Vakfı, 1994).

____ *Gemiler...Süvariler...İskeleler...* (İstanbul: İletişim, 1998).

Uluçay, Çağatay and Enver Karatekin, *Yüksek Mühendis Okulu* (İstanbul: Berksoy Matbaası, 1958).

Unger, Richard W., 'Design and construction of European warships in the seventeenth and eighteenth centuries', in Martine Acerra, José Merino and Jean Meyer (eds), *Les Marines de guerre européennes XVIIème–XVIIIème siècles* (Paris: Presses de l'Université de Paris-Sorbonne, 1985), pp. 21–34.

____ 'Alfred Thayer Mahan, ship design, and the evolution of sea power in the late Middle Ages', *The International History Review* 19/3 (August 1997), pp. 505–21.

Ünlü, Rasim, *İnce Donanma* (İstanbul: Deniz Basımevi, 2005).

____ *Bahriye'nin Haliç Serüveni: İstanbul'un Fethinden Son Divanhaneye* (İstanbul: Deniz Basımevi, 2006).

Uzunçarşılı, İsmail Hakkı, 'Ondokuzuncu asır başlarına kadar Türk-İngiliz münasebatına dair vesikalar', *Belleten* 13 (1949).

____ *Kapıkulu Ocaklari I* (Ankara: TTK, 1943).

____ 'Bahriyya', *Encyclopaedia of Islam: New Edition*, vol. 1 of 10 vols (Leiden: E. J. Brill, 1960), p. 947.

____ *Osmanlı Devletinin İlmiye Teşkilatı* (Ankara: TTK, 1984).

_____ *Osmanlı Devletinin Merkez ve Bahriye Teşkilatı* (Ankara: TTK, 1988).

Von Pivka, Otto, *Navies of the Napoleonic Era* (Newton Abbot: David and Charles, 1980).

Ware, Chris, *The Bomb Vessel: Shore Bombardment Ships of the Age of Sail* (Annapolis, Maryland: Naval Institute Press, 1994).

Winfield, Rif, *The 50-gun Ship* (Great Britain: Caxton Editions, 1997).

Winklareth, Robert J., *Naval Shipbuilders of the World: From the Age of Sail to the Present Day* (London: Chatham Publishing, 2000).

Woodman, Richard, *The Story of Sail* (London: Catham Publishing, 1999).

Yakay, Sinan, *Kdz. Ereğli'de Tersâneciliğin Tarihi ve Tersâneci Ağalar* (İzmit: Kdz. Ereğli Ticaret Odası Yayınları, 2004).

Yakital, Emin, 'Bahriye Mektebi', *TDV Islam Ansiklopedisi*, vol. 4 (İstanbul: Türkiye Diyanet Vakfı, 1991), pp. 509–11.

Yavuz, Celalettin, *Osmanlı Bahriyesinde Yabancı Misyonlar-Çeşme Faciasından Birinci Dünya Harbine Kadar Osmanlı Bahriyesi'nde Çağdaşlaşma Gayretleri* (İstanbul: Dz. İk. Grp. K.lığı Basımevi, n.d.).

Zaloğlu, Mustafa, *Gemici Dili* (İstanbul: Türk Deniz Kuvvetlerini Güçlendirme Vakfı Yayınları, 1988).

# GLOSSARY

***Âhen akreb*** Iron hand
***Âhen çenber*** Iron strap
***Âhenî çilingirkârî mühimmât*** Iron equipment
***Âhen çubuk-ı İsveç*** Swedish iron rod
***Âhen halka-i civata-i araba*** Iron rings of bolts and screws for wagons
***Âhen-i hâm*** Raw/unprocessed iron
***Âhen kanca*** Iron hook
***Âhen kiriş*** Iron beam
***Âhen lenger-i tolos*** Iron kedge anchor
***Âhen maşa-i çatal*** Iron forked tongs
***Âhen palanga-i top*** Iron cable for guns
***Akçe*** A small silver coin (one third of a ***para***)
***Akrebli ve ibreli basîte-i âfâkî*** Elevation wood with hour hand and needle
***Âlât*** Rope
***Âlât-ı gomana-i filuka*** Anchor cable of a ship's boat
***Âlât-ı gomana-i palamar*** Anchor cable for mooring
***Âlât-ı gomana-i sandal*** Anchor cable of a ship's boat
***Âlât-ı gomana-i tolos*** Rope of a small kedge anchor
***Âlât-ı kavalete*** The messenger of a cable
***Âlât-ı saltâ-i planga*** Rope for surging tackle
***Âlât-ı serviçe/servise/selviçe*** Running rigging, cordage and equipment composed of this kind of cordage
***Ambar emini*** The administrator in charge of stores
***Ardıç*** Juniper
***Âriyet kapusu*** Temporary gate
***Arma*** Rigging of a ship
***Arma olunmak*** Being rigged
***Arşın/Arşun*** A unit of length equal to 1 ***zira***, 1 French ***pic***
***Ateş tulumbası*** Fire pump
***Avârız*** An extraordinary tax levied by the government on the ***reaya*** in times of unusual need and payable in cash, kind or services

**Ayak mimarı** Base architect
**Babafingo çubuğu** Topgallant mast
**Bâdbân (yelken)** Sail
**Bâdbân-ı sandal** Sails of a rowing boat
**Bâdbân-ı filuka** Sails of a boat
**Bâdbânî-i kalyon** The chief sail maker
**Bahriye Kânunnâmesi** Naval regulations
**Bahriye Nazırı** Minister of Navy
**Bakırcı esnafı** Copper traders
**Bakır huni** Copper funnel
**Balkovân** Balcony
**Baruthâne** Gunpowder mill
**Basdika/bastika** Snatch block
**Başmimar** Chief architect
**Beş delikli paçavra** Shells with five holes/carcass
**Beyaz top keçesi** White felt for cannons
**Biraga/Brago** The breeching of a ship's gun
**Boçlana** Puzzolane. It was mixed with lime in order to obtain Puzzolane mortar. It easily hardened under the water and had long been used widely in underwater constructions before the introduction of cement
**Bodoslama** Sternpost
**Borina** Bowline
**Bumba** Boom. The yards used horizontally
**Burgu-i top** Cannon drill, augers for guns
**Burgucubaşı** Chief augerer
**Burton** Bertone, a kind of gunboat
**Cârsu tuğlası** Square brick
**Cebehâne-i Âmire** The Imperial Armoury
**Cerrahbaşı** Chief surgeon
**Cıvadıra** Bowsprit
**Cizye** Poll tax payable by non-Muslims
**Cunda** Peak
**Cunda sereni** Studdingsail yard
**Çalpara** A hinged lid made of iron sheet fixed into the mouths of the holes in order not to let sea water leak into ships
**Çam** Pine
**Çâr kûşe pusula** Square compass
**Çarub** Broom
**Çekeleve** A sailing craft used in the Levant, with two short masts that lean forward

***Çenber-i dayyık*** Narrow ring
***Çenber-i macana-i âb*** Rings for water barrels
***Çene*** A slightly round place at the connection of stem and keel
***Çilingirkârî*** Related to the delicate iron works
***Çömlekçi çamuru*** Slop
***Darphâne-i Âmire*** The Imperial Mint
***Defterdâr Efendi*** Treasurer
***Deben-i kazma*** Blade of a pickaxe
***Demir külâh*** Iron cone
***Demir kürek*** Iron shovel
***Demir meşale*** Iron torch
***Demir sabanlı üç dilli makara*** Three-sheaved block with iron stroop
***Demir sabanlı iki dilli makara*** Two-sheaved block with iron stroop
***Demir sabanlı makara-i bastika*** Snatch block with iron stroop
***Dil-i mısrî*** Egyptian sheave
***Dirisa*** To shift the direction of guns etc.
***Dişbudak*** Ash tree
***Donyağı/revğân-ı pîh*** Tallow
***Dubas*** A river ship used in transfer of freights
***Dümen iğnecikleri*** The bearing pintles of the rudder
***Elek*** Sifter
***Emme tulumba*** Suction pump
***Erz*** Rice
***Endâze çıkarmak*** To take a mould of a ship according to the drawings by means of thin pieces of pine
***Endâzeden çıkmak*** This expression is used for the ships put on stocks after their sternposts and broadsides have been raised, levelled, braced and formed. Ships whose construction came to this stage were called ***kafes halinde***.
***Endâze güvertesi*** Wide and flat floors on which the pictures of the ships to be constructed were drawn and according to which their moulds were taken
***Endâzehâne*** Measuring and modelling house
***Ester*** Mule
***Falye/falya*** Touchhole of a muzzleloader
***Fânus*** A round glass case used for protecting the light of a candle, oil/kerosene lamp and etc. from wind
***Fekk-i lenger*** To weigh anchor (to pull the anchor out of water)
***Felenk/filenk*** A cross piece of timber laid down as part of the slip ways for a ship or boat

***Filandre*** Pennant; the long and narrow streamer carried at the head of the mainmast

***Firaşkon/Burton*** A tackle of one single and one double block; a tackle of one double and one triple block; a tackle of two triple blocks; threefold purchase

***Firman*** Imperial decree

***Fitil-i Mısrî*** Wick

***Fula*** Hand glass (a kind of sandglass)

***Fuğla*** Lookout post on the foremast

***Funda*** Heath. A substance consisting of various types of small trees that was burned to dry up boats, galleys and galleons when their hulls were first constructed. It was also used during the caulking process.

***Furun*** Furnace

***Gabya*** Top

***Gabya çubuğu/direği*** Topmast

***Gabya sereni*** Topsail yards

***Gabya yelkeni*** Lower topsail

***Gırçıla/gırcila/gırcala/kırcıla/kırçila*** Marline of the best material. It was usually made of high-quality hemp and used in many ways

***Gırçıla-i manilla*** Manilla marline

***Gırçıla-i Osmânî*** Ottoman marline with tar. It was used in firm and unmovable parts.

***Göke*** Cogge, an obsolete kind of ship, high in the free-board

***Gomana delikleri*** Hawseholes

***Gomena teli*** A ship's chain cable

***Gönye maa tahta*** Set square with wood

***Göz kurşunları*** Circular leads

***Griva/gruva/guruva/grua*** A cathead on a ship

***Gürgen*** Hornbeam

***Ğırar/ğırare*** Sack

***Hadde*** The name of the machine used to produce thin plates and wires out of mines such as copper and iron

***Haddehâne*** Name given to the workshop where copper was processed and developed into thin and fibre form in order to sheathe the hulls and bottoms of the imperial ships

***Ham kendir*** Raw hemp

***Hammaliye*** Porterage

***Harbe*** Halberd

***Hark-ı nâr*** A substance used to dry the copper sheets that are applied for sheathing the hulls and bottoms of ships

***Hartuç (Fişek)*** Cartridge
***Hassa Kurşuncubaşısı*** Chief official in charge of the supply and distribution of lead
***Hatt-ı Hümâyûn*** Imperial edict
***Hekimbaşı*** Chief physician
***Hendesehâne*** The engineering school
***Hil'at*** Robe of honour
***Hortum*** Hose
***Humbara*** Shell
***Humbara havanı*** Shell mortar
***Ihlamur ağacı*** Lime tree
***Irgad/ırgat*** Capstan, windlass
***İbrişim*** Silk
***İkâmet elçileri*** Permanent ambassadors
***İsâğa*** Casting, moulding
***İskandil*** Sounding lead for measuring the depth of the sea
***İskarmoz/iskarmos/iskarmuz*** A rowlock; a tholepin; a ship's rib or timbers; post; seam; futtock. It is a pin or thole inserted vertically into the sides of a boat to allow the oar to be fastened
***İskota*** Sheet of a sail
***İskota makara*** Sheet block
***İspavlo/rişte*** Thin rope used for fixing the worn-out parts of a sail
***İspiralya*** Cabin skylight
***İstifdaç/Üstübeç*** White lead used in painting to obtain paint in desired thickness
***İstralya*** A stay of a ship's mast
***Jengâr*** Poisonous green rust on copper
***Kadem*** A measure of width, which equals to $^1/_2$ ***arşun***
***Kalafat***/Caulking Plugging cracks between planks with such materials as oakum, pitch, tar, tallow and resin to make them waterproof
***Kali/kalay*** Tin
***Kalite*** Galleot, a warship with 19-24 rowing banks
***Kali-yi İngiltere/ingilizî*** British tin
***Kalyon*** Galleon
***Kanâ*** It refers to draught marks or an instrument of the wharf workers for measuring length. 1 ***zira-i mimari*** = 24 ***parmak***, and 1 ***zira*** (formerly used) = 24 ***kanâ***, and ***kanâ*** is a little bigger than ***parmak*** because 1 ***zira-i mimari*** consisted of 24 ***parmak*** = 75 cm = 37 French ***pus***.
***Kanca-i firaşkon*** Hooks for threefold purchase
***Kanca-i griva*** Hooks for cat davit/cathead

***Kanca-i lumbar*** Hooks for gunports

***Kanca-i sandal*** Hooks for boats

***Kancalı torno makara*** Single block with hook

***Kancalı makara-i palanga-i güverte*** Hooked block of deck tackle

***Kandelisa/kandiliça*** Foretackle; girtline; triatic stay

***Kandeliça-i Osmânî*** A kind of rope for sails

***Kantar*** 44 ***okka*** = 56.44 kg

***Kapak*** The double-decked man-of-war with 80 to 110 guns and with two gun decks below the spardeck

***Karaağaç*** Elm

***Karaya oturmak*** To run aground

***Kârgir ızgaralı rıhtım*** Stone-grilled quay

***Kârgir ocak*** Stone hearth

***Karina*** Bottom of a ship or boat

***Karış*** A measurement of length, span. 3 ***karış*** is equal to 1 ***arşın/arşun***

***Kasavele*** Clothesline, especially on warships

***Kaşkavâl*** A fid of a ship's mast or a square bar to support the weight of the topmast

***Katran*** Tar

***Kaveleta*** Messenger (the equipment on the ship, around which cables and chains were coiled in order to pull the anchors)

***Kavilya*** Treenail

***Kazık*** Stake

***Kemere*** A beam under a ship's deck

***Kefçe-i top*** Scoop for loading gunpowder to guns

***Kereste*** Timber

***Keski*** Chisel

***Kestane*** Chestnut

***Keten*** Flax

***Kırlangıç*** An oared ship used for duties such as war or coast guarding, or trade

***Kıyye*** See ***vukıyye***

***Kile*** A unit of measurement used for grains. There were various types of ***kile*** such as ***Istanbul kilesi***, 18 to 20 ***okkas*** (or approximately 25 kg), and ***Ibrail kilesi***, 70 to 80 ***okkas*** (or around 100 kg). In the period of sailing ships, ***kile*** assumed a new meaning and it was used in the same way that we use ship tonnage today. Thirty-six ***kiles*** were equal to one tonnage (***tonilato***)

***Kintal*** Quintal. A unit of weight equal to a hundredweight (112 lb), or formerly 100 lb

***Kirpâs*** Sailcloth

***Kirpâs-ı bâdbân*** Sailcloth

***Kirpâshâne*** Sail-making and storing house

***Kontratavlon*** Lower orlop deck

***Köknar*** Fir

***Kömür-i âhenger*** Coal used by ironworkers

***Kükürt*** Sulphur

***Kufl*** Lock

***Kufl-i asma*** Padlock

***Kulaç*** Fathom, which equals one-third of a ship, 185 cm or 6 ***kadem***. It is generally used for measuring the length of ropes and chains.

***Kuntura mizana*** Small fore-and-aft storm sails

***Kurtlaca/kurdelesa/kordelisa/kordaliça/kurtelaça*** Topmast studdingsail

***Kuru havuz*** Dry dock

***Kuruz*** Wing transom

***Kuşak*** Brace

***Küfe-i kebîr*** Big pannier

***Küfeki taşı*** Coarse sandstone; softish sandstone grit that withstands fire well

***Külçe bakır*** Copper bullion

***Lâma*** Plate

***Lâma demiri*** Flat-rolled iron

***Lâma-i lumbar*** Plate for gunports

***Lahm-ı ğanem*** Mutton

***Landa*** A chain of a shroud on a ship

***Landa demiri*** Chain plate

***Landa-i pateraçe*** Chain plates of backstays

***Lata*** Lath/ledge (a long, narrow, thinnish board made of pine timber)

***Lehim*** Soldering

***Lenger*** Anchor

***Lenger-endâz*** At anchor (used for a ship dropped/cast anchor)

***Lengerhâne*** Anchor house

***Liman reisi*** Port commander

***Lodra*** A unit of weight. 1 ***lodra*** equals to 0.44 ***kıyy***e

***Macuna/maçula maa cerr-i eskâl*** Mechanical crane

***Maça*** Claw hammer, which is a tool of caulkers for removing old planks

***Maden toplu mikrazlar*** Scissors of metal shells

***Mahzen-i çûb*** Timber store in the arsenal

***Mahzen-i sürb/kurşunlu mahzen*** The place where ship and shipyard equipment was kept and stored for later use. Among the equipment were various iron pieces, nails, copper pots, lead plates, hemp, cords, barrels, sail, awning, anchor, cannon, lamp and paper

**Maden toplu mikraslar** Scissors of metal shells

**Makara** Pulley, block

**Makara Dili/Zebân-ı Makara** Sheave generally made of rosewood (**pelesenk**), iron or brass

**Makara-i bastika** Snatch block

**Makara-i torno** Single block, block with one sheave inside

**Mangatsa/kemere** A beam under a ship's deck

**Manivela-ı top** Gun lever

**Mayıstra** Main boom

**Mayıstra sereni** Main yard

**Mayıstra yelkeni** Mainsail

**Melezçam** Larch

**Mertek** Rafter

**Meşe** Oak

**Mihmandâr** Standard bearer

**Mikrâs/z** Scissors

**Minderlik kutn** Cotton for cushion

**Mismâr** Nail

**Mismâr-ı atîk** Old/used nails

**Mismâr-ı makara-i tulumba** Nail used to fasten the parts of blocks of a pump

**Mismâr-ı tulumba** Nails for pumps

**Mismâr-ı yâş** A kind of nail

**Mortoloz**

**Muhassıl** Tax collector

**Musavver kebîr kürre-i semâ** Illustrated celestial globe of a big size

**Müteharrik nemçekârî pusula** Moving compass of Austrian type

**Nakkâş** Muralist

**Nân-ı azîz** Bread

**Nişadır** Ammonium chloride

**Nühâs-ı hâm** Raw copper

**Nühâs kapak** Copper lid

**Nühâs karavana** Copper cauldron

**Nühâs kefçe** Copper ladle

**Nühashâne** Copper processing house

**Ocak** Hearth, stove

**Ocaklık** A method of procurement of some required materials from provinces that were rich in these materials as part of their tax. The provinces were sometimes charged to construct one or two ships as well.

***Okka*** A measure of weight equal to 1.288 kg (see ***kantar***) = 400 ***dirhem***

***Palamar*** Mooring rope

***Palanga/halat takımı*** Tackle

***Palanga-i borina-i makara*** Bowline tackle block

***Palavra*** The main deck of a man-of-war

***Para*** See ***akçe***

***Pateraça*** Back stays

***Patrona-i humayun*** The vice admiral's flagship

***Pelesenk ağacı*** Rosewood

***Pergâr-ı tâm*** A pair of compasses

***Pertavsiz*** Magnifying glass

***Pırnar/pırnal ağacı*** Quercus ilex, holly oak, helm oak, a kind of oak whose wood is used in producing treenail

***Peygamberağacı*** Lignum vitae

***Pirasya*** Brace

***Pirinç*** Brass

***Pirinç ağızlık*** Bras mouthpiece

***Pladora*** Cross plank

***Plakon*** A reinforcing rail of iron; timber band

***Plankete*** Chain shot (heavy balls joined by a chain). They tangled in the enemy ship's rigging and tore it down.

***Poca/boça*** A kind of missile in naval artillery

***Praçol*** Knee

***Praketa*** Ship's log

***Pusula*** Compass

***Puzolan*** Volcanic ash

***Rasâs*** Lead

***Reaya*** The tax-paying Ottoman subject class, as distinct from the military class

***Reis-i evvel*** Executive officer

***Resenci*** Rope maker

***Revğân-ı bezîr*** Linseed oil

***Revğân-ı pih*** Tallow

***Revğân-ı sâde*** Pure oil

***Revğân-ı şem*** Wax

***Revğân-ı zeyt*** Olive oil

***Rîk*** Sand

***Riyâle-i Hümayun*** The rear admiral's flagship

***Rubu' tahtası*** Quadrant
***Rûy-ı mâye*** Zinc ferment or alloy
***Rûh-ı tuitya (Çinko Oksit)*** Zinc white
***Saat-ı rîk*** Hourglass
***Safra*** Ballast
***Sakolya/sakuleta/sakulta*** Cartridge bag
***Salkım*** Grape shot
***Saltâ*** To ease off, surging a rope etc.
***Salya*** To shift from one side to the other
***Samur kürk*** Sable fur
***Sancaklık şali*** A kind of wooden fabric used in the production of colours/flags
***Sandık/ateş tulumbası*** Coffer
***Seferiyye akçesi*** A temporary treasury or certain amount of money provided by the Imperial Mint in order to meet some emergency expenses of military and naval campaigns
***Senderus*** Glue and oil extracted from copal tree
***Seng-i âteşî*** Refractory stone
***Seng-i küfekî*** Grit
***Seng-i molos*** Unhewn stone
***Ser-topi-i kalyon*** Artillery chief on a galleon
***Seren*** Yard
***Seyir defteri/seyir jurnali*** Logbook
***Sihâm Muâcelâtı*** The treasury of the urgent expenses established for campaigns within İrâd-ı Cedîd Treasury
***Sirti/sirtu*** Long-line
***Sonsuz ipli kovalı tulumba*** Chain pump/endless chain
***Sömbeki/gavvâs*** A person who dives into the sea in order to remove anchors and cannons of the old sunken ships
***Sualtı dürbünü*** Underwater glass
***Sudagabu/Sodagabo*** Gunner on a ship
***Sundurma*** Shed, lean-to
***Sülügen(Kırmızı kurşun oksit)*** Red paint, which was put on newly placed iron sheets as coating material
***Sûzen*** Sewing needle
***Sûzen-i bâdbân*** Sewing needle for sails
***Sütûn*** Mast
***Sütûn-ı civadıra*** Bowsprit
***Sütûn-ı mayıstra*** The mainmast
***Sütûn-ı mizana*** The mizzenmast of a sailing ship

***Sütûn-ı tirinkete*** The foremast

***Şalope*** Sloop

***Şayka*** A type of ship used mainly on rivers, especially on the Danube and its tributaries and along the coast of the Black Sea, for transport as well as for defence of river banks. A ***şayka*** with three light cannons was 17–33 ***zira*** long.

***Şehdiye*** A type of two-to-three-masted sailing warship of 23–35 ***zira*** in length

***Tabân*** Heel

***Tâbe-i dest*** Pan with a handle

***Tahta nühâs*** Copper plate

***Tavlama ocağı*** Annealing furnace

***Tavlon*** Lower deck, the orlop deck of a warship

***Tavşan*** A carpenter dealing with delicate pieces of workmanship

***Talimar*** Cutwater of a ship, false stem, the bows, knee of head

***Tedhîn*** To grease

***Tel-i Frengî*** French wire

***Temürhâne*** Iron processing house

***Tente*** Awning

***Tersâne Zindanı*** The prison inside the naval arsenal

***Tersâne-i Âmire*** Imperial Naval Arsenal

***Tersâne-i Âmire Emîni*** The director of the Imperial Naval Arsenal

***Tersâne-i Âmire Tulumbacıbaşısı*** The chief official in charge of supplying and delivering the pumps and related equipment at the Imperial Naval Arsenal

***Tesviye*** Levelling

***Tezgâh*** Workbench

***Tirşe*** Light green

***Tombaz*** Flat-bottomed river ships without decks, pontoon

***Tonos/tolos demiri*** A warping anchor

***Top kundağı*** Gunstock

***Tophâne-i Âmire*** Imperial Cannon Foundry

***Trabago*** A type of ship available in the Adriatic

***Trata-(go)*** Fishing vessel of a small size

***Trinkete sereni*** Fore yard

***Trinkete yelkeni*** Foresail, forestaysail

***Tuğla-i inâd-ı furun*** Support brick for furnace

***Tulumba-i harîk*** Fire pump

***Tunc*** Bronze

***Tunc inecikler*** Bronze bearing pintles

***Tunc zebân*** Bronze sheave

***Tutkal*** An infusable elastic substance composed of gomelica, rubber and neft

***Tutya*** Zinc

***Tüfenk*** Rifle

***Umk*** Depth

***Uskuna*** Schooner

***Üç ambarlı*** Three-decker

***Üstübî*/**Oakum It is the most important substance for the caulking process. It consists of flax, hemp and pieces of worn-out ropes, and it is used to fill the spaces between the timbers of hulls before the process of tarring and applying pitch.

***Varyoz*** Heavy hammer

***Vukıyye = Okka = Kıyye*** = 1.288 kg

***Yeke-i dümen*** Tiller, rudder tiller

***Yunmalı senk-i siyah-ı küfeki*** Washed black sandstone

***Yüz tokmaklı barut çarkı*** Gunpowder wheel with 100 mallets

***Zahire ambarı*** Granary

***Zemîn Kundakları*** Ground gunstocks

***Zift*** Pitch

***Zira-ı mimari*** = 24 ***parmak*** = 37 French ***pus*** = 75.8 cm

# INDEX

**Ships**

**Place Names**

**Name Index**